A SHORT HISTORY OF

MODERN ENGLISH LITERATURE

BY

EDMUND GOSSE

HON. M. A. OF TRINITY COLLEGE, CAMBRIDGE

NEW YORK

D. APPLETON AND COMPANY

1900

PREFACE

THE principal aim which I have had before me, in writing this volume, has been to show the movement of English literature. I have desired above all else to give the reader, whether familiar with the books mentioned or not, a feeling of the evolution of English literature in the primary sense of the term, the disentanglement of the skein, the slow and regular unwinding, down succeeding generations, of the threads of literary expression. To do this without relation to particular authors, and even particular works, seems to me impossible; to attempt it would be to essay a vague disquisition on "style" in the abstract, a barren thing at best. To retain the character of an historical survey, with the introduction of the obvious names, has seemed to me essential; but I have endeavoured to keep expression, form, technique, always before me as the central interest, rather than biography, or sociology, or mere unrelated criticism. In this way only, by the elimination of half the fascinating qualities which make literature valuable to us, could it be possible in so few pages to give anything but a gabble of facts. And the difficulties of omission have been by far the greatest that have assailed me. If any one accuses me of injustice to an author, I must acknowledge with despair that I have been "unjust" to every one, if justice be an exhaustive statement of his claims to consideration. No critical reader can be more indignant at my summary treatment of a favourite of his own than I have been at having to glide so swiftly over mine.   But the procession of the entire theme was the one thing that seemed essential; whether I have in any measure been able to present it, my readers must judge.

The great pressure upon space has been relieved by dividing the history of English literature into two portions.   If this series continues to receive the support of the public, it is hoped that a volume on the archaic section may bring the story down from the earliest times to Robert of Brunne and Laurence Minot.   In my first three chapters I have further lightened my labour by leaving out of consideration what was written in this country in Latin or French, for, although this may be material in dealing with thought in England, it can have but a small connection with the history of expression in the English language.   I make no apology for the prominence given throughout to the art of poetry, for it is in verse that style can most definitely and to greatest advantage be studied, especially in a literature like ours, where prose has mainly been written without any other aim than the naïve transference of ideas or statement of facts, like the prose of M. Jourdain, while our national poetry, which is one of our main national glories, has been a consecutive chain of consciously elaborated masterpieces.

I have to acknowledge, with warm thanks, the kindness of that distinguished mediæval scholar, Prof. W. S. McCormick, of the University of St. Andrews, who has been so obliging as to read the proofs of my early chapters.   For other and more general acknowledgments I must refer to my bibliographical appendix.

July, 1897.

CONTENTS

vii

A SHORT HISTORY OF
MODERN ENGLISH LITERATURE

I

THE AGE OF CHAUCER

1350–1400

IT is now a recognised fact that the continuity of English literature is unbroken from *Beowulf* and Cædmon down to the present day. But although this is not to be denied, it is convenient for practical purposes that we should begin the study of modern English poetry and prose at the point where the language in which these are written becomes reasonably and easily intelligible to us. The old classic writers looked upon Chaucer as " the father of English literature "; we look upon him as a figure midway between the fathers and us, their latest sons, and we are aware that for six or seven centuries before the composition of the *Vision of Piers Plowman* and the *Canterbury Tales*, Englishmen were writing what was stimulating, and national, and worthy of our closest attention. There came a great change in the fourteenth century, but we have been rash in supposing that a completely new thing began at the close of the Middle Ages. The traditions of early English survived, and were merely modified. In Langland we shall presently meet with an author untouched by modern forms and ideas, who wrote in the manner and in the spirit of long generations of less-gifted precursors. The more closely literary history is studied, the less inclined shall we be to insist on a sudden and arbitrary line of demarcation between the old epoch and the new.

Yet, it being convenient to distinguish, for practical purposes, between the Old and the Middle and New English, we do discover in 1350 a date with which we may make shift to begin the study of modern English literature. About that time a modification in English manners was introduced, which was of the highest importance to writers and readers. After the first great plague (1349) the residue gathered themselves together into what was more like a nation than anything which had existed in this country before, and this concentrated people reasserted for itself, what it had partly lost for a while, a national and native language. We may well begin the study of modern literature from the approximate date of the recognition of English as the language of England. Very rapidly after that the general use of French disappeared, while the native dialects were drawn together and moulded into one ; our present grammar, and even our present vocabulary, being largely a creation of the reign of Edward III. English became a highly vitalised condensation of elements hitherto deemed irreconcilable, elements which were partly Teutonic, partly Latin.

With the exclusion of foreign forms of speech, in future to be accepted only if molten into a firm and consistent English, our intellectual life assumes a wholesome insularity. When England was a political term, including Anjou and Aquitaine, the forces of its intelligence were scattered. It retires behind the barrier of its narrow seas, and has no sooner divided itself from the language and interests of Europe than it recreates a literature of its own. The fusion of the native language does not become complete until the end of the century, but it had been working for fifty years previously. In 1362 French ceases to be the legal tongue of the realm, and in 1363 the first English oration is made in Parliament by a minister who will address members no longer in what is really a foreign tongue. All this movement is made in resistance to Court habits and Court prejudices; it is a strictly popular movement, forcing upon the attention of the upper classes the will of the millions who are ruled. The beginning of modern English literature, therefore, is essentially democratic without being revolutionary. It is a result of a break-down of the feudal principle of isolation, and the consequence of a fusion between the nobles and the professional and commercial part of the population.

As we break into the literature of England at 1350, we find ourselves in the midst of a considerable metrical activity, which does not promise at first to arrest our attention with anything very valuable or very salient. The favourite secular reading of the age seems to have been alliterative adaptations, mainly from the French, of the old romances of chivalry. Perhaps the most readable, and certainly a very typical example of these imitations has come down to us in *William of Palerme*, the date of the composition of which is probably about 1355. The activity of the versifiers who carried on this facile manufacture of romances was exercised in two directions: on the one hand they endeavoured to revive the old native measures, and on the other they strove to create a prosody analogous to that already accepted by the Latin nations. Out of the former proceeded Langland, and out of the latter Chaucer. The moment had come for a sharp and final contest between accentuated alliteration and rhyme. It was decided in favour of rhyme by the successes of Chaucer, but in the early part of the transitional period alliteration seemed to be in the ascendant. Many of the metrical romances mingled the two forms, usually in a fashion that was exceedingly ineffective and ungraceful.

The chivalrous and monastic romances of this purely mediæval period were, so far as we can now perceive, of little literary value. They were commonly mere imitations of translations; they owed their plots and even their sentiments to French precursors, and if they are now to be studied, it is solely on account of their interest for the philologist. It is believed that all through the second half of the fourteenth century these paraphrases were excessively numerous, especially in the West-Midland dialect, and their literary insignificance was extreme. They dealt with corrupt and fragmentary legends of the Arthurian cycle, or with allegories which owed their form and substance alike to that *Roman de la Rose*, which had so profoundly impressed itself upon the æsthetic sense of Europe. Every poet felt constrained to retire into a bower or a bed, and there be subjected to a vision which he repeated in verse when he awakened. Not Chaucer, not even Langland, disdained to employ this facile convention.

Among these monotonous romancists, most of them entirely anonymous, there emerges dimly the figure of one who was evidently a poet in the true sense, though not of a force sufficiently commanding to turn the tide of poetry in a new direction. This is the mysterious West-Midland writer, who, for want of a name, we have to call the author of *Sir Gawain and the Green Knight*. His works have come down to us in a solitary manuscript, and no contemporary notice of him has been discovered. There is, indeed, no external evidence to prove that the poet of *Sir Gawain* wrote the *Pearl, Cleanness,* and *Patience,* which accompany it, but the internal evidence is very strong. Not merely are these four poems highly similar in vocabulary and style, but they excel by a like altitude all other romances of their kind and age which are known to exist. There is repeated, moreover, in each of them a unique mood of austere spirituality, combined with a rare sense of visual beauty in a manner in itself enough to stamp the four poems as the work of one man. Until, then, further discoveries are made, we may be content to accept the author of *Sir Gawain and the Green Knight* as the first poet of modern England, and as a precursor, in measure, both of Langland and Chaucer. Mr. Gollancz, who has edited and paraphrased the *Pearl,* surprised at the excellence and complete obscurity of this poet, has hazarded the conjecture that he may be that Ralph Strode (the "philosophical Strode" of Chaucer's *Troilus and Cressida*) whose writings were so universally admired in the fourteenth century and seem to be now completely lost. This is a suggestion of which no more can be said than that it seems almost too good to be true.

There were many romances written on the story of Gawain during the later half of the fourteenth century. Our author took many of his details from the *Perceval* of Chrêtien de Troyes, and extended his poem to more than 2500 lines. It is a wild fairy-tale, full of extravagant and impossible adventures; full, too, of a marvellous sense of physical and moral beauty, the intense combination of which appears to me to form the distinctive feature of this poet. The same qualities, in more stern and didactic form, appear in *Cleanness*, which is a collection of Biblical paraphrases, and in *Patience*, which retells the story of Jonah; but they take fresh lustre in the singularly beautiful elegy on the daughter of the poet, which is called the *Pearl*. This poem, for modern taste a little too gemmed and glassy in its descriptive parts, possesses a delicate moral elevation which lifts it high above all other allegorical romances of its class. I am, however, inclined to set the poetical merits of *Sir Gawain and the Green Knight* higher still. The struggles of the knight to resist the seductions of Morgan la Fay are described in terms which must be attributed to the English poet's credit, and the psychology of which seems as modern as it is ingenious, while over the whole poem there is shed, like a magical dye, the sunset colour of the passing Age of Faith.

It seems on the whole to be probable that the charming poet, whom we do not dare to call Ralph Strode, composed the four works of which we have just spoken, between 1355 and 1360. In his hands the alliterative paraphrase of the fourteenth century reached its most refined expression. But the author of *Sir Gawain* had not the narrative force, nor the author of *Cleanness* the satiric fervour, to inaugurate a new school of English poetry. His sweet and cloistered talent, with its love of vivid colours, bright belts, sparkling jewels, and enamelled flowers, passed into complete obscurity at the approach of that vehement genius of which we have now to speak.

The earliest poem of high value which we meet with in modern English literature is the thrilling and mysterious *Vision of Piers Plowman.* According to the view which we choose to adopt, this brilliant satire may be taken as closing the mediæval fiction of England or as starting her modern popular poetry. *Visio willelmi de petro plowman* is the only title of this work which has come down to us, and the only contemporary hint of its authorship. Although the popularity of the poem was extreme, the writer is not mentioned in a single record. The Court poets were in the ascendant, and preserved each others' names; the author of the *Vision* was outside the pale of fashion, a preserver of antiquated forms, a barbarous opponent of French tendencies in culture. It is necessary, therefore, to make what use we can of reports set down long after his death, and still better, of what revelations he is induced to make in the course of his poem. All these have been carefully examined, and their conjectural result is sufficient to enable us to form a tolerably distinct portrait of one of the greatest writers of the Middle Ages.

There is little doubt that his name was WILLIAM LANGLAND (or William of Langley); that he was born, about 1332, at Cleobury Mortimer, in Shropshire; that he was of humble birth, though not of the humblest; that he was brought up for the Church, but never passed out of the lesser orders; that he suffered the loss of most that was dear to him in the great plague of 1349; that he came up to London and became a canonical singer— became, in fact, a chaunter at St. Paul's, by which he contrived to eke out a poor livelihood for Kit, his wife, and for Nicolette, his daughter. He was a poor man, "roaming about robed in russet," living, unseen, in a

little house in Cornhill. His youth was spent wandering
on the Malvern Hills, which left so deep an impress on
his imagination that he mentions them three times in a
poem otherwise essentially untopographical. It has been
thought that he returned to Malvern at the close of his
life; in 1399 he was probably at Bristol. He fades out
of our sight as the century closes. It was early reported
that he was a Benedictine at Worcester, and a fellow of
Oriel College at Oxford. Neither statement is confirmed,
and the second is highly improbable. Langland was a
man of the people, without social claims of any kind, an
observer of the trend of "average English opinion."

The *Vision of Piers Plowman* has come down to us in
not fewer than forty-five MS. copies. But these, on
collation, prove to belong to three distinct texts. It is
almost certain that Langland wrote the first draft of his
poem in 1362, rewrote it in 1377, and revised it again, with
large additions, somewhere between 1392 and 1398. Of
these, the earliest contains twelve, and the latest twenty-
three *passus* or cantos, the modifications being of so
general a character that the three texts may almost be
considered as distinct poems on the same subject. The
existence of the 1362 text gives Langland a remarkable
precedence among the poets of the age, a precedence
which is not always sufficiently recognised by those who
speak of Chaucer. It is improbable that we possess a line,
even of Chaucer's translation, earlier than about 1368,
while the literary value of Chaucer's work was for twenty
years after 1362 to remain much inferior to Langland's.
In the *Vision of Piers Plowman* the great alliterative school
of West-Midland verse culminated in a masterpiece, the
prestige of which preserves that school from being a
mere curiosity for the learned. In spite of its relative

difficulty, *Piers Plowman* will now always remain, with the *Canterbury Tales*, one of the two great popular classics of the fourteenth century.

While Chaucer and the other Court poets, with an instinctive sense of the direction which English prosody would take, accepted the new metrical system, introduced from Italy and France, Langland remained obstinately faithful to the old English verse, the unrhymed alliterative line of four beats, of which his poem is now the best-known type and example :

> " *And then lùted Lóve in a loùd nótĕ,*
> *Till the ddy dàwned these dàmsels dáncĕd,*"

in its most obvious form ; in its more rugged shape :

> " *I have as much pity of póor men as pédlar hath of cáts*
> *That would kíll them, if he cátch them might, for cóvetise of their skíns.*"

It is a mistake to seek for perfect accuracy in Langland's versification. He hurries on, often in breathless intensity, and he does not trouble to consider whether he has the proper number of " rhyme-letters " (the initial letters of the strong syllables), or whether the syllables themselves are not sometimes weak. The great thing is to hasten forward, to pour forth the torrent of moral passion. The poem should be read aloud, impetuously but somewhat monotonously, and when the reader has grasped the scheme of the metre its difficulties will be found to have disappeared.

The poem which is generically called the *Visio de petro plowman* consists of several portions which are not closely or very intelligibly welded together. It must be remembered that Langland is essentially inartistic : he has no concern with the construction of his poem or the balance of its parts. He has a solemn word to say to

2

England, and he must say it; but the form in which he says it is immaterial to him. He does not address a critical audience; he speaks to the common people, in common verse: he is *vates*, not *artifex*, and for those who trouble themselves about the exterior parts of poetry he has a rude disdain. Even the figure of Piers Plowman, which gives name to the whole, is not once introduced until we are half through the original draft of the poem. Of the three texts, that of 1377 is usually considered the most perfect. This consists of a prologue, in which the allegorical vision is introduced, and of four cantos mainly dealing with the adventures of Meed the Maid; then follow, in three more cantos, the Vision of the Seven Deadly Sins, who repent, and are led to the shrine of Divine Truth by a mysterious ploughman named Piers. This first poem ends, rather abruptly, with a contest between Piers and a worldly priest about the validity of indulgences.

To this, the proper *Vision of Piers Plowman*, are appended the three long poems, in the same metre, named *Do-well*, *Do-bet* (that is *better*), and *Do-best*. These defy analysis, for they proceed upon no distinct lines. *Do-well* is mainly didactic and hortative; its sermons made a deep impression on the contemporary conscience. Modern readers, however, will turn with greater pleasure to *Do-bet*, which contains the magnificent scene of the Harrowing of Hell, which was not equalled for pure sublimity in English poetry until Milton wrote. By this time the reader perceives that Piers Plowman has become a disguise of Christ Himself, Christ labouring for souls, a man with men. In *Do-bet* the stormy gloom which hangs over most of Langland's threatening and denun-ciatory verse is lifted; the eighteenth canto closes in a diapason of lutes, of trumpets, "men ringing to the resurrection," and all the ghosts of spiritual darkness fleeing from the splendour of Easter morning. In *Dobest* the poet's constitutional melancholy settles upon him again. He sees life once more as it is—broken, bitter, full of disappointment and anguish. He awakens weeping, having seen Conscience start on a hopeless pilgrimage in search of the lost and divine Plowman.

In the form of his great work Langland adopts the mediæval habit of the dream. But this is almost his only concession to Latin forms. Alone among the principal writers of his age he looks away from Europe, continues the old Teutonic tradition, and is satisfied with an inspiration that is purely English. That he had read the *Roman de la Rose* and the *Pélerinage* of Deguileville is not to be doubted; recent investigations into the work and life of Rutebeuf (1230 ?–1300 ?) have revealed resemblances between his religious satires and those of Langland which can hardly be accidental. It is now recognised that the vocabulary of the *Vision* contains no fewer French words than that of Chaucer, from which, indeed, it can scarcely be distinguished. But the whole temper and tendency of Langland is English, is anti-French; he is quite insulated from Continental sympathies. He is an example of what thoughtful middle-class Englishmen were in the last years of Edward III., during the great wars with France, and while the plague, in successive spasms, was decimating the country.

The *Vision* is full of wonderful pictures of the life of the poor. Langland was no Wycliffite, as was early supposed; in his denunciations of clerical abuse there was no element of heterodoxy. He saw but one thing, the necessity of upright individual conduct; of this conduct the ploughman on the Malvern Hills was one with Pope or Christ—a living representation of that essential Truth which is deity. The main elements in his stormy volubility are sincerity and pity. Piers is "Truth's pilgrim at the plough"; he is obliged to expose the rich in their greediness, their cruelty, their lasciviousness. Nor does he see the poor as spotless lambs, but their sorrows fill him with a divine pity, such a tenderness of heart as modern literature had not until that time expressed, such as modern life had until then scarcely felt. Another view of *Piers Plowman* M. Jusserand acutely notes when he says that it "almost seems a commentary on the Rolls of Parliament." It is an epitome of the social and political life of England, and particularly of London, seen from within and from below, without regard to what might be thought above and outside the class of workers. It is the foundation of the democratic literature of England, and a repository of picturesque observations absolutely unique and invaluable.

The firmness with which Langland began, and the inflexibility with which he continued his life's work in poetry, strangely contrast with the uncertain and tentative steps which his greater coeval took in the practice of his art. It is now generally believed that the birth of GEOFFREY CHAUCER must have taken place not long before and not long after 1338; if this be the case, he was probably about six years the junior of Langland. But Chaucer was thirty-five years of age before he saw his way to the production of anything really valuable in verse. His career first throws light on his literary vocation when we learn that, in 1359, he took part in Edward III.'s famous invasion of France. He was taken prisoner in a skirmish in Burgundy, and was ransomed by the King; after nearly a year on French soil Chaucer returned to England. It is not easy to overrate the importance of this expedition, made at the very age when the perceptions are most vivid. France set its seal on the genius of the poet, and already, we cannot doubt, the bias of his mind was formed. He was the personal servant of the King's daughter-in-law; he must have shown himself courtly, for he presently becomes *valet de chambre* to Edward himself. In this his early youth, while Langland is identifying himself in poverty with the ploughmen of the Malvern Hills, Chaucer is taking for life the stamp of a courtier and a man of fashion.

He developed an ardent admiration for the chivalrous and courtly poets of the France of his own day; he read, and presently he imitated, Machault, Guillaume de Deguileville, Eustache Deschamps, and the less-known master whom he calls "Graunson, flower of them that make in France." He takes their emblems, their blossoms, their conventional forms, and prepares to introduce them, with unparalleled elegance, to gentle readers in England. But still more than these his contemporaries, he admires the old masters of allegory, Lorris and Meung, whose *Roman de la Rose,* in not less than twenty-two thousand verses, had now for nearly a hundred years been the model and masterpiece of all mediæval French poetry. To study French verse in 1360 was to find the prestige of the *Roman de la Rose* absolutely predominant. Poetry could scarcely be conceived of, save in relation with that laborious allegory, so tedious to us in its primitive psychology, so intensely fascinating and seductive to the puerile imagination of the Middle Ages. It was natural that Chaucer's first essay should be to place this masterpiece in English hands, and accordingly a translation of the *Romaunt of the Rose* is the earliest known production of the English poet.

That he completed this labour of love is uncertain. Deschamps, in a famous ballad addressed to that " grant translateur, noble Geoffroy Chaucier," compliments him on having scattered the petals and planted the tree of the Rose in the Island of the Giants, Albia. But it is now believed that only the first 1705 lines of the translation which we possess are Chaucer's, and even these have been questioned. He certainly translated, about 1366, an *A, B, C,* from Deguileville of Chalis ; this we possess, and an original poem of about the same date, the *Complaint unto Pity*, interesting because in it we find the earliest known example of that very important national stanzaic form, the *rime royal* of seven lines on three rhymes. In 1369 the Duchess Blanche of Gaunt died, and Chaucer celebrated her virtues in a long octosyllabic poem, in the course of which he told the story of Alcyone and Ceyx. This is his first appearance as a leading English writer, although it is more than possible that he had already written creditable works which time has neglected to spare.

In the *Book of the Duchess* the hand of Chaucer is still untrained, but that element of freshness, of April dewiness and laughing brightness, which was to continue to be his primal quality, is already prominent. Even on so sad an occasion he cannot keep out of his elegy the pure blue blaze of noon, the red and white of fallen flowers, the song of birds, the murmur of summer foliage. The great John of Gaunt is himself introduced, in a turn of the forest, and the poet with delicate tact persuades him to describe his wife and so regain composure. Chaucer owed much to Machault in the external machinery of this poem, which extends to thirteen hundred lines, but the pathos and the charm are all his own. That he wrote many other juvenile poems before he reached the age of thirty or thirty-five, may be taken for certain, but they are lost to us. It is possible that the loss is not serious, for Chaucer was still in bondage to the French, and it is highly unlikely that he dared, as yet, to sail away from the convention of his masters.

He did not learn to be an original poet until he had passed through France and left it behind him. In 1372 he went on the King's business to Genoa and Florence, and this was the first of several Italian expeditions, in the course of which his eyes were singularly opened to the budding glories of the Renaissance, and his ears tuned to the liquid magic of Italian verse. It may be conjectured that he was chosen for this mission because of his unusual acquaintance with the Italian tongue. It is difficult not to be convinced that he enjoyed the conversation of Petrarch, though if he had known Boccaccio personally he would hardly have called him Lollius ; he certainly brought back to England the first echo of the fame of Tuscan poetry and the first warmth of its influence on European letters. Both these poets scarcely survived Chaucer's first visit to their country. The ten years, however, from 1372 to 1382 have left little mark on Chaucer's actual production, so far as it has come down to us. We may attribute to the close of that decade the *Complaint of Mars* and the *Parliament of Fowls*, poems of no very great value in themselves, but interesting as showing that Chaucer had completely abandoned his imitation of French models, in favour of a style more fully his own, and more in harmony with classical and Italian taste.   In the latter of these pieces the study of Dante and of Boccaccio is undisguised.   Still, it is curious to observe that at the age of about forty-five, one of the greatest poets of Europe had, so far as we know, composed absolutely nothing which could give him prominence in literary history.

The excitement caused by the great democratic or socialistic rising of 1381 was followed by, and perhaps resulted in, a marvellous quickening of intellectual life in England.   There was an immediate revival in all the branches of literature, and it is to this approximate date that we owe the *Bible* of Wycliffe and the romance of *Sir John Mandeville;* now Gower, observing that "few men indite our English," set down the Latin of his *Vox Clamantis* in order that he might compose a long poem in English "for King Richard's sake."   Chaucer, too, who so long while had been falteringly learning and attempting to practise the art of song, ventured, about 1382, on the composition of the *Troilus and Cressida*, the first work in which the magnificence of Chaucer reveals itself.   This was an adaptation of *Il Filostrato* of Boccaccio, in five long books of rime royal.   It has been shown that Chaucer was not content with a translation from the Italian, which would have occupied but a third of his poem, but that more than half is, so far as we can discover, entirely his own invention.   He used the text of Boccaccio, whom he mysteriously names "Lollius," as a centre round which to weave the embroideries of his own fancy, and it is a critical error to dismiss *Troilus and Cressida* as a mere paraphrase.   It is essentially an original poem of great value and significance.   The careful study of this *epos* has revealed the fact that Chaucer's knowledge of

Italian literature was not slight and superficial, as had been supposed, but profound. He quotes, in the course of *Troilus and Cressida*, from Dante, Petrarch, Benoît, the *Teseide* of Boccaccio, and the Latin *Trojan History* of Guido delle Colonne. While fascinated by the vigour of these new sources of inspiration, he seems to have wholly laid aside his study of his old beloved but languid poets of France.

It may fairly be said that the narrative love-poetry of England, which has developed in so many and so rich directions, practically opens with Chaucer's delicate, melancholy *Troilus and Cressida*. In the last book of this work so little trace is found of that jollity and gust of life which are held to be the special characteristics of this great poet, that it has been conjectured that Chaucer was now passing through some distressing crisis in his private life. This sadness is certainly continued in what is his next contribution to literature, the unfinished but extended visionary poem called the *House of Fame*. This piece is written in octosyllabic rhymed verse, such as Barbour had employed in the *Bruce* some ten years earlier. It bears very numerous traces of the careful study of Dante; but no Italian poem has been discovered of which it can be considered a paraphrase. In the *House of Fame* Chaucer is seen to have gained great ease and skill, to have learned to proceed without reference to any model or master, and to have discovered how to use that native fund of humour which he had hitherto kept in abeyance. In short, it is here that we first begin to catch the personal voice of Chaucer, a sound such as English literature had never heard before in all the centuries of its existence.

The spring of 1385 is the date now believed to be that

at which Chaucer composed his next great work, the admirable *Legend of Good Women.* It consists of a prologue, followed by nine (or rather ten) stories of virtuous classical heroines. The style of this poem exemplifies a sudden advance in Chaucer's art, for which it is difficult to account; and there is evidence that it was regarded with astonishment by contemporary readers, as something which revealed a beauty hitherto undreamed of. Here also he first adventures upon the definition and evolution of character, the ten "good women" being distinguished from one another by numerous traits of psychology, delicately observed. It is to be noticed, moreover, that it is in the *Legend of Good Women* that Chaucer first employs his greatest gift to English prosody, the heroic couplet of five beats each line.

> " *A thousand timës have I heard men tell*
> *That there is joy in heav'n and pain in hell*"—

so the Prologue opens, and this is the earliest of many tens of thousands of "correct" ten-syllable couplets in English. It is here that Chaucer adopts the daisy as his flower of flowers, inventing a pretty legend that Alcestis was transformed into a marguerite. But this blossom had been adopted before his time by Machault and others, Margaret being a common Christian name in the royal house of France. Chaucer owed the idea of this poem to Boccaccio, but in the treatment of it there is little or no trace of exotic influences. He had now learned to walk alone, without even a staff to support his footsteps. We hasten on, however, because the *Legend of Good Women,* admirable and charming as it is, seems to the general student to be but the vestibule leading us to and preparing us for the vast and splendid temple of the *Canterbury Tales.*

It is believed that Chaucer was approaching his fiftieth year when it occurred to him to illustrate the daily life of his age in England by means of a series of metrical tales fitted into a framework of humorous reflection and description. The phrase of Dryden cannot be bettered: Chaucer took "into the compass of his *Canterbury Tales* the various manners and humours of the whole English nation." He had been gradually rejecting the laboured tradition of the past; he had been gradually freeing himself from the vain repetitions, the elegant, bloodless conventions, the superficial and artificial graces of the mediæval minstrels. He had, after long labour, and careful comparative study of Italian models, contrived to create a form, a method of expression, which was extremely distinguished and entirely individual to himself. One thing remained undone, namely, to put this new manner of writing at the disposal of a thoroughly new and a thoroughly national subject. This he would now, about 1386, begin to do, and by that act would rise into the first order of the world's poets.

It is the opinion of Mr. Skeat that the first of the *Canterbury Tales* to be conceived was the Monk's Tale, and that this was originally designed to form part of a Legend of Good Men, which was presently merged in the larger work. There can be no question that Chaucer was long engaged in collecting material for his great panoramic poem before he began to put the parts of it into such sequence as they now possess. Moreover, we cannot doubt that he had by him abundant stores of verse, composed earlier, and with no thought of the

Canterbury Tales. Mr. W. S. McCormick points out as examples of this incorporated matter, the " Legend of St. Cecile," which required no change, and "Palemon and Arcite," which had to be rewritten. Until Henry Bradshaw, with his brilliant critical instinct, discovered or divined the plan on which the *Canterbury Tales* must have been executed, the work appeared simply chaotic. Further investigation has so far cleared up the plan, that we are now able to realise fairly well how the edifice rose in the architect's imagination, although but a fragment was ever built. It is fortunate, indeed, that Chaucer lived to complete the Prologue, which is not merely one of the most enchanting of all poems, but is absolutely essential to us in any consideration of the aim of its author.

From the Prologue we learn that Chaucer's idea was to collect at the Tabard Inn a number of persons, representative of all ranks and classes in his day, all proposing to start together on a pilgrimage. Each pilgrim

> " *In this voyage shall tellen talēs twain—*
> *To Canterbury-ward, I mean it so,*
> *And homeward he shall tellen other two,*"

each pilgrim, therefore, telling four tales in all. This would have implied the writing of at least a hundred and twenty narrative poems, and it seems astonishing that Chaucer, whose health, we may surmise, was already failing, and who looked upon himself as an old man, should have been ready to adventure upon so vast an enterprise. As it is, we possess about twenty-five finished tales, a great mass of poetical literature, and as much, perhaps, as we could now study with profit ; yet, as we should always realise, not a fourth part of what the poet planned. That the writings of Chaucer (*Troilus and Cressida* being the main exception) form a succession of fragments, each abandoned as if in a fury of artistic impatience to make room for a more ambitious scheme, and that the last and most splendid is the most fragmentary of all, these are, indeed, pathetic considerations. Like Leonardo da Vinci in another art, the zeal of Chaucer was insatiable, and in trying to secure all the perfections he brought no important enterprise to completion.

The pilgrims start in merriment from the Tabard, but they never arrive at Canterbury ; the supper which mine host was to give to the best teller was never eaten and never ordered. The pilgrim who spoke first was the Knight, whose tale of " Palemon and Arcite" had doubtless been for some time in the poet's desk, since it exemplifies the imitation of Boccaccio which Chaucer had by 1387 outworn ; it is the poet's grandest achievement in his Italian manner. This tale has a noble remoteness from the ordinary joys and sorrows of mankind ; it is suitably placed in the mouth of " a very perfect, gentle knight" ; but Chaucer, whose one design was to escape from the superfine monotony of fourteenth-century literature, and to speak in variety and freshness to the common reader, immediately relieves the strain by permitting the rude Miller, with his coarse and humorous tale, to burst in. These transitions are managed with great tact, and, no doubt, if Chaucer had completed his design, they would have been universal ; some dignified or feminine figure would doubtless have separated the Miller from the Reeve. We have an instance of Chaucer's feeling in this matter in the case of the Prioress's Tale, where the poignant story of Hugh of Lincoln is preluded by the Shipman's gross and "merry" anecdote, and succeeded by the portentous parody of " Sir Thopas." The tendency of the age had run too heavily in the direction of lugubrious and fatal narratives ; Chaucer, keenly alive to the wants of the general reader, sees that the facetious element must no longer be omitted, nay, must actually preponderate, if the *Canterbury Tales* is to be a great popular poem. Hence it is probable that as he progressed with the evolution of his scheme, tragedies were more and more excluded in favour of fun and high spirits, and that the complexion of the work was growing more and more cheerful up to the moment when it was suddenly stopped by Chaucer's death. It is particularly to be noted that Chaucer brings a specimen of every then familiar form of literature into his scheme — animal stories, fabliaux comic and serious, chivalric romances, Italian legends, ballads, sermons, traveller's tales or magic, Breton lays ; in short, whatever could be expected to form the intellectual pabulum of his readers was so much grist to his mill, drawn in to increase the variety and widen the scope of his variegated picture of life.

Chaucer is the last and in certain aspects the greatest of the mediæval poets of Europe. Boccaccio had seen the need of popularising the sources of poetry, of breaking down the thorny hedge of aristocratic protection which guarded the rose of imagination from vulgar hands ; but it was Chaucer who let the fresh winds of heaven into that over-perfumed and over-privileged enclosure. As Dante and Petrarch had immortalised the spiritual dignity and delicacy of the Middle Age, as Villon was to record in words of fire the squalid sufferings of its poor, so Chaucer summed up the social pleasures and aspirations of its burgher class in verses that remained without a rival. In an age preoccupied with ideas and images, Chaucer, by extraordinary good luck, had the originality to devote himself to character. Practically without a guide, and restrained by the novelty and difficulty of his task, he did not achieve his true work until old age had come upon him, and we are tantalised to find him taken from us at the very moment when he had at last achieved a complete mastery over his material. What Chaucer might not have produced had he lived ten years longer no one can endure to conjecture.

For what he has left us, fragmentary and tentative though it be, our gratitude should be unbounded. This is by far the greatest name in our literature until Shakespeare be reached. In the last ten years of the fourteenth century, Chaucer not merely provided us with a mass of enchanting verse, but he lifted the literature of his country out of its barbarous isolation and subserviency, and placed it in the foremost rank. It was not Chaucer's fault if a feebler race, succeeding him, let England slip back into a secondary or even a tertiary place. When he died, barely over sixty years of age, in 1400, not one writer in Europe surpassed him in reputation, not one approached him in genius. The advance which he had made in psychology was immense ; it was actually premature, for no one was discovered, even in Italy, who could take advantage of his intelligent pre-eminence, and reach from that standpoint to still higher things. If the fifteenth century in Italy failed to take advantage of the examples of Petrarch and Boccaccio, still more truly may we say that in England it neglected to comprehend the discoveries of Chaucer. His splendid art was misunderstood, his quick and brilliant insight into human nature obscured, and a partial return to barbarism succeeded his splendid poetic civilisation. Appreciate his contemporaries and followers as we will, the closer our comparative study is, the more completely do we become convinced of the incomparable pre-eminence of Chaucer.

The prosody of Chaucer's later and more elaborate works is not, as was so long supposed, an arbitrary or a loose one. Even Dryden knew no better than to discover in the verse of the *Canterbury Tales* "a rude sweetness of a Scotch tune"; it is obvious that he was quite unable to scan it. It was, on the contrary, not merely not "rude," but an artistic product of the utmost delicacy and niceness, a product which borrowed something from the old national measure, but was mainly an introduction into English of the fixed prosodies of the French and the Italians, the former for octosyllabic, the latter for decasyllabic verse. The rules of both, but especially the latter, are set, and of easy comprehension; to learn to read Chaucer with a fit appreciation of the liquid sweetness of his versification is as easy an accomplishment as to learn to scan classical French verse, or easier. But it must be remembered that, in its polished art, it was a skill fully known only to its founder, and that, with Chaucer's death, the power to read his verses as he wrote them seems immediately to have begun to disappear. Chaucer gave English poetry an admirable prosody, but it was too fine a gift to be appreciated by those for whom it was created.

An absence of critical judgment, at which it is needless to affect surprise, led the contemporaries and successors of Chaucer to mention almost upon equal terms with him his friend and elder JOHN GOWER. To modern criticism this comparison has seemed, what indeed it is, preposterous, and we have now gone a little too far in the opposite direction. Gower is accused of extreme insipidity by those who, perhaps, have not read much of the current poetry of his day. He is sinuous, dull, uniform, but he does not deserve to be swept away with scorn. Much of his work has great historical value, much of it is skilfully narrated, and its long-winded author persists in producing some vague claim to be considered a poet. Gower was probably ten or fifteen years older than Chaucer. His early French verse has mainly disappeared; but we possess his Latin *Vox Clamantis*, and, what is much more important, his English poem in 30,000 verses, the *Confessio Amantis*. Of this there are two existing versions, the first dedicated to Richard II., and composed about 1383, in which Chaucer is mentioned with friendly compliment; the other dedicated to Henry IV., and possessing no mention of Chaucer, the date being about 1393.

The *Confessio Amantis* consists of a prologue and eight books, in octosyllabic rhymed verse. The prologue is a strange prophetical performance, in the course of which the poet sketches the history of the world. In the body of the poem, the author, as a lover in despair, receives a visit from Venus, who commends him for confession to Genius, her priest. The lover's statement of his symptoms and experience fills seven of the books, the eighth being occupied by his cure and absolution. The statement is constantly interrupted by the disquisitions of Genius, who tells one hundred and twelve stories by way of illustration of the passions. Those who depreciate Gower should recollect that this was the earliest large compendium of tales produced in the English language. Gower's use of English was far from being so consistent or so firm as that of Chaucer. He wavered between

3

French, Latin, and English, and was an old man before he persuaded himself to employ the new composite tongue. He was an aristocrat, and it was with hesitation that he persuaded himself to quit the courtly French tongue. About 1399 Gower wrote an English poem in rime royal, the *Praise of Peace*, and lived on, *cæcus et senex*, until 1408, the admirer and panegyrist of Henry IV. to the last.

The Northern dialect was illustrated by a great number of writers, most of them anonymous, and either retaining the alliterative forms of verse, or trying to adapt them to romance metres. Among these, to HUCHOWN are attributed the romances of *Sweet Susan* and the *Great Geste of Arthur*. Whether the fine Scottish paraphrase of *Lancelot of the Lake*, which Mr. Skeat has printed, is due to the same vague Huchown, or Hugh, is uncertain. There was a whole crop of Gawain and Arthur romances in the Northern dialect ; but by far the most considerable poet of Scotland in the fourteenth century was JOHN BARBOUR, Archdeacon of Aberdeen, who repeatedly visited France, and who, in a limited and inelastic but quite undeniable shape, accepted or independently invented a Southern prosody, not unlike that of Chaucer, but founded in imitation of the *Roman de la Rose*. It would seem that the writings of Barbour were once extremely numerous, but only those of his late age survive. About 1375, being then probably sixty years old, he began his long historical romance of the *Bruce*, which we still possess, which enjoyed an immense popularity, and which is usually considered one of the glories of Scottish literature. Barbour also wrote a *Book of Troy*, of which fragments are preserved, and after he was seventy composed, in conventional paraphrase, a *Legend of the Saints*, of which more than thirty thousand verses have been printed. He was evidently a very abundant writer, since the names of other important works of his have come down to us.

It is by the *Bruce* alone, however, that we have to judge Barbour. This is not a mere chronicle in octosyllabic rhymed verse; it is a national epic of real value. Barbour is not a brilliant writer, and, in strange contradistinction to the Scotch poets who followed him, he is austerely bare of ornament. He tells a patriotic story very simply and fluently, with a constant appeal to chivalrous instincts, and with a remarkable absence of all mythological machinery. The *Bruce*, which is now commonly divided into twenty long books, is the chief literary relic of old Scotland, and has, perhaps, never ceased to make a successful appeal to the *ingenium perfervidum Scotorum.* The intensity of Barbour's sense of the value of political independence, expressed in lines such as

> "*Ah! freedom is a noble thing . . .*
> *He lives at ease that freely lives,*"

adds a sympathetic beauty to his otherwise somewhat bald and dry historical narratives. His absence of pedantry, his singular passion for truth in an age given up to vagueness about fact, and his large grasp of events, make us regret Barbour's tantalising lack of inspiration. At the close of his life he indited that enormous translation of the *Legenda Aurea* which has been already mentioned, and which they may read who can.

In spite of the great importance and popularity of Langland's *Vision*, the retrograde and insular manner of writing did not hold its own against the new prosody and the influences from Italy and France. Much, however, was still written in the early alliterative manner, and an anonymous Wycliffite, in the very last years of the century, produced a powerful satire, entitled *Piers the Ploughman's Creed*, extending to more than eight hundred verses. It is thought that to the same hand we owe the *Ploughman's Tale*, long bound up among the poems of Chaucer, to whose language and manner of writing it bears no resemblance. The *Creed* is the better piece of the two ; it is imitative of Langland, but its great vivacity of style, and its value as illuminating the condition of the middle and lower classes, and the dissensions in the English Church, can scarcely be exaggerated. In this poem the ploughman has no supernatural character or attributes. The description of a rich Dominican convent is perhaps the best-known specimen of a powerful poem to the importance of which, strangely enough, Pope was the first to draw attention. The author, though he had not the vehement energy of Langland, was a close and picturesque observer of manners. The date of the *Creed* has been conjectured as 1394, and that of the *Tale* as some years earlier than 1399. Another work of somewhat the same class, *Richard the Redeless*, an expostulation with Richard II., has now pretty definitely been assigned to the old age of Langland himself. It is to be supposed that a vast amount of occasional verse of this national kind was produced, but did not survive till the invention of printing.

As early as the twelfth century we find evidences of the performance in England of pageants and miracle plays in which the rudiments of the modern drama must have been observable. The earliest existing specimens, however, date from the fourteenth century, and we are able to judge of the literary value of these mysteries from the cycle of York Plays, forty-eight of which are preserved in an almost contemporary MS. We find the drama here no longer in a perfectly primitive state ; it is freed from the liturgical ritual and manipulated by the hands of laymen. It is difficult to assign a date to the York Plays, but they are conjectured to have been composed between 1350 and 1380. They are written in rhyme, and most of them in stanzas ; they deal with passages of the Bible, treated in such a way as to lead us to believe that what we possess is but a fragment of a vast dramatisation of the Scripture narrative, composed for a popular stage, and played by the city guilds in Corpus Christi week. The historical and linguistic interest of these miracle pageants, of course, greatly exceeds their purely literary value. It would be absurd to take them too seriously as dramatic poems ; yet there is not merely much vivacity and humour in their comic scenes, but an occasional felicity of expression when they deal with the solemn portions of the story which they popularised. There were also Corpus Christi mysteries at Beverley, Chester, Woodkirk, and Coventry.; the Reformation put a stop to them all.

The splendid revival of poetry in England during the fourteenth century was accompanied by no similar awakening in prose. Our authors continued to affect the same lisping, stumbling speech to which earlier generations had accustomed themselves. It is no ill task for a student to compare the prose treatises of Chaucer with his poetry, the latter so supple, brilliant, and vital, the former so dull and inert. The prose of the second half of the fourteenth century is almost entirely translated ; hardly any original performance of an English mind in it is worthy to be named.

About 1387 there was composed a prose treatise, entitled

the *Testament of Love*, which Mr. Bradley, with extraordinary ingenuity, has shown to have been written, probably
in prison, by THOMAS USK, a London citizen who fell
under the displeasure of the Duke of Gloucester, and was
barbarously executed.   It is a rambling sort of psychological autobiography, in imitation of Boethius.   Usk
praises that " noble, philosophical poet," Chaucer, while
in his prologue he derides the habit of composing all
serious matters in Latin or in French, and recommends
his own book as a conspicuous innovation, so that he
may be thought to have been before the age in critical
insight.   But to read the *Testament of Love* is to tramp
across acres of dry sand.   The art of being interesting in
prose of English invention was yet to be discovered.

Two translations, the one lay, the other sacred, represent at its highest level of excellence the prose of the end
of the century.   The most picturesque production of the
age is certainly the former of these, that geographical
romance called the *Travels of Sir John Mandeville.*   These
spurious memoirs of a traveller who did not travel, were
written in French, as is now believed, by a certain Bearded
John of Burgundy, the pseudonym, perhaps, of an Englishman who had fled from his own country and lived
under that disguise at Liège.   The original text was not
circulated until about 1371 ; the admirable English version is some years later.   *Sir John Mandeville* is a tissue
of plagiarisms from early travellers, carefully woven
together by a person who has enjoyed little personal
opportunity of observation.   This absurd book, which
gulled the age to an amazing degree, is full of charm in
its original form, and tells its incredible tales in the best
mediæval manner ; it has always been a storehouse of
romantic anecdote.   It was of great service to the national

speech, since, whoever the translator was, he wrote a
more graceful and fluent prose than any Englishman
had done before him.

A still more epoch-making event in English prose was
the formation of that paraphrase of the Vulgate which is
known as *Wycliffe's Bible*. This was a composite work,
which occupied several heterodox hands from about
1380 to 1388. JOHN WYCLIFFE'S career as a reforming
Churchman had already reached its apogee before it
appears to have occurred to him, possibly under the
influence of Langland's great poem, that to appeal to
the masses of the English nation it was necessary to write
in their own language, and not, as he had hitherto so
effectively done, in Latin. His energy was thereupon,
during the four remaining years of his life, set on the
cultivation of the vernacular, and, above all, on the editing, for the first time, of a complete Bible in English.
He seems to have set his friend Nicholas of Hereford to
translate the Old Testament, and when that disciple, to
escape recantation, fled to Rome in 1382, his work was
found to be complete up to the middle of Baruch.
Wycliffe himself finished the Apocrypha, his version of
the New Testament being already done. He died in
1384, leaving his pupil and curate John Purvey, the
librarian of the Lollards, to revise the whole translation,
a task which was completed in 1388. The general
Prologue to the whole Bible is believed to be the work
of Purvey; but the entire question of the authorship of
the Wycliffite books remains very obscure.

It is impossible to overestimate the gift of Wycliffe to
English prose in placing the Bible at the command of
every common reader. But the value of Wycliffe as an
independent writer may easily be exaggerated. If we

compare his New Testament with the work of Nicholas of Hereford, we may conjecture that Wycliffe had a certain conception of style undreamed of by his wooden disciple. But his own manner is exceedingly hard and wearisome, without suppleness of form. His sentences—except, occasionally, in his remarkable *Sermons*—follow certain Latinised formulas with fatiguing monotony. The danger which beset English prose at this time was that it might continue to lie inert in the state of clumsy flatness into which the decay of Anglo-Saxon influences, and the too-slavish following of Latin educational literature, had plunged it. As a matter of fact, it did lie there for some centuries, very slowly and very uncertainly rising in the wake of English verse to the dignity of harmonious art.

II

THE CLOSE OF THE MIDDLE AGES

1400–1560

IT is difficult to find any political or social reason for the literary decadence of the close of the Middle Ages, but the fact is patent that the reigns of the three Henries in England were marked by a strange and complete decline in the arts of composition. Not a single work of signal merit, whether in prose or verse, distinguishes the first half of the fifteenth century, and we are forced, in order to preserve the historical sequence, to record the careers and writings of men who at no other period would demand particular attention in a survey so rapid as this. In consequence, it is imperative that we should dwell a little on the productions of Occleve and Lydgate, although the original talent of these versifiers was small and their acquired skill almost contemptible. They are interesting, less from their pretensions to imagination than from this semi-official position as recognised makers of verse, carrying on the tradition of poetry, though with none of its ecstasy and charm.

That Occleve and Lydgate were so imperfect in their grasp of those principles of poetry which Chaucer had formulated as to be unable to produce verse which had a superficial resemblance to his, is the more curious when we consider that they had enjoyed, or certainly might have enjoyed, the advantage of that master's personal instruction.   Each of them was evidently more than thirty when Chaucer died.   Of the two, THOMAS OCCLEVE may have. been slightly the elder.   Neither had any real conception of the aim of Chaucer's work, or of the progress in intellectual civilisation which he had made.   Even to remain where Chaucer left them was too much for these feeble bards to achieve; they crept back into the barbarism of mediocrity.   They imitated with great humbleness those very Frenchmen whom Chaucer had outgrown and had left behind him, and in their timid, trembling hands English literature ceased to command the respect of Europe.   .   .

Their very peculiar prosody, which offers far greater difficulty than those of Langland and Chaucer, is only intelligible if we conjecture that they never understood or early forgot the meaning of Chaucer's elaborate and scientific versification.   Occleve, who had been close to Chaucer, had a greater appreciation of the new smoothness and grace than JOHN LYDGATE, who had a most defective ear, and knew it.   His verses are not to be scanned unless we suppose that he refused to follow Chaucer in the employment of a solid and coherent Southern prosody, but endeavoured to combine the use of rhyme and a measure of stanzaic form, with some remnant of the old national verse, retaining its strong accents and its groups of redundant syllables.   Lydgate's native speech was Suffolk, and he used throughout life Saxon forms and habits of locution which were unfamiliar and even uncouth to a courtly London ear.   Many critics, of whom the poet Gray was the earliest, have attempted to explain away the seeming rudeness of Lydgate, and to minimise the mean impression which he gives.   But no argument will make his metrical experiments appear successful, nor remove the conviction, of which he was himself conscious, that his ear was bad and tuneless.

Occleve was a frivolous, tame-spirited creature, tainted with insanity. He is fond of chatting about himself, and, among other confidences, informs us that Chaucer wished him to be properly taught, but that the pupil "was dull, and learned little or naught." Occleve speaks so humbly of his own poetical performances that it would be harsh to dwell on their tedious character. The *De Regimine Principum* (*The Governail of Princes*), which seems to date from 1411, is written in Occleve's favourite rime royal, and gives us as clear an impression of the man himself, of his style, of his views regarding contemporary history, and of his attitude towards the new English language, as could be gained by a laborious study of the remainder of his long-winded, monotonous works. It is a brave spirit which tires not before the five thousand lines of the *De Regimine* are closed, and one wonders whether Henry V., for whose use the poem was composed, ever became familiar with its contents. The author, who represents himself as "ripe unto the pit" with the results of an unseemly life, and as so cowardly that he only backbites those whom he dislikes, had certainly not fallen into the sin of pride. We forgive much to him, because he preserved for us the coloured portrait of Chaucer.

It is no great praise of Lydgate to say that he had a brisker talent than Occleve: Although he is careful to speak of Chaucer with constant respect, he is hardly, as Occleve was, his pupil. He rather imitates, often quite servilely and as though Chaucer had never written, the great French romantic poets of the fourteenth century.

A large part of Lydgate's life was spent in the Benedictine monastery of Bury St. Edmunds, from which he made occasional excursions to Oxford and Paris. The fecundity of Lydgate was phenomenal; Ritson, who deciphered his manuscripts until he must have hated the poet's very name, catalogued two hundred and fifty of his poems; it is said that at his death his existing verses must have exceeded 130,000 in number. No one living has read Lydgate in his entirety, and but few of his works have yet been edited. The excessive prolixity and uniformity of his style, which never rises and cannot fall, baffles all but the most persistent reader. His *Troy Book* is a translation from the Latin of Guido delle Colonne; his *Temple of Glass* a continuation of the *House of Fame;* his *Falls of Princes* an imitation of a French paraphrase of Boccaccio, but little distinction of style can be perceived, whether the laborious epic is adapted from Italian or English or French sources. The *Falls of Princes,* printed in 1494, and accepted in the sixteenth century as a mediæval classic, has been the most popular of the longer poems of Lydgate. It is believed to have been completed as late as 1438, and it displays in interesting ways the rapid development and modernisation of the English tongue. The student who desires to receive a favourable impression of the talent of Lydgate may be recommended to select the prologue of this enormous poem; he will be rewarded by a conventional but pleasing eulogy of Chaucer. Lydgate, as Gray says, "wanted not art in raising the more tender emotions of the mind," and, on occasion, he can be diffusely picturesque.

It is not probable that the entire works of Lydgate will ever be made accessible to readers, nor is it to be conceived that they would reward the labours of an editor. But although it must be repeated that Lydgate is an author of inferior value, excessively prosy and long-winded, and strangely neglectful both of structure and of melody, a selection could probably be made from his writings which would do him greater justice than he does to himself in his intolerable prolixity. He has a pleasant vein of human pity, a sympathy with suffering that leads him to say, in a sort of deprecating undertone, very gentle and gracious things. He is a storehouse of odd and valuable antiquarian notes. His *Pur le Roy*, for instance, is a rich and copious account of the entry of Henry VI. into London in 1422; better known is his curious satire of *London Lackpenny*. Lydgate belongs—it is vain to deny it—to a period of retrogression and decay. But he had his merits, and the way to appreciate his verses is to compare them with the wretched, tuneless stuff put forth by his pupils and followers, such as Benedict Burgh.

A poet, Sir THOMAS CLANVOWE, who had studied the manner of Chaucer with greater care than Lydgate, and had a more melodious native talent than Occleve, wrote about 1403 a short romance in an almost unique five-line stanza, *The Cuckoo and the Nightingale*, in which the author, although "old and unlusty," falls asleep by a brook-side in May and hears the birds philosophising. Even in this mellifluous piece, which flows on like the rivulet it describes, the metrical laws of Chaucer are found to be in solution. Here occurs that reference to Woodstock which long led astray those who supposed Chaucer to be the author of this poem. Longer and much later, and still less like the genuine master, is the over-sweet, tedious romance in more than two thousand octosyllabic verses, boldly called *Chaucer's Dream*, though

Chaucer is not in any way concerned in it. It is a paraphrased translation of a vague, flowery story about a
pilgrimage to an island of fair ladies ; it contains a succession of pretty mediæval pictures painted in faint, clear
colours, like the illuminations in a missal, pale and delicate, in its affectation of primitive simplicity.

Of all poems of the fifteenth century, however, that
which is most faithful to the tradition of Chaucer, and
continues it in the most intelligent way, is the *King's Quair*
(or Book). The history of this work is as romantic as
possible, and yet probably authentic.[1] JAMES 1. of
Scotland, in 1405, not being yet eleven years old, was
treacherously captured by the English, in time of truce,
off Flamborough Head, and had been confined, first in
the Tower, then in Windsor Castle, for eighteen years,
when, seeing Johanne de Beaufort walking in the garden
below his prison window, he fell violently in love with
her. The match pleased the English Court ; they were
married early in 1424, and proceeded as King and Queen
to Scotland. The poem we are now discussing was
written in the spring and early summer of 1423, and it
describes, in exquisitely artless art, the progress of the
wooing. This poet was murdered, in conditions of
heartless cruelty, in 1437. We possess no other indubitable work of his except a Scotch *ballade*.

The King's Quair, in more primitive periods of our
literary history, was accepted as a contribution to Scotch
poetry. But Dr. Skeat was the first to point out that
although the foundation of it is in the Northern dialect, it

---

[1] In 1896 a very ingenious attempt was made by Mr. J. T. T. Brown to
throw doubt on the authenticity of the *King's Quair ;* but it cannot be said
that any convincing evidence against the accepted tradition was produced. Mr.
Brown's arguments were negative, and have been ably met by M. Jusserand.

is carefully composed, as if in a foreign language, in the
elaborate Midland or Southern dialect as used, and
perhaps not a little as invented, by Chaucer. James I.,
indeed, is completely under the sway of his great predecessor; no poet of the century repeats so many phrases
copied from, or introduces so many allusions to, the
writings of Chaucer as he does. He was immersed, it is
evident, in the study and almost the idolatry of his
master; the first violent emotion of his sequestered life
came upon him in that condition, and he burst into song
with the language of Chaucer upon his lips. In spite of
this state of pupilage, and in spite of his employment of
the old French machinery of a dream, allegorical personages and supernatural conventions, the poem of James I.
is a delicious one.   His use of metre was highly intelligent; he neither deviated back towards the older
national prosody, like Lydgate, nor stumbled aimlessly
on, like Occleve; he perceived what it was that Chaucer
had been doing, and he pursued it with great firmness,
so that, in the fifty or sixty years which divided the latest
of the *Canterbury Tales* from *The Flower and the Leaf,*
the *King's Quair* is really the only English poem in
which a modern ear can take genuine pleasure.

In its analysis of moods of personal feeling, the *King's
Quair* marks a distinct advance in fluent and lucid expression.   The poem is full, too, of romantic beauty; the
description of the garden, of the mysterious and lovely
being beheld wandering in its odorous mazes, of the
nightingale, "the little sweetë nightingale" on "the
smalë greenë twistis," is more accomplished, of its kind,
than what any previous poet, save always Chaucer, had
achieved.   The pathos of the situation, our sympathy
with the gallant and spirited royal poet, the historic

exactitude of the events so beautifully recorded, the curious chance by which its manuscript was preserved unknown until the end of last century—all combine to give the *King's Quair* a unique position in English literature.   Alas ! as Rossetti sings :

> " *Alas ! for the woful thing*
> *That a poet true and a friend of man*
> *In desperate days of bale and ban*
> *Should needs be born a king.*"

These lines remind us of the *Ballads* which form so large and so vague a department of our national literature.   It is difficult to know where to place the romantic ballads, most of which have come down to us in a language and a metre which cannot be much earlier, at earliest, than the end of the sixteenth century.   The original types of these national poems may have existed in the fifteenth century, but their antiquity is certainly a matter of speculation.   Not so dubious, however, is the approximate date of the less beautiful but curious and significant ballads of the Robin Hood cycle.   The latest general opinion about these is that they were brought together, in something like their present form, soon after 1400.   The earliest reference to the hero is found in *Piers Plowman ;* but a Scottish chronicler, writing in 1420, gives 1283 as the date when

> " *Little John and Robin Hood*
> *Waythmen were commended good ;*
> *In Inglewood and Barnesdale*
> *They used all this time their travail.*"

We may conjecture that soon after 1300 there began to be composed ballads about a mythical yeoman who had taken to the forest in Yorkshire a generation earlier ;

that all through the fourteenth century these ballads
continued to be made and repeated—"harpèd at feasts"—
until, soon after 1400, some crowder of superior poetical
skill selected the best, and composed the *Geste of Robin
Hood;* and that throughout the fifteenth century other
Robin Hood ballads were made, less original and authoritative than those in the *Geste,* and that these latest are
what we principally possess at present.

In the *Geste of Robin Hood,* which is a long poem of
456 stanzas, we possess the earliest and most genuine
version of the narrative now existing. Here we find the
good yeoman, Robin Hood, a proud and courteous outlaw, who has taken to the wood in Barnesdale. His
companions are Little John, William Scarlet or Scathe-
locke, and Much, the miller's son. Robin lives by hunting the King's deer, and by gallantly robbing such barons,
archbishops, and abbots as venture through his forest.
But he is generous, and if a knight who is in trouble
crosses his path, he will not let him go till they have
dined together. The great enemy of Robin Hood and
his men is the Sheriff of Nottingham, who represents
the terrors of the common law. The proud sheriff
accosts Little John, who says that his own name is Richard
Greenleaf, and is accepted into the sheriff's service; he
betrays his master to Robin Hood under the forest, and
the poor sheriff is bound and humiliated. It is a blow
to our sentiment of romance, which has taught us since
our childhood to picture Robin Hood sitting at a venison
pasty, in the heart of Sherwood Forest, in company with
his sweetheart and wife, Maid Marian, to learn that
this lady is totally unknown to the genuine old ballads.
There were ancient stories about Friar Tuck and Maid
Marian, but not in connection with Robin Hood; nor

4

were these stories, so far as we know, told in verse. The earliest ballad in which Robin Hood and Maid Marian are mentioned together is a very poor doggerel piece, probably later than the time of Shakespeare. We may notice that in the oldest ballads the scene is laid, indifferently, in Barnesdale Forest, near Pontefract, and fifty miles off in Sherwood Forest, near Nottingham. It has been conjectured that there were originally two cycles of ballads, the one a Barnesdale set, the other a Sherwood set, and that the compiler of the *Geste of Robin Hood* helped himself to material from each of them.

Lancastrian prose exemplifies the same conditions of intellectual weariness and decadence which depressed Lancastrian poetry ; but the decline is less marked, because in the preceding century verse had flourished brilliantly, while prose had not flourished at all. After 1400 we begin to see the English language more freely, though scarcely more gracefully, used, and for direct purposes, not merely or mainly in the form of translations. A very active and audacious talent was employed by REGINALD PECOCK in confuting the errors of those disciples of Wycliffe who were styled " Lollards." He brought his attacks to a climax in 1449, when he was made Bishop of Chichester, and compiled his *Repressor of overmuch Blaming of the Clergy*. His other main production, the *Book of Faith*, is of somewhat later date. His sophistical ingenuity ultimately brought him to confusion and shame. The matter of Pecock is paradoxical and casuistical reasoning on controversial points, in which he secures the sympathy neither of the new thought nor of the old. That he wrote in English to secure a wider audience, and that he is on the whole fairly simple and direct in style, are symptoms of a general advance of English as an accepted language fit for literary and yet popular exercises. Still, the fate of the brilliant Bishop of Chichester proves that the time was not ripe for the discussion in English of any but the most obvious and harmless themes. Had Pecock confined himself to the Latin language, he might have closed a splendid career at Canterbury, instead of expiring like a starved lamp under the extinguisher of his prison at Thorney.

We see Pecock bring the vernacular into the service of theological controversy, and we find another eminent divine, JOHN CAPGRAVE employing it for purely historical purposes. The exact date of the composition of Capgrave's *Chronicle of England* is uncertain ; he was probably at work upon it through the second quarter of the century ; it closes with the year 1417. He is a much less rapid and audacious writer than Pecock. The attitude of Capgrave's mind is archaically mediæval, and he possesses in large measure that blight of monotony and tameness which mars almost all Lancastrian literature. His historical importance is immense, especially if his Latin writings are taken into consideration ; but from the mere point of view of development of English style, Capgrave is negligible. Yet, so miserable is the poverty of the first half of the fifteenth century, when we have mentioned Pecock and Capgrave, there is no other prose writer to be named. English prose was still in its embryonic condition. In a familiar class, the *Paston Letters*, which date from 1422 onwards, offer us a precious opportunity of judging in what manner ordinary people of position expressed themselves in the discussion of daily experience.

The second half of the fifteenth century was in England

even more desperately barren of poetry than the first. In its absolute sterility, one solitary poem of merit demands attention, as much for its rarity as its positive charm. Some woman, whose name has not been preserved, wrote after 1450, but in close discipleship of Chaucer, the beautiful little allegorical romances of *The Flower and the Leaf* and the *Assembly of Ladies*. She took the idea of the former from Eustache Deschamps, who had composed three such poems, in one of which he gave the prize to the leaf, and in another to the flower; but the English piece begins as a translation of Machault's *Dit du Vergier*. It is accordingly wholly French in tone and character, and, coming at the very close of the Middle Ages, lights up, with a last flicker of imitation, the indebtedness of English mediæval poetry to France. The charm of *The Flower and the Leaf* is, however, very considerable ; the anonymous poetess has a singularly graceful fluency, and she does not exaggerate, as do some of her Scottish successors, the ornaments of phraseology. Her poem well sums up the eclectic mediæval mannerism. It opens with the praise of spring. Before sunrise the writer goes into a grove, where, listening for the nightingale, she turns down a narrow path and comes to an arbour. She hears a music of sweet voices, and sees advance a troop, "a world of ladies," with one noblest figure, waving a branch of agnus castus, in the midst of them. Then there appear to her strange men-at-arms, a gorgeous cavalry, who arrive, part, and joust. When the fight is over, the ladies advance, and lead the victors to a giant laurel-tree. These people were all in white; but as they disappear, a company in green comes strolling up, also marvellously adorned. But the sun burns the flowers, and the ladies too; and then comes down a storm of wind and rain. The white come to the succour of the green, and all pass away in company. The poetess is left to the solemn presence of Diana and of Flora, and must choose between the Flower and the Leaf. "Unto the Leaf I owe mine observance," she answers, and the romance is over. The strange, delicate, unsubstantial poetry of mediæval chivalry is over, too, in these pretty and melodious exercises in rime royal, the only considerable gift to early English literature made by a woman. It is interesting to observe that she betrays the half-century of developing language which divides her from Chaucer's death by her archaistic, that is to say, no longer perfectly natural, use of metrical ornament.

From the miserable emptiness of English poetry after 1450, it is agreeable to turn to Scotland, where the art was cultivated in some oddity and artificiality of form, indeed, but, on the whole, with singular success. Save in the one respect of the almost idolatrous study of Chaucer, the course of poetry in Scotland seems to have run in a totally independent channel. The Scotch poets of the Renaissance are connected with the mediæval tradition, not by any Southern links, but by certain chroniclers who closely imitated Barbour, and who are only to be distinguished from him by their more modern use of language. About 1420 ANDREW OF WYNTOUN, a monk of St. Serf's, on Lochleven, completed an *Original Chronicle of Scotland*, in nine books of octosyllabic verse; he treated the subject from the "origin" of the world. Wyntoun's history is less amusing than his fabulous legends, which he tells eagerly and gaily, with a garrulous credulity.

We pass on for some forty years, and, at the threshold

of the literary poetry of Scotland, are arrested by a survivor of the old didactic chronicle-school. BLIND HARRY, or Henry the Minstrel, composed about 1460, in the Northern dialect, a long *Acts and Deeds of Sir William Wallace*, in which, for the first time, the heroic couplet was employed by a Scotch poet. Blind Harry was therefore, no doubt, acquainted with the writings of Chaucer, who invented that form of verse, but he displays no other Southern characteristic. His *Wallace* is the direct descendant of the *Bruce* of Barbour. This minstrel shows a certain advance in the freedom of his narrative, and in the psychological treatment of the hero he exhibits an occasional liveliness which may or may not be wholly voluntary, since the exigencies of rhyme drive him occasionally to strange shifts. He is singularly prosy, and not infrequently incoherent; yet there is an air of sincerity and good faith about the *Wallace* which commands respect. Blind Harry, however, has none of the moral elevation of Barbour, and is, in fact, a writer of scant importance to any but philologists and historians.

Henryson must have been writing about the same time as Blind Harry, but a century seems to divide them in literary temperament. The latter belonged to the Middle Ages; the former was a child of the Renaissance, and its introducer into Scottish poetry. Of the life of ROBERT HENRYSON little is known; it is conjectured that he was born about 1425, and died about 1506. He was notary-public, and perhaps schoolmaster, at Dunfermline, and Dunbar tells us that he died there. Allusions to the Abbey of Dunfermline, and to walks "down on foot by Forth," add faintly to the picture we form of a merry, philosophical bard. Every critic quotes the stanza in which Henryson describes how he brightens the fire, wraps himself up, "takes a drink his spirits to comfort," and buries himself in the *quair* or volume in which glorious worthy Chaucer wrote of fair Cressid and lusty Troilus. This is one of those vivid, personal pictures, so sadly rare in our early literature, in which the veil of time seems suddenly rent for a moment to let us look upon the great dead masters face to face.

It would be absurd to represent Henryson as habitually lifted to such heights of felicitous expression; yet he is commonly vivid, natural, and observant to a degree beyond any predecessor save Chaucer, whom he intelligently followed. In some of his poems he is purely allegorical, in the old French way. In *Orpheus and Eurydice*, which comes down to us through a unique copy printed in 1508, a narrative in rime royal is followed by a moral in the heroic couplet, and all tends to show that Orpheus is the better spirit of man, which twitches the strings of the harp of conscience and bids our foolish appetites return heavenward. The moral nature of Henryson deems that Chaucer had dealt too tenderly with the errors of passion, and in a pitiful and dolorous *Testament of Cressid* he shuts the door of mercy severely upon her. In *Robin and Makyne*, breaking through the tradition of solemn iambics for all subjects, Henryson bursts forth into a light lyrical measure of a charming pastoral gaiety. This ballad is the Scotch counterpart of the *Nutbrown Maid*, an excellent English pastoral ballad or lyrical eclogue of doubtful date.

Henryson's principal feat was that of translating, or rather paraphrasing, *Æsop's Fables* into Scottish rime royal. Æsop had been printed in Latin in 1473, and in Greek in 1480; Caxton Englished the *Fables* from the French in 1483. It is believed that Henryson was independent of English influences, and his version may date from about 1478. Of these fables a prologue and thirteen narratives are all that have come down to us, and this is much to be regretted, since in the realistic vigour of these stories Henryson is at his best. All are worth studying ; the hasty reader may be recommended particularly to "The Cock and the Jasp" and "The Uplands Mouse and the Burgess Mouse." No greater compliment can be paid to the latter than is paid by M. Jusserand, who, although a Frenchman, prefers Henryson's version to that of Lafontaine. In this agreeable dominie of Dunfermline, we first meet with the rustic vein, the homeliness in pastoral imagination, which has continued to be characteristic of Scotch literature, and which culminates in Burns.

A poem of poignant beauty and pathos, the *Lament for the Makers,* written by Dunbar about 1507, reveals to us the fact that a whole school of reputable poets flourished in Scotland at the Courts of James III. and James IV. What we possess of the Scots poetry of that epoch is so excellent in kind that we may well mourn that the writings of Sir Mungo Lockhart of the Lea, Quintin Shaw, "good gentle" Stobo, and the rest of them have completely disappeared. Of the list of poets, apparently belonging to his own age or to the generation immediately preceding," "good Master" Walter Kennedy is the only one of whose work we have any substantial fragments. These present to us the idea that he was a link between Henryson and Dunbar, but inferior in merit to both of them. We gather, indeed, that Dunbar was recognised at once as the first poet of the age, and we may console ourselves by believing that in the ninety or a hundred poems of his which we are fortunate enough to possess, we hold the fine flower of Scotch Renaissance poetry. Dunbar, let it be plainly said, is the largest figure in English literature between Chaucer and Spenser, to each of whom, indeed, he seems to hold forth a hand.

The life of WILLIAM DUNBAR is very imperfectly known to us. It is probable that he was born in 1460, and that he died soon after 1520. He was a Lothian man, educated at St. Andrews. After the murder of James III., in 1488, Dunbar seems to have passed over to France, as a secular priest, preaching his way through Picardy to Paris, where a great many young Scotch-men, some of them afterwards to be eminent, were then studying. He seems to have travelled widely, visiting even Holland, Spain, and Norway. In 1500 we find him back in Scotland, and attached for the remainder of his life to James IV. as Court poet, taking, among the many versifiers of the age, the predominant appellation of "Rhymer of Scotland" or Poet Laureate. In this capacity he was present in London to negotiate the marriage of James IV. and Margaret Tudor, in 1502; for which ceremony Dunbar composed the most ambitious of his existing works, *The Thistle and the Rose*. In 1507 the art of printing was introduced into Scotland by Andrew Miller of Rouen, and among the earliest productions of the press was a collection of Dunbar's poems, including the *Golden Targe* and the *Flyting of Dunbar and Kennedy*, 1508. He seems to have survived Flodden field in 1513, but the remainder of his life is very vague.

Extreme richness and brightness of diction are the characteristic qualities of Dunbar's verse. He is the first to break up and cast behind him the monotonous conventions of mediæval style. His range is very wide, sweeping from solemn hymns and lyrics of a poignant melancholy to invectives and comic narratives of the broadest merriment. Without doubt he specially prided himself on his elaborate allegorical romances, in which he gave free access to those "lusty roses of rhetoric" with which he loved to adorn his verse. These allegories are of the old familiar French school, distinguished only by the extremely ornate and melodious verbiage of Dunbar. There is less courtliness and more nature in the comic lyrics of Dunbar, the sprightliness and vigour of which are clouded for modest readers by their remarkable freedom of language. Fortunately the dark Northern dialect and the eccentricities of Dunbar's spelling are veils to hide our blushes. In the *Testament of Andrew Kennedy*, a humorous will in verse, the influence of Villon upon Dunbar has been perhaps a little hastily traced. The pictures which this poet gives of the Court life are curiously rough and coarse, heightened in colour, no doubt, by the poet's singular gift for satire. The vituperative verses of Dunbar, written apparently with the maximum of violence and of good temper, remind us of the tourneys of the Italian Humanists. They were merely exercises in abusive rhetoric indulged in among excellent friends. One of the best-known of Dunbar's poems, the *Dance of the Seven Deadly Sins*, is of the graver satirical class. Some of his religious pieces are not only of a true sublimity, but display that lyrical element in him which was so new in British poetry of artifice.

In reaching Dunbar we find that we have escaped from the dead air of the late Middle Ages. The poetry of this writer is defective in taste—rhetorical, over-ornate; he delights to excess in such terms as "crystalline," "redolent," "aureate," and "enamelling." He never escapes—and it is this which finally leads us to refuse the first rank to his gorgeous talent—from the artificial in language. He does not display any considerable intellectual power. But when all this is admitted, the activity and versatility of Dunbar, his splendid use of melody and colour, his remarkable skill in the invention of varied and often intensely lyrical metres, his fund of animal spirits, combine to make his figure not merely an exceedingly attractive one in itself, but as refreshing as a well of water after the dry desert of the fifteenth century in England. It is a matter for deep regret that the early verse of this great writer is lost, one fears beyond all hope of its recovery. The analogy of Dunbar with Burns is very striking, and has often been pointed out; but the difference is at least that between a jewel and a flower, the metallic hardness of Dunbar being a characteristic of his style which is utterly out of harmony with the living sensitiveness of his greater successor. This metal surface, however, is sometimes burnished to a splendour that few poets have ever excelled; for intricate and almost inaccessible elaboration of rhyme-effects, Dunbar's *Ballad to Our Lady* is one of the most extraordinary feats in the language.

The consideration of the Scotch poets of the Renaissance has, however, carried us a little way beyond their English contemporaries. In poetry there was nothing that could compete for a moment, not merely with Dunbar, but with the lesser writers of his school; but in prose there took place, about 1470, a very remarkable revival, analogous to the sudden development of poetry just one hundred years earlier. At the extinction of the Lancastrian dynasty, modern English prose, hitherto a mere babbling of loose incoherent clauses, began to take form and substance. It is evident from various indications that the awkwardness and deadness of English prose had struck many persons of influence at the Yorkist Court. Caxton tells us of the anxiety which the King's sister, Margaret, Duchess of Burgundy, felt for the cultivation of a pure English. One of the first who attempted to reform the use of the vernacular was the aged Lancastrian Lord Chancellor, Sir JOHN FORTESCUE, who, having written pregnantly and abundantly in Latin, began, when he was probably approaching eighty years of age, to compose in English, and produced, in 1471, a *Declaration upon Certain Writings out of Scotland,* a retractation of his Lancastrian arguments and an acknowledgment of Edward IV. A year or two later, it would seem, Fortescue wrote his more important treatise, the *Difference between an Absolute and a Limited Monarchy.* He deserves the praise of being our earliest political historian. Fortescue is one of our greatest Latin authorities on constitutional law, and as a writer on definitely national themes in a purely colloquial English he is an innovator among those who wrote, if not in Latin or French, in a style obviously translated from one of those tongues. His sentences are short, but abrupt and inelegant ; he performs his task, and we acknowledge his courage, but we cannot pretend to enjoy the manner of delivery.

The man, however, to whom English prose owes its popular vehicle is WILLIAM CAXTON, whose *Recueil of the Histories of Troy,* translated in 1471 from the French of Raoul Lefevre, was printed by his own hand at Cologne. In 1476 he brought his press over to Westminster, and began his career as the Aldus of England; the first-fruits of his printing-press being the *Dictes of the Philosophers,* 1477, by the second Earl RIVERS, who also deserves "a singular laud and thanks" as one of the pioneers of our prose. Caxton, besides the immortal fame which he won as the introducer of printing into England, was a lucid and idiomatic writer, whose style may be observed in various translations, as well as in shorter and more original "prologues" and "epilogues." It is highly to Caxton's credit that he saw that English prose, in order to become an instrument worthy of the language, must be vitalised. What passed for Lancastrian prose had been dead, heavy, cold as a clod, and as opaque. Caxton, without any very great genius for writing, was at least vivid and amusing. When he excuses himself for scribbling, unauthorised, an epilogue to Lord Rivers's *Dictes*, saying that "peradventure the wind had blown over the leaf," Caxton introduces a playfulness, a lightness of touch that had been hitherto unknown in English prose. He was a man, not of genius, but of industry and taste, born at a fruitful moment.

Not Fortescue, nor Rivers, nor Caxton, however, can compare with the writer who first achieved the feat of writing English prose that should have the charm of English verse. To the great name of Sir THOMAS MALEORE or MALORY it would scarcely be possible to pay too high an encomium. Unhappily, of his person we know absolutely nothing; he was "the servant of Jesu both day and night," and that shadow in the mist of piety is all we see of the immortal author of the *Morte d'Arthur*. For two centuries past the legends of Arthur and his Table Round had permeated the English fancy; verse romances, translated or imitated from the French, each engaged with some fragment or other of the vast mysterious story, had been the popular reading of gentle and simple. Malory came forward, at the moment when English prose felt itself able at last to compete with verse, and presented to the new dynasty a compilation of the whole Arthurian cycle, selected and arranged with infinite art, and told in a style that was as completely novel as it was beautiful and effective.

Much has been said of an English epic of Arthur, and Spenser, Milton, Dryden, and Tennyson in turn essayed or approached it. Each of them was, or would have been, indebted to the old chronicle of Malory; it is questionable if any of them has, or would have, excelled him. He came at the moment when the charm of these exquisite tales of chivalry was taking its sunset colours. No longer credulously believed, it was necessary that stories which were already beginning to be questioned, the real propriety of which was fading with the passage of those Middle Ages, of which they were the purest expression, should be clarified of their coarsest improbabilities, their wildest outrages upon credence, and that their appeals to sentiment, to beauty of idea, should be carefully gathered into a posy. In 1470 much was still believed that we reject, much still passed for gospel truth that we can hardly put up with in a fairy-tale. Men's minds were passing through a transition, from the child-like credulity of the Middle Ages to the adolescent ignorance of the Renaissance. However much Malory might pare away, he might be trusted to preserve enough to astonish a modern reader.

To say that Malory's style is better than that of any of his predecessors is inadequate, for, in the broad sense, he had no predecessors. English prose, as a vehicle for successive and carefully distinguished moods of romantic mystery, plaintive melancholy, anger, terror, the intoxicating fervour of battle, did not exist before he wrote the *Morte d'Arthur*. His sentences are short, but they have nothing of the dryness of Fortescue's; if he is languid, it is because he desires to produce the impression of languor, not, like Caxton, because he is inherently a light weight in literature. The effect which Malory has produced on generations of English readers is greater than we are accustomed to realise. He tinges the whole English character; he is the primal fount of our passion for adventure, and of our love of active chivalry. The tales he tells are old; the Britons, as William of Malmesbury tells us, had been raving about Arthur for centuries, when he felt it his duty to reprove them. Since then the beautiful, fantastic cycle had grown and grown, till it covered the whole imagination of Western Europe as with a dewy cobweb. But it was Malory, and not any Frenchman or Celt, who drew the bright lines together, and produced, out of such evanescent material, one of the great books of the world.

Under the House of York the art of writing English verses became almost extinct. John Kay, Edward IV.'s royal poet, paraphrased exclusively from Latin, and he was succeeded by Bernard André, who wrote in French. The work done by Langland and Chaucer threatened to be entirely undone, and English poetry was once more ready to submit to the tyranny of Continental Europe. With the accession of the Tudor dynasty a change for the better came in, and the reign of Henry VII. was illustrated by certain writers, not of the first excellence, but yet deserving great praise for having taken up the tradition of English imaginative writing. Hawes, Barclay, and Skelton were almost exactly contemporaneous, and all three began to write after the visit of Dunbar to London, on the occasion of the marriage of James IV., in 1503. It is hardly fantastic to attribute to the example of the highly lettered and poetic Court of Scotland the sudden revival of English verse after more than half a century of total obscuration.   In nothing else, however, do Skelton, Barclay, and Hawes, three very distinct types, resemble one another.

A very interesting link between Lydgate and Spenser is formed by STEPHEN HAWES. The only work of his which demands our notice is the long allegory of the *Pastime of Pleasure,* in six thousand verses of rime royal, finished about the year 1506, and printed three years later by Wynkyn de Worde. This poem is of peculiar interest as being an elaborately artificial attempt to re-suscitate the mediæval romance of allegorical chivalry, which was by that date entirely out of fashion. Stephen Hawes, with calm disdain for modern Tudor taste, goes back to the mode of two hundred years earlier, and in-vents a poem in the manner of Jean de Meung. The speaker of this piece is called Grande Amour, and he walks distractedly in a glorious valley full of flowers, till at moonrise he finds himself at the foot of a copper image, and lies down there to sleep. The lady Fame appears to him, attended by her greyhounds, Governance and Grace, and tells him that far away, in the magical town of Music, lives La Belle Pucelle, but that the way to this castle perilous is defended by giants. She leaves him, and he wanders on until he sees the turrets and battle-ments of the fortress of Moral Document. He slays giants, storms the castle, and after serving apprentice-ships with the ladies Grammar, Logic, and Rhetoric, he pushes on to the city of Music and finds La Belle Pucelle. Their meeting in the garden is prettily described; but many things get mixed together, and the poem, now half ended, loses all coherence. The hero vanquishes many giants and releases many ladies with his sword Clara Prudence ; then marries, grows old and dies, while Time and Eternity compose his epitaph.

> "*For though the dayë be never so long,*
> *At last the bells ringeth to evensong,*"

is the only couplet commonly remembered of this languid and artificial poem, affected and tedious to a degree, and yet strangely permeated with the sense of romantic beauty. Hawes was an extravagant admirer of Lydgate, whose prosodical heresies affect his measure unfavourably.

ALEXANDER BARCLAY, who, although "born beyond the cold river of Tweed," used the Southern dialect, and wrote at Ottery St. Mary, in Devonshire, did useful if somewhat humble work by paraphrasing in English several of the Latin eclogues of Æneas Sylvius and of Mantuan, and Brandt's huge Suabian satire of the *Narrenschiff* or *Ship of Fools*. But Barclay was a dull and clumsy versifier, and far more interest attaches to the strange experiments in metre of his "rascal" rival, JOHN SKELTON. In 1489 this curious person was created Poet Laureate at the University of Oxford, and in 1493 made laureate to the King at Cambridge, being habited for the occasion in a green and white dress, with a wreath of laurel, and the word *Calliope* embroidered in golden letters of silk on his gown. From the earliest infancy of the Duke of York (afterwards Henry VIII.) Skelton was his tutor, and Erasmus called him the *decus et lumen* of British letters. He has the reputation of disgusting ribaldry, but when he chooses to be sober, Skelton is delicately ornate to affectation. His great claim to our notice is that he was the first to break up the monotony

5

of English verse. His *Chaplet of Laurel* is a piece of laborious allegory which Hawes might have signed, but the real talent of Skelton lies in his wild and breathless short-line poems, half romance, half burlesque, of which *Philip Sparrow* is the type. The *Chaplet of Laurel* itself is broken by odd, frenzied lyrics, one of which is the famous

> " *Merry Margaret,*
> *As midsummer flower,*
> *Gentle as falcon,*
> *Or hawk of the tower.*"

This rattling verse lent itself to the poet's fierce diatribes against Wolsey, who drove his tormentor at last into sanctuary in Westminster Abbey for the remainder of his life. There are amazing passages in *Colin Clout* and the *Tunning of Elinour Rumming* which go far to justify Pope's unkind epithet of "beastly Skelton." Warton has aptly described this poet's versification as "anomalous and motley," but it was a powerful solvent of the stiff, tight, traditional metre of the fifteenth century.

By this time the brief summer-time of the Renaissance in Scotland had been brought to a sudden close at Flodden, but in the meanwhile much had been produced in the wild and coarse, but highly intelligent Court of James IV. which it would doubtless greatly interest us to read. But in Scotland there was a far slighter chance of the preservation of a literary product than in the south of England, and even the introduction of the printing-press did not suffice to ensure survival to the mass of Scotch poetry, whose authors are to us nothing now but names. Probably we possess the best of all in Dunbar, whose brilliant virility and splendour of fancy are not repeated in GAVIN DOUGLAS, the famous Bishop of Dunkeld, whose gifts the Scottish critics have been inclined a little to overrate. His is, however, a picturesque personality; a son of Archibald " Bell the Cat," Earl of Angus, educated at St. Andrews and Paris, identified with all the stormiest intrigues of his age, the poetical bishop appeals to the fancy as the hero of a stirring romance. But his original poems, his laborious allegories the *Palace of Honour* and *King Heart*, are of a kind now familiar and even wearisome to us in our descent of the Middle Ages, and in the gorgeousness of his verbiage Douglas only repeats, without surpassing, Dunbar. His fancy, however, inflamed by the reading of the classics, adopts humanist forms, and his picture of Love, no infant genius, but a man with square limbs, clad in green, like a hunter, is no mediæval deity.

After the disaster of Flodden in 1513, the part taken by Douglas became a very prominent one. In these distracting times he had turned to the classics, and was translating Ovid to comfort himself. His famous version of the *Æneid* belongs to 1512–13. Under James V. his fortunes rose: he was made Abbot of Aberbrothock and Bishop of Dunkeld, and for many years " all the Court was ruled by the Earl of Angus and Mr. Gawain Douglas, but not well." How he fought for the Archbishopric of St. Andrews, and how his turbulent ambition overreached itself; how he fled to Wolsey, and died of the plague in Lord Dacre's house in London in 1522, are parts of the romance of literary history. His *Virgil* is written in heroic couplets, with " prologues " in stanzaic form prefixed to the books; these prologues have been praised for the graceful studies of conventionalised natural objects which they present. But Gavin Douglas is most interesting as a writer in whom we can watch the change from the mediæval to the humanist attitude in the act of abruptly taking place.

It is not necessary to dwell at any length on the work of Sir DAVID LYNDESAY, James V.'s Lyon King-of-arms, in whom the brilliant school of Scotch Renaissance poetry closes. Lyndesay's interests and instincts were not artistic, and it is plain that he wrote in verse mainly because it was the only convenient weapon to his hand. He continued to compose allegories in the outworn taste of his predecessors, but even this insipid form concealed a reforming enthusiasm for current politics and the spleen of a practical satirist. He attacked ecclesiastical corruption, and was a supporter of Knox, in rough language and with a terrible fluency lashing all the sins and follies of his age. The rapid reader, whom the bulk of Lyndesay's works might alarm, may discover what manner of man and what manner of poet he was by reading the *Testament and Complaint of the Papingo*, or dying parrot.

The reign of Henry VIII. is illustrious in the history of literature for the progress which it encouraged in English prose. Verse made little mark in the early years of the reign ; but the King himself was solicitous about the improvement and free use of prose, and was aided in his designs by men of competent genius. In particular, the violent constitutional changes which had marked the fifteenth century naturally called for a school of historians. It is true that the art of political history, so long held in the traditional grasp of the chronicler, was not to be learned in a day. The critic of the progress of literature observes with extreme interest the change which is introduced by the perception by English writers of the genius and mission of Froissart. The early Tudor historians, of whom Edward Hall and Robert Fabian are the most notable, show, in their consciousness of the fact that the authorities do not always agree, a glimmering of the historic instinct. But they are dull and credulous. To Fabian the placing of a new weather-cock on the steeple of St. Paul's or the tale of dishes at a city feast is a momentous matter. Hall, who begins to tell a story better than Fabian, often loses the point of it in some silly detail. Both, as it has been observed, improve as they reach a later date.

It is difficult to understand why, in an age so constantly in relation with France, it should have taken more than a century for the genius and influence of Froissart to have made themselves felt in England. A historian so cognisant of English affairs should, one would suppose, naturally attract English readers, but it is evident that, after the independent reformation of the English language in the fourteenth century, the knowledge of French rapidly went out of fashion. John Bourchier, Lord BERNERS, was Governor of Calais when, about 1520, Henry VIII. desired him to perform that translation of the *Croniques* which was printed by Pynson in 1523; and although Berners was already an elderly man, and had not, so far as we know, enjoyed any practice in literature, his native talent was such, and his mind so accurately tuned to that of Froissart, that the translation he produced marked an epoch in the writing of English history, and was a notable addition to the still rare monuments of harmonious prose.

Of scarcely less importance was the work to which the same translator next turned, the rendering into fluent and picturesque prose of the romance of *Huon de Bordeaux*, the great popularity of which settled for English readers the form of much of the elfin chivalry, even by that time no longer credible or possible, but highly stimulating to the imagination, which still moves a childish fancy; and in the pages of Berners's *Huon*, the fairy monarch, Oberon, first stepped on the shores of England.

A deepening of the sense of religion and a quicker intellectual life, such as the incidents of Henry VIII.'s reign tended to encourage, left their direct mark upon literature in England. Men like Linacre and Colet returned from Italy. Men like Erasmus came to us, with their hearts and brains inflamed with new ideas, and it was the lads who listened at their feet who were to be the pioneers of thought in the coming age of reform. These humanists, unfortunately, in their desire for Catholic sympathy, trusted too much to Latin, and not enough to the vernacular. It is to be regretted that Sir THOMAS MORE, the greatest humanist, perhaps the greatest intellect of his time, gave so much to Europe that was meant for England. His masterpiece, the *Utopia*, was not published by himself, but in his excellent Life of *Richard III.* we see reflected on English history, for the first time, the pure light that Berners had so happily borrowed from Froissart. Hallam has, however, gone too far, both positively and relatively, in calling this "the first example of good English language." The same writer has described More's *Richard III.* as "the first book I have read through without detecting any remnant of obsolete forms." It is difficult to comprehend what Hallam meant by "obsolete," for More employs the phraseology of his own time not less freely than, for instance, Bishop Fisher does in his sermons. It is right, however, to recognise in More an easy, fluid grace which had been very rare before him, and is frequent in his writings.

But More is not more lucid or simple than his arch-adversary, WILLIAM TYNDALE, to whom we owe the inestimable gift of an English *New Testament* in 1526,[1] followed in 1535 by an entire *Bible*, in which Miles Coverdale co-operated. In fact, it is dangerous to use comparative terms of praise and blame to these masters of early Tudor prose. The language was rapidly developing, and they moved with it. They shared its shortcomings and its advantages; they were carried onward in the rush of its advance. But the introduction into every English household of the *Bible*, translated into prose of this fluid, vivid period, is, after all, by far the most important literary fact of the reign of Henry VIII. It coloured the entire complexion of subsequent English prose, and set up a kind of typical harmony in the construction and arrangement of sentences.

It would be an error, however, to exaggerate the general condition of prose in Tudor times. It had thrown off a large proportion of the stiffness and dulness of mediæval language, and it had learned from Malory, Berners, and More the art of rising on occasion to pathetic, and even splendid eloquence. The work of Coverdale and Cranmer, appealing as it did to the million, rendered the arrangement of English thoughts in fine English language a not unfamiliar feat. We owe much to the theological writers of the middle of the sixteenth century, and to none more than to the committee of divines who, under Cranmer's guidance, gave

---

[1] It is important to notice that Tyndale's translation of the New Testament was quite independent both of Wycliffe and of Wycliffe's original, the Vulgate. Erasmus had by this time printed the Greek text, and it was directly from that source—although unquestionably with constant reference to Luther's German version of 1522—that Tyndale performed his work.

us, in 1549, the exquisite adaptation of homilies and collects called the *Book of Common Prayer*. It is remarkable, however, that translation is still predominant, and that the mannerism of the foreign author and the genius of his language still impresses itself upon the English translator. Harmonious as Cranmer is, he becomes homely, and even rough, when he leaves the liturgical diction which he borrowed from the Latin of the Catholic Church. The straightforward colloquial wit of Latimer is often very inspiring, and we thrill to-day at Foxe's plain and poignant stories, but neither in Foxe nor in Latimer do we find what is truly called style.

At an age when most was borrowed, and all was experimental, it was very curious to see how the condition of English prose struck our earliest academic critic, THOMAS WILSON, in his *Art of Rhetoric*, 1553. He speaks of the English of the time in other terms than those which we, looking forward and backward, are now inclined to use ; but he asserts certain laws which it is easy for us to see were those which most of the Tudor writers of that age, men as unlike as Cavendish and Ascham, Bale and Leland, were unanimous in following. Writers, according to Wilson, ought "to speak as is commonly received," and who does that more than Latimer ? They are not "to seek to be overfine, nor yet overcareless," and we are reminded of the wholesome, elegant roughness of the *Toxophilus* (1545). "To speak plainly and nakedly after the common sort of men in few words" is the motto of this simple critic, and in no work of that or any age is this ideal more bluntly lived up to than it is in GEORGE CAVENDISH'S breezy and familiar *Life of Wolsey*. But, again, Wilson speaks of some who "seek so far for outlandish English that they forget altogether their mother's language," and we are reminded of the lay translators, who were not always or often so reserved, or so comparatively chastened, in their vocabulary as was Sir THOMAS NORTH in his version of Amyot's *Plutarch*.

The *Art of Rhetoric* tells us that there was already an affectation of archaism — "the fine courtier will talk nothing but Chaucer." He notes, too, the pedantry of the Humanists, so crammed with classical allusion and quotation "that the simple can but wonder at their talk"; the fashion for tasteless neologisms, for the constant planting of some awkward "inkhorn term," not one out of a score of which was destined to strike root and live, even for a generation. All these are faults and follies, and Wilson critically derides them. We can trace them one by one in the minor authors of the age. But these eccentricities, these affectations, if we will, displayed an almost feverish preoccupation with the art of writing. Success might not often crown the effort, but the effort is made; we are far already from that deadness of the fifteenth century, when the chronicler tells his dreary sentences, mumbling and dropping them like the beads of an old conventional rosary. By 1550 the language has become highly vitalised, and although we cannot yet say that any great ease has been gained in the manœuvring of sentences, though grand thoughts are enveloped still in cumbrous phrases, and the measure is still monotonous and rough, the road is being busily made which will presently lead us up to Hooker and to Bacon.

When Wilson spoke, however, of the "fine courtiers who will talk nothing but Chaucer," was he not rather thinking of that very striking archaistic poem, the *Court*

of Love, which was actually attributed to Chaucer himself
in the edition of 1561 ?   This poem has been the theme
of much discussion.   It was probably not written earlier
than 1540, and it is unintelligible, unless we regard it as
a deliberate and purely imitative attempt to resuscitate
the mediæval romance in a humanistic age. With the
earlier poems formerly attributed to Chaucer we can see
that the anonymous authors intended no fraud, but that
the excellence of their accidental productions led subsequent editors, in their laxity, to fasten to the car of the
greatest mediæval poet everything which seemed to them
fairly worthy to share in his triumph.   But this explana-
tion does not cover the *Court of Love,* a mock-antique of
nearly fifteen hundred lines, the versification and language
of which instantly bewray it to a philologist as certainly
later than the Middle Ages.   It seems plain that in this
remarkable poem we have a conscious literary exercise,
almost a forgery, from the hand of a very clever poet,
who was a student of James I. and of Lydgate as well as
of Chaucer.

Who this poet was we can at present offer no conjecture.   " Philogenet, of Cambridge, Clerk," is the author,
but under this pseudonym he has remained undetected
by modern criticism.   The imitation of the Chaucerian
manner is close, but the writer has an ease and a melodious
flow of versification denied to Hawes or Barclay, so far
as we can judge by their existing works ; and, in spite
of its intentional archaism, the *Court of Love* reads as
though it was written a generation later than the *Pastime
of Pleasure.*   It contains a considerable number of words
of the "aureate" class, otherwise mainly used by the poets
of the Northern dialect, and I have elsewhere suggested
that it is the work of a Scotch poet deliberately writing

in the English tongue. The author begs that "metricians" will excuse his little skill, but the curious point is that in respect of metre he is far more accomplished than any other poet of the first half of the sixteenth century, with the doubtful exception of Skelton. We must look at the *Court of Love* as a literary exercise, not without analogy to the paintings of the pre-Raphaelites, in which a modern artist, rebelling against the tendencies of his own age, resolutely returns to discarded ideals and obsolete forms of art. Another such exercise, of still later date, is the Scotch poem of the *Court of Venus*, by ROLLAND. With these puzzling compositions the schools of mediæval poetry in Great Britain definitely close.

Simultaneously with this archaistic revival, which was of no real importance, there was a movement in the opposite direction which was of a revolutionary character, and which led directly to the adoption of new and final rules in English prosody. The historic evidences of this highly important movement are, unhappily, lost to us. We can hardly reconstruct, even by conjecture, what were the ties which bound together the group of brilliant young poets whose work, most of it posthumous, was published by Tottel in his well-known miscellany of *Songs and Sonnets* in 1557. We know that Sir THOMAS WYATT the elder, and Henry Howard, Earl of SURREY, were the leaders of the school. Sir Francis Bryan was another member, but we know not which were his contributions. All these were dead when the volume of 1557 was, as is supposed, edited by NICHOLAS GRIMALD, who inserted many of his own poems. Lord Vaux was another of the "uncertain authors," and so, it is believed, were John Heywood, Barnabee Googe, and Churchyard, who, alone of the whole group, survived until the age of Shakespeare. It is evident that all these men could hardly be considered contemporaries, and the verse collected by Tottel must have been composed at various times within the space of some thirty years. It represents, no doubt, a selection of the poems produced by poets of widely-different habits and degree, but all in the new manner, in defiance of mediæval tradition.

Among these new poets the earliest are the greatest. The merit of Surrey and Wyatt so far surpasses that of their successors that they have, to some excess, monopolised the credit of innovation. Wyatt, born in 1503, was much the oldest of the group; he was an active diplomatist and traveller, and evidently a man whose mind was peculiarly open to foreign influences. He died in 1542. As to the Earl of Surrey, in spite of his high lineage, his eminence as a writer, and the romantic incidents of his life and death, we are singularly ignorant of the facts of his earlier career. He was perhaps born in 1516; he was certainly executed on Tower Hill, in circumstances of bewildering obscurity, in January 1547. Tradition declares that, like Wyatt, but in more fantastic conditions, Surrey visited Italy in his youth. In the legends of a later generation the poet was represented as conducted by Cornelius Agrippa through the mazes of necromancy, and shown his Geraldine in a magic mirror. All this, and more, is valuable only as proving the hold which the romantic idea of Surrey had taken on the popular mind. Wyatt is understood to have nursed a hopeless passion for Queen Anne Bullen, whose brother George was one of the group of new poets. The whole movement seems inspired by an uneasy amorous chivalry, seeking modern forms for its expression.

In this our tantalising ignorance of the events which

led to the composition of the poems, we are driven to an examination of the poems themselves. This, at first sight, seems to help us little, since they are strung together without any revelation of chronological order. Those of Wyatt, Surrey, and Grimald are, however, by great good fortune, distinguished from the anonymous mass, and as we examine these more closely, certain indications become plainly visible. In the volume of 1557, the earliest verses are those of Surrey, and they claim this pre-eminence from their excellent value. Surrey was, without question, the most flexible talent in the group, and in all probability the one who pointed out the road to the others. It is certain that he was precocious, and he may have been writing as early as 1536, that is to say, six years before the death of Wyatt. There seems evident in the majority of Wyatt's poems a timidity which contrasts with the boldness of Surrey, and, although it must be confessed that the dates present us with great difficulties, we have the impression that Surrey was the master-spirit, as he was certainly the purer and finer poet. It is not desirable, however, to distinguish too closely between those two great harbingers of modern lyrical poetry. Wyatt seems to have borrowed most from France, Surrey most from Italy, and the latter was at that moment the more fruitful source of inspiration.

It was noted by the editor of 1557 that the whole group of new poets excelled in the art of writing "in small parcels." By this he meant in short lyrics, as contrasted with the lumbering and pompous forms of mediæval poetry. We are prepared to find the new writers eager to adopt from Continental literature such metres and types as should be most useful to them in carrying out this design, and accordingly we find the contributions of Surrey opening with an essay in *terza rima*, the earliest in the language. To Wyatt and to Surrey conjointly is due the honour of having introduced the sonnet from Italy, and, what was to be of less importance, the rondeau from France. It is not impossible that the sonnet also may have come to Wyatt from France, and not directly from Italy, since these were the days of Mellin de St. Gelais and of Clément Marot. In another publication, issued a fortnight after the *Miscellany*, Tottel printed some translations of Virgil done by Surrey into blank verse. The adoption of this metre shows the quickness and delicacy of Surrey's taste, for it was but very recently invented in Italy, and the *Sofinisba* of Trissino (1515) was the only work in which it had attained any prominence. Surrey, whose instinct for prosody was phenomenal, must have met with this play, or possibly with Sannazaro's timid essay in the *Arcadia*, and at once transplanted blank verse from a soil in which it would never flourish, to one in which it would take root and spread in full luxuriance.

It is to Surrey and Wyatt, then, that we owe the direction our modern lyric poetry has taken. Their songs and sonnets are of a Petrarchan character; they begin, in English, that analysis of the malady of love, that impulsive, singing note of emotion, which has since enriched our literature with some of the loveliest lyrics in the world. Their own work was not, in comparison with what presently succeeded it, of the highest excellence. They were forerunners, progenitors—they prophesied of better things. Their elegies are easy and flowing, their songs graceful, their sonnets (especially Surrey's) remarkable for the daring with which real scenes and persons are introduced into the impassioned descant.

Wyatt is sometimes a little weighed down by remnants of the mediæval vocabulary and movement, and his ear is singularly uncertain ; but when he pours out such a strain of tender song as " Forget not yet," and we compare this with anything that had preceded it in English of the same class, we have to acknowledge his extreme sensitiveness to valuable exotic models. In this high service to poetry, Grimald (who was possibly an Italian by birth—Niccolò Grimaldi) took a part which has scarcely received due attention. He was two or three years younger than Surrey, and he wrote, at his best, with more smoothness of melody than either of the elder friends. His lyric beginning "What sweet relief" was not equalled again until the Elizabethan age, and Grimald was particularly happy in the use of a rhymed couplet of alternately twelve and fourteen syllables, which was intended, perhaps, to represent the French alexandrine. This curious measure, which was not Grimald's invention, became excessively popular during the next half-century, sank into doggerel jingle, was cast out with mockery, and has never been used since 1600. Such are the whimsical fates of metrical innovations, for the sonnet and blank verse, which long seemed to have sunken into oblivion under the popularity of this twelve-fourteen measure, only waited until its brief day had closed to rise into honoured and permanent use.

The period between 1530 and 1545 probably includes all that was of primary importance in this first renaissance of English poetry. What strikes us in it pre-eminently is its complete emancipation from the mediæval traditions which had bound all previous writers of verse. It was the earliest British recognition of the new laws which European lyric had made for itself, but it was essentially a premature recognition of it. ·The accentuation of English was still uncertain, although a comparison of the iambic line of Wyatt and of Surrey suggests that a marked solidification of metre took place after 1535.   Neither of these poets was great; skilful, elegant, eminently enlightened and unattached, they lacked the force of thought and richness of imagination which might have stamped their innovations on popular practice.   So that the school of Wyatt and Surrey remains something isolated and ineffectual, breaking with a posy of delicate flowers and a few graceful playthings the great empty space which divides the mediæval from the Elizabethan age.   It is not, however, in any way correct to say that Wyatt and Surrey were "precursors" of the latter.   If they prophesied of anything, it was of a graceful age of humanistic and Petrarchan poetry, gentle, smooth, and voluble, such as came to France, but was excluded from England by a forcible evolution of national spirit in a quite different direction.

III

THE AGE OF ELIZABETH

1560–1610

THE accession of Queen Elizabeth, in 1558, was immediately followed by such a quickening of the political, social, and religious life of England as makes a veritable epoch in history. In literature, too, we are in the habit of regarding the development and range of those "spacious" times as having been extraordinary. Ultimately, indeed, nothing that the world has seen has been more extraordinary, but this expansion of the national temperament did not by any means reach the sphere of letters at once. For the first twenty years of the Queen's reign English literature was apparently stationary in its character, unadorned by masterpieces, and oblivious of distinction in style. If we look more closely, however, we may see that these years, inactive although they seem, were years of valuable preparation, education, and whetting of the national appetite.

The sentiment of the early Tudors, in all things connected with the mind, had been narrow and opposed to the movements of Continental thought. But Elizabeth, although her vehement Protestantism might seem to cut her off from European sympathy, was in reality much more drawn to its intellectual manifestations than her predecessors had been. It would be more to the point, perhaps, to say that her subjects were drawn into the general life of the world more than theirs had been. Everywhere new emotions, a new order of thought, were abroad, and what had passed over Italy long before, and had seized France half a century earlier, now invaded England. With the death of Mary, the bondage of the Middle Ages was finally broken through ; a rebellion against the ascetic life was successful ; a reaction against exclusive attention to religious ideas set in, almost with violence, among men of a literary habit of mind. Calvinism, a new phase of the ascetic instinct, made a footing in England, but it advanced slowly, and allowed literature time to develop by the side of it. In short, there obtained, from wider knowledge of the material world, from slackening theological torment, from a larger commerce with mankind, a reassertion of human nature, a new pleasure in the contemplation of its joys, its passions, its physical constitution. It is to this altered outlook upon life and man that we owe the glories of Elizabethan literature.

But these glories were not able to display themselves at once. In the tradition of English writing, especially of English verse, everything was still primitive and feeble, uncertain and inconsistent. The lyrics of Wyatt and Surrey had given a suggestion of a path which poetry might take, but a pretty copy of verses here and there flashing in the midst of a sea of jingling prose, did not show that even the gentle lesson of *Tottel's Miscellany* had been practically learned. We have but to compare what was written in England in 1560 with the slightly earlier literature of Italy, or even of France, to see that this country still languished in a kind of barbarism. To contrast the madrigals and epigrams of Marot, which it

is perfectly fair to compare with work of the same class
produced by the early Elizabethans, is to draw a parallel
between the product of an accomplished and in his way
perfectly modern master, and the stumblings of ignorant
scholars, who, eager to learn, yet know not what they
should be learning.

The best that can be said, indeed, of the early Elizabethans is, that they were conscious of their deficiencies,
and that they spared no pains in groping after self-educa-
tion. They avoided no labour which might help them
to improve the English language, to make its vocabulary
rich enough and its syntax supple enough for the designs
they had before them. But it is very strange for us to
observe how little their vigour was aided by intelligence
or their activity by sureness of touch. Humanism came
upon the nation, but in forms curiously foreign to the
rest of Europe ; it came in an almost infantine curiosity
to become acquainted with the ideas of the ancient
classics, without taking any trouble to reproduce the
purity of their style or to preserve the integrity of their
language. England was flooded with "translations" in
prose and verse ; it has become the fashion of late to
find surprising merits in the former, but no one has yet
been bold enough to champion the latter. Lovers of
paradox may hold that Adlington (1566) is a picturesque
writer on lines dimly suggested by Apuleius, or that
Heliodorus is sufficiently recognisable in the "witty and
pleasant" pages of Underdowne (1569). But in dealing
with verse we are on firmer ground, and it may safely be
asserted that viler trash, less representative of the original,
less distinguished in language, less intelligent in intention,
is not to be found in the literature of the world, than in
the feeble, vague, and silly verse-translations from the

classics which deformed the earlier years of Elizabeth's reign. Phaer (1558) would be the worst of all translators of Virgil were he not surpassed in that bad eminence by the maniac Stanyhurst (1582). As for the group of gentlemen who put Seneca into rhyme—the Newtons and Nevilles and Studleys and Nuces—they, in their own words, "linked lie, with jingling chains, on wailing Limbo shore," the complete mockery of every stray reader who comes across them. Arthur Golding, who paraphrased the *Metamorphoses* of Ovid (1565–67), was the best of this large class of verse-translators of the early part of the reign; he possessed no genius, indeed, but a certain limpidity and sweetness in narrative lifts him out of the "limbo" of the Jasper Heywoods and the Churchyards.

This labour of translating occupied a vast number of persons at the Universities and the Inns of Court, where, as we are told in 1559, "Minerva's men and finest wits do swarm." Much, possibly the majority of what was written, never reached the printing-press at all. More interesting, perhaps, but scarcely more meritorious than the work of the translators, were the attempts at original or imitative poetry. The earliest name is that of Barnabee Googe, whose most important poem, the *Cupido Conquered,* shows, like the *Temple de Cupido* of Marot (the comparison is cruel for Googe), a tendency to return to mediæval forms of allegory, and to the school of the *Roman de la Rose.* George Turbervile, a translator from Mantuan and Boccaccio, wrote so-called "songs and sonnets" (1567) of his own. The *Romeus and Juliet* of Arthur Broke has the interest of having certainly been enjoyed by Shakespeare. These and other minor poets of this experimental period were greatly hampered by their devotion to the tiresome couplet of alternate six and seven beats, a measure without a rival in its capacity for producing an effect at once childish and pedantic. But it is in the frequent and popular miscellanies of this age, and particularly in the *Paradise of Dainty Devises* (1576) and the *Gorgeous Gallery of Gallant Inventions* (1578), that the triviality and emptiness of early Elizabethan verse-style may be most conveniently studied. Poetry was in eager request during these years, but the performance was not ready to begin ; the orchestra was tuning up.

One musician, indeed, there was who produced for a very short time a harmony which was both powerful and novel. The solitary poet of a high order between Dunbar and Spenser is THOMAS SACKVILLE, afterwards Lord Buckhurst and Earl of Dorset. Born in 1536, he went early to Oxford, and became locally celebrated for "sonnets sweetly sauced," which have entirely disappeared ; we may conjecture that they were of the school of Wyatt. In 1561 there was played at Whitehall the "great mask" or tragedy of *Gorbuduc*, by Sackville and his friend Norton. Finally, the second or 1563 edition of the narrative miscellany called *A Mirror for Magistrates* contained two contributions, an "Induction" and a story of "Henry Stafford, Duke of Buckingham," from the pen of Sackville : it is supposed that these were written about 1560. In the latest of these compositions the poet, addressing himself by name, says that it was his purpose "the woeful fall of princes to describe" in future poems ; but this he was prevented from doing by his absorption in political and public life. He rose to the highest offices in the state, living on until 1608, but is not known to have written another line of verse.

Sackville's poetical life, therefore, closed at about the same age as Keats's did ; he is among "the inheritors of unfulfilled renown." His withdrawal from the practice of his art probably delayed the development of English literature by a quarter of a century, since of Sackville's potentiality of genius there can be no question. What he has left to us has a sombre magnificence, a stately fulness, absolutely without parallel in his own age. The poetlings around him were timid, crude, experimental, but Sackville writes like a young and inexperienced master perhaps, yet always like a master. He shows little or not at all the influence of Wyatt and Surrey, but with one hand he takes hold of the easy richness of Chaucer and with the other of the majesty of Dante, to whose *Inferno* the plan of his *Induction* is deeply indebted. In his turn, Sackville exercised no slight fascination over the richer, more elaborate and florid, but radically cognate fancy of Spenser ; and even Shakespeare must have read and admired the sinister fragments of the Lord High Treasurer. Scarce an adjective here and there survives to show Sackville faintly touched by the tasteless heresies of his age. His poetry is not read, partly because of its monotony, partly because the subject-matter of it offers no present entertainment; but in the history of the evolution of style in our literature the place of Sackville must always be a prominent one.

It is to be noted, as a sign of the unhealthy condition of letters in this hectic age, that although it produced experiments in literature, it encouraged no literary men ; that is to say, the interest in books was so faint and unsettled, that no one man was persuaded to give his life to the best literature, or any considerable portion of his life. The only exception may seem to be that of GEORGE

GASCOIGNE, whose talent needed but to have equalled his ambition to reach the highest things. Unfortunately, his skill was mediocre, and though he introduced from Italy the prose comedy, the novel, and blank verse satire, and was the first translator of Greek tragedy and the earliest English critic—success in any one of which departments might have immortalised him—he was tame and trifling in them all. He was still writing actively when, in 1577, he died prematurely, at the age of forty. Nash, in the next generation, summed up the best that can be said for Gascoigne in describing him as one "who first beat the path to that perfection which our best poets have aspired to since his departure."

What has been said of the verse of the early Elizabethan period is in some measure true of its prose, with the exception that bad taste and positive error were less rampant because there was much less ambition to be brilliant and less curiosity in experiment. The prose of this period is not to be sharply distinguished from that of the earlier half of the century. It presents to us no name of a creator of style, like Cranmer, and no narrator with the vivacity of Cavendish. ROGER ASCHAM, who survived until 1568, was the leading writer of the age in English ; his influence was strenuously opposed to the introduction of those French and Italian forces which would have softened and mellowed the harshness of the English tongue so beneficially, and he was all in favour of a crabbed imitation of Greek models, the true beauty of which, it is safe to say, no one in his day comprehended in the modern spirit. It is impossible to call Ascham an agreeable writer, and pure pedantry to insist upon his mastery of English. His efforts were all in an academic direction, and his suspicion of ornament was in diametric opposition to the instinct of the nation, as to be presently and in the great age abundantly revealed. Meanwhile to Ascham and his disciples the only thing needful seemed to be " to speak plainly and nakedly after the common sort of men in few words." North sacrificed, indeed, all distinction, but secured a merry species of vigour, in his paraphrase of Amyot's translation of Plutarch. A deserved popularity was won by Day's 1563 translation of the Latin of Foxe's so-called *Book of Martyrs* and by Holinshed's familiar *Chronicles*, of which Shakespeare made abundant use. In a sketch less hurried than this must be, the laborious compilations of Grafton and of Stow would demand an attention which we dare not give to them here. All these compositions were of value, but the progress of English prose is not apparent in any of them.

On no point of literary criticism have opinions differed more than as to the place of JOHN LYLY in the development of style. Extravagantly admired at the time of its original publication, ridiculed and forgotten for two centuries, the *Euphues* (1579–80) has recovered prestige only to have its claims to originality contested. It has been elaborately shown that Lyly owed his manner and system to the Spaniard Guevara, and his use of English to Lord Berners, while the very balance of his sentences has been attributed to imitation of the *Prayer-Book*. In all this there seems to me to be too much attention paid to detail ; looking broadly at the early prose of Elizabeth's reign, it is surely impossible not to recognise that a new element of richness, of ornament, of harmony, an element by no means wholly admirable, but extremely noticeable, was introduced by Lyly ; that, in short, the publication of *Euphues* burnishes and suddenly animates

—with false lights and glisterings, if you will, but still animates—the humdrum aspect of English prose as Ascham and Wilson had left it. Splendour was to be one of the principal attributes of the Elizabethan age, and *Euphues* is the earliest prose book which shows any desire to be splendid.

It is a very tedious reading for us, this solemn romance of a young Athenian of the writer's own day, who visits Naples first and then England. But to the early admirers of *Euphues*, its analysis of emotion, its wire-drawn definitions of feeling, its high sententiousness, made it intensely attractive. Above all, it was a book for ladies; in an age severely academic and virile, this author turned to address women, lingeringly, lovingly, and he was rewarded as Richardson was two centuries later, and as M. Paul Bourget has been in our own day. Of the faults of *Euphues* enough and to spare is said in all compilations of criticism. Lyly's use of antithesis is always severely reproved, yet it broke·up successfully the flat-footed dulness of his predecessors; his method of drawing images from fabulous zoology and botany is ridiculed, and deservedly, for it degenerates into a trick; yet it evidences a lively fancy; his whole matter is sometimes styled "a piece of affectation and nonsense," yet that merely proves the critic to have never given close attention to the book he condemns. The way Lyly says things is constantly strained and sometimes absurd, but his substance is always noble, enlightened, and urbane, and his influence was unquestionably as civilising as it was extensive. As to his Euphuism, about which so much has been written, it was mainly a tub·to catch a whale,—a surprising manner consciously employed to attract attention, like Carlylese. It had no lasting effects, fortunately, but for the time it certainly enlivened the languid triviality of the vernacular.

Of infinitely greater importance was the revolution effected in poetry, in the same eventful year 1579, by the publication of the *Shepherd's Calender* of EDMUND SPENSER.   With this book we begin a new era; we stand on the threshold, not of a fashion or a period, but of the whole system of modern English poetry. The strange obscurity which broods over most of Elizabethan biography—where the poetry was every-thing and the poet little regarded — lifts but seldom from the life of Spenser.   He may have been born in 1552; some translations of his from Petrarch and Joachim du Bellay, already showing the direction of his reading, were printed in 1569; from 1570 to 1576 he was at Cambridge, where he fell into a literary, but ex-tremely tasteless and pedantic set of men, who, neverthe-less, had the wit to perceive their friend's transcendent genius; and during three obscure years, while we lose sight of him, we gather that he was bewitched by the charming form and character of Sir Philip Sidney, his junior by two years.   The influence of Sidney was not beneficial to Spenser, for that delightful person had accepted the heresy of the Cambridge wits, and was striving to bring about the " general surceasing and silence of bald rhymers," and the adoption in English of classic forms of rhymeless quantitative verse, entirely foreign to the genius of our prosody.

For a moment it seemed as though Spenser would succumb to the authority of Sidney's Areopagus, and waste his time and art on exercises in iambic trimeter. But at the end of 1579 came the anonymous publication of the *Shepherd's Calender,* and in the burst of applause which greeted these lyric pastorals, the danger passed. The book consisted of twelve eclogues, distantly modelled on those of Theocritus, and more closely upon Virgil and Mantuan ; they were in rhymed measures of extreme variety, some of the old jingling kind, from which Spenser had not yet escaped, others of a brilliant novelty, conveying such a music as had yet been heard from no English lips. "June" is the most stately and imaginative of these eclogues, while in " May " and " September" we see how much the poet was still enslaved by the evil traditions of the century. The *Shepherd's Calender* is momentous in its ease and fluent melody, its novelty of form, and its delicate grace. Throughout England, with singular unanimity, " the new poet" was hailed with acclamation, for, as Sidney quaintly put it two years later, "an over-faint quietness" had "strewn the house for poets," and the whole nation was eager for song. Yet we must remember that the positive value of these artificial pastorals of 1579 might easily be, and sometimes has been, overrated.

Spenser now disappears from our sight again. We divine him employed in the public service in Ireland, associated there with Raleigh, and rewarded by the manor and castle of Kilcolman. We get vague glimpses of the composition, from 1580 onwards, of a great poem of chivalry, in which Spenser is encouraged by Raleigh, and in 1590 there are published the first three books of the *Faerie Queen*. From this time forth to the end of his brief life, Spenser is unchallenged as the greatest of the English poets, no less pre-eminent in non-dramatic verse among his glorious coevals than Shakespeare was presently to be in dramatic. He published in 1591 his *Complaints*, a collection of earlier poems ; *Colin Clout's*

Come Home Again in 1595, *Amoretti and Epithalamia* in the same year, three more books of the *Faerie Queen* and the *Four Hymns* in 1596. The close of his life was made wretched by the excesses of the Irish rebels, who burned Kilcolman in October 1598. Spenser, reduced to penury, fled to England, and died " for lack of bread " in London, on the 16th of January 1599.

It is by the *Faerie Queen* that Spenser holds his sovereign place among the foremost English poets. Taken without relation to its time, it is a miracle of sustained and extended beauty ; but considered historically, it is nothing less than a portent. To find an example of British poetry of the highest class, Spenser had to search back to the Middle Ages, to Chaucer himself. So great was the change which two centuries had made in language, in prosody, in attitude to life, that Spenser could practically borrow from Chaucer little or nothing but a sentimental stimulus. The true precursors of his great poem were the Italian romances, and chiefly the *Orlando Furioso.* It is not to be questioned that the youth of Spenser had been utterly enthralled by the tranquil and harmonious imagination of Ariosto. In writing the chivalrous romance of the *Faerie Queen*, Spenser, although he boasted of his classical acquirements, was singularly little affected by Greek, or even Latin ideas. There was no more of Achilles than of Roland in his conception of a fighting hero. The greatest of all English poems of romantic adventure is steeped in the peculiar enchantment of the Celts. It often seems little more or less than a *mabinogi* extended and embroidered, a Celtic dream tempered with moral allegory and political allusion. Not in vain had Spenser for so many years inhabited that " most beautiful and sweet country," the Island of Dreams

and melancholy fantasy. Cradled in the richness of
Italy, trained in the mistiness of Ireland, the genius of
Spenser was enabled to give to English poetry exactly
the qualities it most required. Into fields made stony
and dusty with systematic pedantry it poured a warm
and fertilising rain of romance.

The first three books of the *Faerie Queen* contain the
most purely poetical series of pictures which English
literature has to offer to us. Here the Italian influence
is still preponderant ; in the later books the Celtic spirit
of dream carries the poet a little too far into the realms
of indefinite fancy. A certain grandeur which sustains
the three great cantos of Truth, Temperance, and Chastity
fades away as we proceed. It would be, indeed, not
difficult to find fault with much in the conduct of this
extraordinary poem. The construction of it is loose and
incoherent when we compare it with the epic grandeur
of the masterpieces of Ariosto and Tasso. The heroine,
Queen Gloriana, never once makes her appearance in
her own poem, and this is absurd. That a wind of
strange hurry and excitability seems to blow the poet
along so fast that he has no time to consider his grammar,
his rhymes, or even his continuity of ideas, but is obliged,
if the profanity be permitted, to " faggot his fancies as
they fall "—this is certainly no merit ; while the constant
flattery of Elizabeth has been to some fastidious spirits
a stumbling-block.

But these are spots in the sun. The rich and voluptuous colour, the magical landscape, the marvellous
melody, have fascinated young readers in every generation, and will charm the race till it decays. More than
any other writer, save Keats, Spenser is interpenetrated
with the passion of beauty. All things noble and comely

appeal to him ; no English poet has been so easy and yet so stately, so magnificent and yet so plaintive. He is pre-eminent for a virile sweetness, for the love and worship of woman, for a power of sustaining an impression of high spectacular splendour. What should constitute a gentleman, and in what a world a gentleman should breathe and move—these are his primary considerations. His long poem streams on with the panoply of a gorgeous masque, drawn through the resonant woodlands of fairyland, in all the majestic pomp of imitative knight-errantry. And then his music, his incomparable harmony of versification, the subtlety of that creation of his, the stanza which so proudly bears his name—the finest single invention in metre which can be traced home to any English poet ! All these things combine to make the flower of Edmund Spenser's genius not the strongest nor the most brilliant, perhaps, but certainly the most delicately perfumed in the whole rich garden of English verse.

The splendid achievement of Spenser saved our literature once and for all from a very serious danger. Ascham, whose authority with the university wits of the succeeding generation was potent, had deliberately stigmatised rhyme as barbarous. This notion exercised many minds, and was taken up very seriously by that charming paladin of the art, Sir PHILIP SIDNEY. His experiments may be glanced at in the pages of the *Arcadia,* and they were widely imitated. They followed, but were of the same order as the stilted Seneca tragedies, to which we shall presently refer, and, like them, were violently in opposition to the natural instinct of English poetry. Spenser would now have none of these "reformed verses," and in one of his early pieces, "The Oak and the Briar," went far to vindicate by his practice a freedom of prosody which was not to be accepted until the days of Coleridge and Scott. Of the works of Sidney himself, it is difficult to know how far they influenced taste to any wide. degree, for they were mainly posthumous. To the *Astrophel and Stella* we shall presently return. The *Arcadia*—that "vain, amatorious poem," as Milton calls it, a heavy pastoral romance in poetical prose and prosy verse, founded on the lighter and more classical *Arcadia* of Sannazaro—though written perhaps in 1580, just after the publication of *Euphues*, was not printed until 1590. The most valuable work of Sidney, who purposed no monument of books to the world, was the *Defense of Poesy*, an urbane and eloquent essay, which labours under but one disadvantage, namely, that when it was composed in 1581 there was scarcely any poesy in England to be defended. This was posthumously printed in 1595.

There was, however, one department in poetry of superlative importance, in which neither Spenser nor even Sidney took a prominent part. It is strange that the former, with all his accomplishments in verse, left the pure spontaneous lyric, the μελος, untouched ; the latter, essaying it on pedantic lines and in a perverse temper, produced the grotesque experiments embedded in the *Arcadia*, the effect of which on subsequent literature was wholly evil. Neither of these great men gave due recognition to a new thing, quite unknown in the English of their own early youth, which revolutionised the speech and style of the nation, and which has done more than anything else to stamp on subsequent English poetry its national character. This was the Song, as introduced, almost simultaneously, and as by an unconscious impulse, by a myriad writers in the last decade but one of the sixteenth century. The successes of English verse had hitherto been of a stately kind; the forms used had scarcely ever been at all felicitous if they strayed from the rigid mediæval stanzas and rhythms. Lyric had awakened in Italy and then in France without encouraging even its direct imitators in England, such as Surrey and Wyatt, to any but a timid elegance. It may be broadly said that, until 1580, the only examples of lyric in English had been fragments or offshoots of rude folk-song.

The change of note is one of the most extraordinary and the least accountable phenomena in the history of literature. Quite abruptly, we find a hundred poets able to warble and dance where not one could break into a tune or a trot a year or two before. It is difficult to assign priority or an exact date in this matter. If Sidney wrote—

> " *Weep, neighbours, weep, do you not hear it said*
> *That Love is dead?* "

(which was not printed until 1598) as early as some critics suppose, he does, in spite of his pedantries, deserve a place among the precursors. We are more sure of Lyly, whose

> " *Cupid and my Campaspe play'd* "

was in print in 1584. Among the anthologies, the earliest in which the true song-note is faintly heard is Clement Robinson's *Handful of Pleasant Delights*, also of 1584. The claim of Constable is now known to rest upon a misprint, and the date of Campion's first songs, which, in 1601, had so passed from hand to hand that they had

grown " as coin cracked in exchange," is uncertain. An
examination of Greene's romances, in which poetry of all
kinds was included, shows a sudden alteration, a brisk
exchange of the old dull trudge for brilliant measures
and lively fancy about the year 1588, and in 1589 Lodge
abruptly throws aside his cumbersome pedestrian style.
Without falling into a dogmatic statement, these indications will suffice to show when the reformation, or rather
creation, of English song occurred.

What caused it ? No doubt the general efflorescence
of feeling, the new enlightenment, the new passion of
life, took this mode of expressing itself, as it took others,
in other departments of intellectual behaviour. But this
particular manifestation of tuneful, flowery fancy seems
to have been connected with two artistic tendencies, the
one the cultivation of music, the other the study of recent
French verse. The former is the more easy to follow.
The year 1588 was the occasion of a sudden outburst of
musical talent in this country ; it is, approximately, the
date of public recognition of the exquisite talent of Tallis,
Bird, and Dowland, and the foundation of their school
of national lute-melody. This species of chamber-music
instantly became the fashion, and remained so for at least
some quarter of a century. It was necessary to find
words for these airs, and the poems so employed were
obliged to be lucid, liquid, brief, and of a temper suited
to the gaiety and sadness of the instrument. The demand created the supply, and from having been heavy
and dissonant to a painful degree, English lyrics suddenly
took a perfect art and sweetness. What is very strange
is that there was no transition. As soon as a composer
wanted a trill of pure song, such as a blackcap or a
whitethroat might have supplied, anonymous bards,

7

without the smallest training, were able to gush forth
with—

> " *O Love, they wrong thee much*
> *That say thy sweet is bitter,*
> *When thy rich fruit is such*
> *As nothing can be sweeter.*
> *Fair house of joy and bliss,*
> *Where truest pleasure is,*
> *I do adore thee;*
> *I know thee what thou art,*
> *I serve thee with my heart,*
> *And fall before thee*"

(a little miracle which we owe to Mr. Bullen's researches);
or, in a still lighter key, with—

> " *Now is the month of maying,*
> *When merry lads are playing,*
> *Each with his bonny lass,*
> *Upon the greeny grass;*
> *The Spring, clad all in gladness,*
> *Doth laugh at Winter's sadness,*
> *And to the bagpipe's sound*
> *The nymphs tread out their ground.*"

This joyous semi-classical gusto in life, this ecstasy in
physical beauty and frank pleasure, recalls the lyrical
poetry of France in the beginning of the sixteenth century, and the influence of the Pléiade on the song-
writers and sonneteers of the Elizabethan age is not
questionable. It is, however, very difficult to trace this
with exactitude. The spirit of Ronsard and of Reny
Belleau, and something intangible of their very style, are
discerned in Lodge and Greene, but it would be dangerous to insist on this. A less important French writer,
however, Philippe Desportes, enjoyed, as we know, a
great popularity in Elizabethan England. Lodge says
of him that he was " ordinarily in every man's hands,"

and direct paraphrases of the amatory and of the religious verse of Desportes are frequent.

The trick of this light and brilliant sensuous verse once learned, it took forms the most various and the most delightful. In the hands of the best poets it rapidly developed from an extreme naïveté and artless jigging freedom to the fullest splendour of song. When Lodge, in 1590, could write—

> " *Like to the clear in highest sphere,*
> *Where all imperial beauty shines,*
> *Of self-same colour is her hair,*
> *Whether unfolded or in twines;*
> > *Heigh ho, fair Rosaline!*
> *Her eyes are sapphires set in snow,*
> *Refining heaven by every wink;*
> *The gods do fear whenas they glow,*
> *And I do tremble, when I think,*
> > *Heigh ho, would she were mine!*"

there was no technical lesson left for the English lyric to learn. But the old simplicity remained awhile side by side with this gorgeous and sonorous art, and to the combination we owe the songs of Shakespeare and Campion, the delicate mysteries of *England's Helicon*, the marvellous short flights of verbal melody that star the music-books down to 1615 and even later. But then the flowers of English lyric began to wither, and the jewels took their place; a harder, less lucid, less spontaneous method of song-writing succeeded.

Meanwhile, in close connection with the creation of the Elizabethan lyric, the development of the sonnet had been progressing. It passed through a crisis in 1580, when THOMAS WATSON published his singularly successful *Hecatompathia*, a volume of a hundred sonnets in a vicious form of sixteen lines. In spite of the popularity of this overrated volume, the metrical heresy did not gain acceptance, and Watson himself, in a later collection, rejected it. In 1580 and 1581 Sidney was writing sonnets in a shape not dangerously differing from the accepted Italian standards, but he also encouraged the composition of quatorzains, poems of fourteen lines ending in a rhymed couplet. Unfortunately, this spurious form became generally accepted in England, in defiance of all Continental precedent. It received imperious sanction from the practice of Shakespeare and Spenser, and, in spite of efforts made by Donne and others, this false sonnet was in universal employment in England until the time of Milton.

Perhaps in consequence of this radical error of construction, which is fatal to the character of the poem, the vast body of Elizabethan sonnets, of which more than a thousand examples survive, suffers from a monotony of style, from which even the gracious genius of Spenser was not entirely able to escape in his *Amoretti*. Of course, infinitely the most valuable of these sonnet-cycles—the only one, indeed, which still lives—is that in which Shakespeare has enshrined the mysteries of a Platonic passion of friendship, fervid and wayward to the frontier of inverted instinct, which has been and always will be the crux of commentators. Yet even here it is to be noted that when Shakespeare leaves the solitary relation which was moving him, at this certain moment, so vehemently, he loses his magic and his melody and falls into the same affected insipidity and monotony as the other sonneteers of the age. The *Astrophel and Stella* of Sidney, posthumously printed in 1591, let loose this new fashion of amorosity upon the world, and the period during which the rage for cycles of quatorzains lasted may be defined as from 1592 to about 1598.

All this time, a prodigious new birth had been making its appearance in English literature. A living drama was created, which, almost without a childhood, sprang into magnificent maturity. In the Middle Ages, the vernacular mysteries had enjoyed their day of popularity in England as in other parts of Europe, and of these miracle plays we still possess four cycles. After fifteenth-century "miracles" had come the sixteenth-century "moralities" and "moral interludes," which were the connecting link between the Mediæval and the Renaissance stage. The latest of the inglorious mediæval playwrights had been JOHN HEYWOOD, whose rollicking *Interludes* were probably acted between 1520 and 1540; after his time the "morality" was an acknowledged survival, no longer in sympathy with the needs of the age. Much has been written, and much is doubtless still to be discovered, with regard to English drama between the *York Mysteries* and *Gorbuduc*, but it lies outside the scope of our inquiry. These "miracles" and "merry plays" were almost entirely devoid of purely literary merit, and were mainly of service in preserving in England the habit of witnessing and enjoying public performances on the stage.

Between the decay of the moralities and the foundation of a genuine native drama, an attempt was made to introduce into England a dramatic literature founded directly on the ancients,—on the comedy of Plautus and the tragedy of Seneca. This effort ultimately failed in this country as completely as it succeeded in France, but it must be remembered that it made a gallant struggle for existence during thirty years. Of these pseudo-classical plays the earliest and most remarkable is the farce of *Ralph Roister*

Doister. This was written by the Head-master of Eton, Dr. Nicholas Udall, about 1551, and was, therefore, almost exactly contemporaneous with the opening of modern comedy in France, in the *Eugène* of Jodelle (1552). If these two plays are compared, their similarity of system is remarkable ; each depends on the exploitation of a single farcical incident, adapted from the classical form to local conditions, with a certain simple insistence on analysis of character. It is curious to examine these two almost childish farces, which have a good deal in common, and to reflect that from these apparently cognate seedlings there presently sprang trees so widely distinct as Shakespeare and Molière. But it would perhaps be more correct to say that the seedling of which *Ralph Roister Doister* was the cotyledon never really reached maturity at all, but withered incontinently away. Other Terentian or Plautan plays were Still's *Gammer Gurton's Needle* (1566) and Gascoigne's prose version of Ariosto's *Gli Suppositi* (1561).

We have already spoken of the rage for translating Seneca which invaded England at the beginning of Elizabeth's reign. The anti-romantic spirit of these tragedies, with its insistence on correctness and simplicity of plot, was contemplated by the English nation as by the French, but while the latter accepted, the former rejected it. The *Gorboduc* of Sackville is mainly interesting as showing how the spirit of Seneca could harden into stone or plaster a romantic genius of the most ductile order. Thomas Hughes (1587) endeavoured to make a positive *pastiche* of Seneca in an Arthurian tragedy. Scholars and wits of the academic type persisted in trying to force this exotic and entirely unsympathetic product on unwilling English ears, and no less a poet than Samuel Daniel, in the full Shakespearean heyday, polished in the true Senecan manner a stately *Cleopatra* (1592) and a stiff *Philotas*. But the classical tradition, thus amply presented, was deliberately and finally rejected by English taste.

We have now reached the most extraordinary event in the history of English literature—the sudden creation of a secular, poetic drama—in the exercise of which letters first became a profession in this country, and in the course of the intensely rapid development of which the greatest writer of the world was naturally evolved. It is necessary to warn the general reader that the processes of this development are extremely obscure, and that almost all its early events are dated and correlated solely by the conjectures of successive commentators, who have to base their theories on atoms of fact or of still less solid report. The dates supplied by the ordinary books of reference are here exceedingly misleading, for the year may be that either of the first performance, or of the registration, or of the publication of each piece, and the first and last of these may be divided by many years. For instance, the extremely important tragedy of *Dr. Faustus* was not printed until 1601, but it was acted in 1588; still more notably, several of Shakespeare's early plays were still in MS. six years after his death. We get our information from rudely kept and imperfect registers, or from the diary of a single manager. Yet it is believed that between 1580 and 1640 not fewer than two thousand distinct plays were acted in England, and of these more than five hundred are extant. Through this vast crowd of imperfect witnesses, often with scarcely a clue, the student of Elizabethan drama has to thread his path. The researches of several students, extremely valuable and original as they are, suffer from the lack of a sense of the frail tenure of irrefutable fact on which their systems are built up. The discovery of a single journal kept from 1585 to 1600 might turn our dramatic histories to something like waste paper. It seems proper to point out that while no part of our inquiry is of a more romantic interest, none is more uncertain and conjectural in its detail.

It appears, however, that the result of the experiments in farce and in Senecan melodrama, of which brief mention has been made above, was, at first, confined to the production of an abundance of rough and incoherent plays, often no more than a succession of unconnected scenes, addressed mainly to the eye. It is probable that we possess a highly favourable example of these incoherent pieces in the *Arraignment of Paris*, by GEORGE PEELE, in which a classical story is faintly treated, with occasional passages of extraordinary suavity of blank verse and grace of fancy. We retain, moreover, eight so-called court-comedies by Lyly, produced between 1580 and 1590. These, mainly written in prose, are allegorical and doubtless political satires, not at all dramatic in character, although broken up into dialogue, and to be considered rather in connection with the *Euphues* than as plays. Lyly, notwithstanding, had his influence in the romanticising of the English stage.

Out of the unpromising chaos of which these were the floating islands which have preserved the most consistency, there unexpectedly sprang the solid group of important writers who immediately preceded Shakespeare, and were, in fact, our first real dramatists, the earliest to conceive of tragedy and comedy in their modern sense. During the plague of 1586 all theatres were closed, and it seems almost indubitable that when they reopened they were catered for by playwrights to whom the idea of a new art had meanwhile presented itself, and who had discussed its methods in . unison. Of these, some, like Kyd and Peele, had been writing at an earlier time, in the old vague way ; others, principally Greene, Lodge, and the anonymous author of that brilliant domestic drama, *Arden of Feversham,* in all probability now opened their dramatic career. In some vague way, the original leadership in the new fashion of writing seems attributable to THOMAS KYD, who had been a translator not merely of Seneca, but of · the French Senecan, Garnier, and now saw the error of his theories. Kyd is a sort of English Lazare de Baïf, the *choragus* who directed the new dramatists and led them off. His early plays have disappeared, and Kyd's archaic *Spanish Tragedy,* acted in 1587, shows him still in the trammels of pseudo-classicism. This fierce play, nevertheless, is pervaded by a wild wind of romantic frenzy which marks an epoch in English drama. In Peele's *King David and Fair Bethsabe,* perhaps a year or two later, there is a surprising advance in melody and the manipulation of blank verse.

Far more important, however, in every way, appears to have been the action of ROBERT GREENE on drama. Here again, unfortunately, much is left to conjecture, since, while the novels of Greene have been largely preserved, his plays have mainly disappeared. It has been taken for granted, but on what evidence it is hard to tell, that his early dramas, produced perhaps between 1583 and 1586, were of the Senecan order, and that Greene was converted to the new tragical manner by Kyd, or even by Marlowe, who was several years his junior.

This theory is founded upon the close resemblance to the style of *Tamburlaine* met with in the *Orlando* and the *Alphonsus* of Greene ; but we cannot be assured that the phenomenon is not a converse one, and the result of Marlowe's improvement upon Greene's rough essays.   It is the undoubted merit of the older writer, that, though he lacks vigour, concentration, and selection, he is more truly the forerunner of the romantic Shakespeare than any other of the school.   In Greene, the new spirit of Renaissance sensuousness, so unbridled in Marlowe, is found to be restrained by those cool and exquisite moral motives, the elaboration of which is the crowning glory of Shakespeare.   Faint and pale as Greene's historical plays must be confessed to be, they are the first specimens of native dramatic literature in which we see foreshadowed the genius of the romantic English stage.   If we turn to France again, where a moment ago we found Jodelle so near to our own Udall, we see that in one generation the two schools have flown apart, and that while Greene and Kyd are prophesying of Shakespeare with us, Grévin and Larivey have already taken a stride towards Molière.

By far the most brilliant personage in this pre-Shakespearian school, however, was CHRISTOPHER MARLOWE. Born in the same year as Shakespeare, he showed much superior quickness of spirit, and was famous, nay, was dead, almost before the greater writer had developed individual character.   Between 1587 and 1593 Marlowe was certainly the most prominent living figure in English poetry, with the single exception of Spenser.   Long obscured by prejudice against the ultra-romanticism of his style and the heterodoxy of his opinions, it may be that of late Marlowe has been celebrated with some exaggeration of eulogy. He has been spoken of as manifestly in the first order of poets, as of like rank with Æschylus, and greater than Corneille. That his genius, cut off in his thirtieth year by the hand of a murderer, had unfathomable possibilities, is not to be denied. His treatment of blank verse, which, though he habitually uses it monotonously and deadly, he can at a moment's notice transform into a magnificent instrument of melody, amounts, in these exceptional instances, to a positive enchantment. He breaks loose from the prison of mediæval convention in thought and style as no Englishman had been able to do before him. He was an "alchemist of eloquence," as Nash called him, who had discovered several of the rarest secrets of magic in literature. To a rare degree he exemplified the passion, the virility, the audacious, and, indeed, reckless intellectual courage of the new English spirit. His epic paraphrase of *Hero and Leander* shows him as intelligently enamoured of plastic beauty as his tragedy of *Edward II.* proves him alive to the long-forgotten art of dramatic psychology.

His was, indeed, a majestic imagination, and yet, judging Marlowe by what we actually possess of his writings, we need to moderate the note of praise a little. By the side of what Shakespeare was immediately to present to us, the grandiloquence of *Tamburlaine* seems childish, the necromantic scenes of *Faustus* primitive and empty, the execution of the well-conceived *Jew of Malta* savage and melodramatic. Only in reaching *Edward II.* do we feel quite persuaded that Marlowe was not merely a poet of amazing fire of imagination and melody of verse, but also a consummate builder of plot and character. This drama is probably almost exactly of the same date as the *Two Gentlemen of Verona*, and was written at the same age. There can be no question that in 1593 the performance and even the promise of Marlowe were greater than that of Shakespeare, who seems to take a leap forwards the moment that his formidable rival is removed. All that can be now said is that, had both poets died on the same day, it is certain that Marlowe would appear to us the greater genius of the two. He is spasmodic and imperfect, his felicities are flashes in a coarse and bombastic obscurity of style, his notions of construction are barbarously primitive ; yet he preserves the perennial charm of one who has been a pioneer, who has cried in the wilderness of literature.

The old notion that WILLIAM SHAKESPEARE was an untaught genius, warbling his wood-notes wild, has long been discarded. We now perceive that he was "made" not less than "born"; that, whether "born" or "made," he was the creature of his time, and of a particular phase of his time, to such an extent that he seems to us not so much an Elizabethan poet as Elizabethan poetry itself. His very life, of which enough is known to make him personally more familiar to us than are most of his less illustrious compeers, is more typical than individual in its features. In Shakespeare an heroic epoch culminates ; he is the commanding peak of a vast group of mountains. It is therefore vain to consider him as though he stood alone, a solitary portent in a plain. More than any other of the greatest poets of the world, he rises, by insensible degrees, on the shoulders and the hands of a crowd of precursors, yet so rapidly did this crowd collect that our eyes are scarcely quick enough to perceive the process. It is perhaps useful, in so very summary a sketch as this, to take the date of Marlowe's death, 1593, and start by seeing what Shakespeare had by that time done.

He was twenty-nine years of age. If he had come up from Stratford in 1586, he had been already seven years in London, but no mention of his name survives earlier than Christmas 1593. He had published nothing, but was then preparing *Venus and Adonis* for the press. How had these seven years, then, during which Marlowe had been so active and so prominent, been employed by Shakespeare? Unquestionably in learning the secret of his art and in practising his hand on every variety of exercise. It seems likely that he had become an actor soon after his arrival in London, probably joining that leading company, "the Lord Strange's men," when it was formed in 1589. Early in 1592 the Rose Theatre was opened on the Bankside, and Shakespeare continued, no doubt, to act there until the more commodious Globe could receive his colleagues and himself in 1599. Mr. Sidney Lee believes that as early as 1591 the actor began to be a dramatist. There is no evidence of great precocity on Shakespeare's part. What he abandoned early, he never learned to excel in; as an example, it may be pointed out that he remains inferior both to Spenser and to Marlowe in the province of rhymed narrative. To the great business of his life, the composition of plays, he applied himself at first as an apprentice. There can be little question that all his early dramatic work consisted in the revising and completing of sketches by older men. These older men would, no doubt, in the main be anonymous playwrights, whose works are now as extinct as their names. But Shakespeare would also imitate and recast the dramatic sketches of those poets of an older generation who had started the new comedy and the new tragedy in England. From Peele, from Greene, from Marlowe most of all, he would borrow, and that without stint or scruple, exactly what he needed to form the basis of his own composite and refulgent style.

That criticism has been too pedagogic in attempting to fix what must, for lack of documentary evidence, be left uncertain in detail, need not prevent us from admitting that certain hypotheses about the early Shakespeare are, at least, highly probable. The struggle between rhyme and blank verse, gradually ending in the triumph of the latter, is certainly an indication of date not to be despised. That other hands than that of Shakespeare are to be traced in the plays attributed to his youth must be allowed, without too blind a confidence in plausible conjectures as to the authorship of the non-Shakespearian portions. By the light of what patient investigation has achieved, we find Shakespeare, by 1593, identified with five or six plays, three of which may be held to be, practically, his unaided and unsuggested work, *Love's Labour Lost*, the *Comedy of Errors*, and the *Two Gentlemen of Verona*. In these we particularly note the struggle still going on for mastery between rhyme and blank verse, and the general effect is one of brightness, grace, and prettiness; the key of feeling is subdued, the deeper wells of human passion are left untroubled. Each of these plays—even the *Two Gentlemen*, which suggested greater things—leaves an impression of sketchiness, of slightness, on the mind, when we compare it with later masterpieces.

It is difficult not to be persuaded that in 1593 something of critical import happened which revealed his own genius to Shakespeare. Marlowe died; the jealousy of the surviving elder playwrights broke out angrily against the Joannes Factotum from Stratford; the play-houses were closed on account of the plague; it is just possible that Shakespeare went to Germany and Italy. Several of these causes, perhaps, combined to intensify his intellectual vitality. His company, now under the patronage of Lord Hunsdon, set to work again early in 1594. Shakespeare printed *Venus and Adonis*, a romance of the vain pursuit of unwilling adolescent beauty. This was perhaps the period of the agony of the *Sonnets;* but Shakespeare soon left transitory and tentative things behind him, and prepared for that solemn and spectacular energy on the results of which the world has been gazing in wonder ever since, that vigour which was to be exercised for eighteen years upon the consummation of English poetry. Between 1593, when drama was still in its essence primitive, and the close of the century, Shakespeare gave his attention mainly to history-plays and to idyllic comedies, reaching in the latter the highest level which this species of drama has attained in any language; *Midsummer Night's Dream* (1595) leading us on by romantic plays, each more exquisite than the last, to a positive culmination of blossoming fancy in the *As You Like It*, of 1599.

With *All's Well that Ends Well* and *Julius Cæsar* a new departure may be traced. Shakespeare seems suddenly to take a more austere and caustic view of life, and expresses it in sinister romance, or, more triumphantly, in tragedy of the fullest and most penetrating order. In 1601 he took an old play of *Hamlet*, perhaps originally written by Kyd, and rewrote it, possibly not for the first time. This final revision has remained by far the most durably popular of Shakespeare's works upon the stage. He had now reached the very summits of his genius, and if we oblige ourselves to express an opinion as to the supreme

moment in·his career, the year 1605 presently offers us
an approximate date. We stand on the colossal peak of
King Lear, with *Othello* on our right hand and *Macbeth*
on our left, the sublime masses of Elizabethan mountain
country rolling on every side of us, yet plainly dominated
by the extraordinary central cluster of aiguilles on which
we have planted ourselves. This triple summit of the
later tragedies of Shakespeare forms the Mount Everest
of the poetry of the world. If *Macbeth* dates from 1606,
there were still four years of splendid production left to
the poet, work of recovered serenity, of infinite sweetness,
variety, and enchantment, but, so far as concerns grasp
of the huge elements of human life, a little less heroic
than the almost supernatural group of tragedies which
had culminated in *King Lear.* And then, probably in
the spring of 1611, the magician, fresh from the ringing
melodies of *A Winter's Tale* and of the *Tempest*, with
all his powers and graces fresh about him, breaks his
staff, leaves his fragments for Fletcher to finish, and
departs for Stratford and the oblivion of a civic life.
After five years' silence — incomprehensible, fabulous
silence in the very prime of affluent song—Shakespeare
dies, only fifty-two years of age, in 1616.

From 1593 to 1610, therefore, the volcanic forces of
Elizabethan literature were pre-eminently at work.
During these seventeen years Spenser was finishing the
Faerie Queen, Bacon and Hooker were creating modern
prose, Jonson was active, and Beaumont and Fletcher
beginning to be prominent. These, to preserve our mountain simile, were majestic masses in the landscape, but the
central cone, the truncation of which would reduce the
structure to meanness, and would dwarf the entire scheme
of English literature, was Shakespeare. Very briefly, we

may remind ourselves of what his work for the press in those years consisted. He published no dramatic work until 1597. The plays to which his name is, with more or less propriety, attached, are thirty-eight in number; of these, sixteen appeared in small quarto form during the poet's lifetime, and the title-pages of nine or ten of these "stolen and surreptitious" editions, originally sold at sixpence each, bear his name. We have the phenomenon, therefore, of a bibliographical indifference to posterity rare even in that comparatively unlettered age. It is curious to think that, if all Shakespeare's MSS. had been destroyed when he died, we should now possess no *Macbeth* and no *Othello*, no *Twelfth Night* and no *As You Like It*. In 1623 the piety of two humble friends, Heminge and Condell—whose names deserve to be carved on the forefront of the Temple of Fame—preserved for us the famous folio text. But the conditions under which that text was prepared from what are vaguely called Shakespeare's "papers" must have been, and obviously were, highly uncritical. The folio contained neither *Pericles* nor the *Two Noble Kinsmen*, yet participation in these is plausibly claimed for Shakespeare. What other omissions were there, what intrusion of lines not genuinely his ?

This question has occupied an army of investigators, whose elaborate and conflicting conjectures have not always been illuminated with common sense. More than a hundred years ago, one of the wittiest of our poets represented the indignant spirit of Shakespeare as assuring his emendators that it would be

> "*Better to bottom tarts and cheesecakes nice*
> *Than thus be patched and cobbled in one's grave,*"

and since that date whole libraries have been built over

8

the complaining ghost. Within the last quarter of a century, systems by which to test the authenticity and the chronology of the plays have been produced with great confidence, metrical formulas which are to act as reagents and to identify the component parts of a given passage with scientific exactitude. Of these "verse-tests" and "pause-tests" no account can here be given. That the results of their employment have been curious and valuable shall not be denied; but there is already manifest in the gravest criticism a reaction against excess of confidence in them. At one time it was supposed that the "end-stopt" criterium, for instance, might be dropped, like a chemical substance, on the page of Shakespeare, and would there immediately and finally determine minute quantities of Peele or Kyd, that a fragment of Fletcher would turn purple under it, or a greenish tinge betray a layer of Rowley. It is not thus that poetry is composed; and this ultra-scientific theory showed a grotesque ignorance of the human pliability of art.

Yet, although the mechanical artifice of this class of criticism carries with it its own refutation, it cannot but have been useful for the reader of Shakespeare that this species of alchemy should be applied to his text. It has dispersed the old superstition that every word printed within the covers of the folio must certainly be Shakespeare's in the sense in which the entire text of Tennyson or of Victor Hugo belongs to those poets. We are now content to realise that much which is printed there was adapted, edited, or accepted by Shakespeare; that he worked in his youth in the studios of others, and that in middle life younger men painted on his unfinished canvases. But there must be drawn a distinction between Shakespeare's share in the general Elizabethan dramatisation of history, where anybody might lend a hand, and the creation of his own sharply individualised imaginative work. If the verse-tester comes probing in *Macbeth* for bits of Webster, we send him packing about his business ; if he likes to analyse *Henry VI.* he can do no harm, and may make some curious discoveries. With the revelation of dramatic talent in England there had sprung up a desire to celebrate the dynastic glories of the country in a series of chronicle-plays. It is probable that every playwright of the period had a finger in this gallery of historical entablatures, and Shakespeare, too, a modest artisan, stood to serve his apprenticeship here before in *Richard III.* he proved that his independent brush could excel the brilliant master-worker Marlowe in Marlowe's own approved style. He proceeded to have a chronicle in hand to the close of his career, but he preserved for this class of work the laxity of evolution and lack of dramatic design which he had learned in his youth ; and thus, side by side with plays the prodigious harmony of which Shakespeare alone could have conceived or executed, we have an epical fragment, like *Henry V.*, which is less a drama by one particular poet, than a fold of the vast dramatic tapestry woven to the glory of England by the combined poetic patriotism of the Elizabethans. Is the whole of what we read here implicit Shakespeare, or did another hand combine with his to decorate this portion of the gallery ? It is impossible to tell, and the reply, could it be given, would have no great critical value. *Henry V.* is not *Othello.*

One of the penalties of altitude is isolation, and in reviewing rapidly the state of literary feeling in England in Elizabethan and Jacobean times, we gain the impression that the highest qualities of Shakespeare remained invisible to his contemporaries. To them, unquestionably, he was a stepping-stone to the superior art of Jonson, to the more fluid and obvious graces of Beaumont and Fletcher. Of those whose inestimable privilege it was to meet Shakespeare day by day, we have no evidence that one perceived the supremacy of his genius. The case is rather curious, for it was not that anything austere or arrogant in himself or his work repelled recognition, or that those who gazed were blinded by excess of light. On the contrary, it seemed to his own friends that they appreciated his amiable, easy talent at its proper value ; he was "gentle" Shakespeare to them, and they loved both the man and his poetry. But that he excelled them all at every point, as the oak excels the willow, this, had it been whispered at the Mermaid, would have aroused smiles of derision. The elements of Shakespeare's perfection were too completely fused to attract vulgar wonder at any one point, and those intricate refinements of style and of character which now excite in us an almost superstitious amazement did not appeal to the rough and hasty Elizabethan hearer. In considering Shakespeare's position during his lifetime, moreover, it must not be forgotten that his works made no definite appeal to the reading class until after his death. ·The study of " Shakespeare" as a book cannot date further back than 1623.

For another century the peak of the mountain was shrouded in mists, although its height was vaguely conjectured. Dryden, our earliest modern critic, gradually perceived Shakespeare's greatness, and proclaimed it in his *Prefaces*. Meanwhile, and on until a century after Shakespeare's death, this most glorious of English names had not penetrated across the Channel, and was abso-

lutely unrecognised in France. Voltaire introduced
Shakespeare to French readers in 1731, and *Hamlet*
was translated by Ducis in 1769. Here at home, in the
generations of Pope and Johnson, the magnitude of Shakespeare became gradually apparent to all English critics,
and with Garrick his plays once more took the stage.
Yet into all the honest admiration of the eighteenth
century there entered a prosaic element ; the greatness was felt, but vaguely and painfully. At the end of
the age of Johnson a generation was born to whom, for
the first time, Shakespeare spoke with clear accents.
Coleridge and Hazlitt expounded him to a world so
ready to accept him, that in regarding the great Revival
of 1800 Shakespeare seems almost as completely a
factor in it as Wordsworth himself. In the hands of
such critics, for the first time, the fog cleared away
from the majestic mountain, and showed to the gaze
of the world its varied and harmonious splendour.
That conception of Shakespeare, which is to-day universal, we owe, in a very great measure, to the intuition
of S. T. Coleridge.

It was the poet-critics of one hundred years ago who
made the discovery that Shakespeare was not an unaccountable warbler of irregular rustic music, but the
greatest of the poetic artists of the world ; that in a certain way he sums up and fulfils the qualities of national
character, as Dante and Calderon, Molière and Goethe
do, but to a still higher and fuller degree. It was they
who first made manifest to us that in the complex fulness
of Shakespeare's force, its equal potency in passion and
beauty and delicate sweetness, in tragic rage and idyllic
laughter, in acrid subtlety and infantile simplicity, we
have the broadest, the most substantial, the most elaborate

specimen of poetical genius yet vouchsafed to mankind. Whatever there is in life is to be found in Shakespeare; there rises the culminating expression of man's happiest faculty, the power of transfiguring his own adventures, instincts, and aspirations in the flushed light of memory, of giving to what has never existed a reality and a durability greater than the gods can render to their own habitations.

The deep study of Shakespeare is a disastrous preparation for appreciating his contemporaries. He rises out of all measurement with them by comparison, and we are tempted to repeat that unjust trope of Landor's in which he calls the other Elizabethan poets mushrooms growing round the foot of the Oak of Arden. They had, indeed, noble flashes of the creative light, but Shakespeare walks in the soft and steady glow of it. As he proceeds, without an effort, life results; his central qualities are ceaseless motion, ceaseless growth. In him, too, characteristics are found fully formed which the rest of the world had at that time barely conceived. His liberality, his tender respect for women, his absence from prejudice, his sympathy for every peculiarity of human emotion—these are miraculous, but the vigour of his imagination explains the marvel. He sympathised because he comprehended, and he comprehended because of the boundless range of his capacity. The quality in which Shakespeare is unique among the poets of the world, and that which alone explains the breadth, the unparalleled vivacity and coherency of the vast world of his imagination, is what Coleridge calls his "omnipresent creativeness," his power of observing everything, of forgetting nothing, and of combining and reissuing impressions in complex and infinite variety. In this godlike

gift not the most brilliant of his great contemporaries
approached him.

With the turn of the century a reaction against pure
imagination began to make itself felt in England, and
this movement found a perfect expositor in BEN JONSON.
Born seven years later than Shakespeare, he worked, like
his fellows, in Henslowe's manufactory of romantic drama,
until, in consequence of running a rapier through a man
in 1598, the fierce poetic bricklayer was forced to take
up an independent position. The immediate result was
the production of a comedy, *Every Man in his Humour*,
in which a new thing was started in drama, the study of
what Jonson called "recent humours or manners of men
that went along with the times."   In other words, in the
midst of that luxurious romanticism which had culminated in Shakespeare, Ben Jonson set out to be what
we now call a "realist" or a "naturalist."   In doing
this, he went back as rigidly as he could to the methods
of Plautus, and fixed his "grave and consecrated eyes"
on an academic scheme by which poetry was no longer
to be a mere entertainment but a form of lofty mental
gymnastic. Jonson called his solid and truculent pictures of the age "comic satires," and his intellectual
arrogance combining with his contempt for those who
differed from him, soon called down upon his proud and
rugged head all the hostility of Parnassus. About the
year 1600 Jonson's pugnaciousness had roused against
him an opposition in which, perhaps, Shakespeare alone
forbore to take a part. But Jonson was a formidable
antagonist, and when he fought with a brother poet, he
had a trick, in a double sense, of taking his pistol from
him and beating him too.

A persistent rumour, constantly refuted, will have it

that Shakespeare was one of those whom Jonson hated.
The most outspoken of misanthropes did not, we may be
sure, call another man "star of poets" and "soul of the
age" without meaning what he said; but there may have
been a sense in which, while loving Shakespeare and
admiring his work, Jonson disapproved of its tendency.
It could hardly be otherwise. He delighted in an iron
style, hammered and twisted; he must have thought that
Shakespeare's "excellent phantasy, brave notions, and
gentle expressions" had a flow too liquid and facile.
Jonson, with his Latin paraphrases, his stiff academic
procession of ideas, could but dislike the flights and
frenzies of his far less learned but brisker and airier
companion. And Jonson, be it remembered, had the
age on his side. To see *Julius Cæsar* on the boards
might be more amusing, but surely no seriously minded
Jacobean could admit that it was so instructive as a performance of *Sejanus* or of *Catiline,* which gave a chapter
of good sound Roman history, without lyric flowers or
ornaments of style, in hard blank verse. Even the
ponderous comedies of Ben Jonson were put forth by
him, and were accepted by his contemporaries, as very
serious contributions to the highest culture. What other
men called "plays" were "works" to Jonson, as the old
joke had it.

Solid and of lasting value as are the productions of
Jonson, the decline begins to be observed in them.
Even if we confine our attention to his two noblest
plays—the *Fox* (1605) and the *Alchemist* (1610) — we
cannot but admit that here, in the very heyday and
glory of the English Renaissance, a fatal element is
introduced. Charm, ecstasy, the free play of the emotions, the development of individual character—these are

no longer the sole solicitude of the poet, who begins to dogmatise and educate, to prefer types to persons and logic to passion. It is no wonder that Ben Jonson was so great a favourite with the writers of the Restoration, for he was their natural parent. With all their rules and unities, with all their stickling for pseud-Aristotelian correctness, they were the intellectual descendants of that poet who, as Dryden said, "was willing to give place to the classics in all things." For the next fifty years English poetry was divided between loyalty to Spenser and attraction to Ben Jonson, and every year the influence of the former dwindled while that of the latter increased.

Not the less does Ben Jonson hold a splendid and durable place in our annals. His is the most vivid and picturesque personal figure of the times; he is the most learned scholar, the most rigorous upholder of the dignity of letters, the most blustering soldier and insulting dueller in the literary arena; while his personal characteristics, "the mountain belly and the rocky face," the capacity for drawing young persons of talent around him and captivating them there, the volcanic alternations of fiery wit and smouldering, sullen arrogance, appeal irresistibly to the imagination, and make the "arch-poet" live in history. But his works, greatly admired, are little read. They fail to hold any but a trained attention; their sober majesty and massive concentration are highly praiseworthy, but not in a charming direction. His indifference to beauty tells against him. Jonson, even in his farces, is ponderous, and if we acknowledge "the flat sanity and smoke-dried sobriety" of his best passages, what words can we find for the tedium of his worst? He was an intellectual athlete of almost un-

equalled vigour, who chose to dedicate the essentially
prosaic forces of his mind to the art of poetry, because
the age he lived in was pre-eminently a poetic one.
With such a brain and such a will as his he could not
but succeed.   If he had stuck to bricklaying, he must
have rivalled Inigo Jones.   But the most skilful and
headstrong master - builder cannot quite become an
architect of genius.

There is no trace of the strict Jonsonian buskin in
FRANCIS BEAUMONT and JOHN FLETCHER; as even contemporary critics perceived, they simply continued the
pure romanticism of Shakespeare, and they seemed to
carry it further and higher.   We no longer think their
noon brighter than his "dawning hours," but we admit
that in a certain sense the great Twin Brethren proceeded beyond him in their warm, loosely-girdled plays.
They exaggerated all the dangerous elements which he
had held restrained ; they proceeded, in fact, downwards,
towards the inevitable decadence, gay with all the dolphin colours of approaching death.   It is difficult to
assign to either writer his share in the huge and florid
edifice which bears their joint names.   Their own
age attributed to Fletcher the "keen treble" and to
Beaumont the "deep bass" — comedy, that is, and
tragedy respectively.   Modern investigation has found
less and less in their work which can be definitely
ascribed to Beaumont, who, indeed, died so early as
1616.   It is generally believed that the partnership lasted
no longer than from 1608 to 1611, and that the writing
of only some dozen out of the entire fifty-five plays was
involved in it.   Were it not that the very noblest are
among these few, which include the *Maid's Tragedy* and
Philaster, A King and No King and the *Knight of the*

Burning Pestle, we might almost disregard the shadowy name of Beaumont, and treat this whole mass of dramatic literature as belonging to Fletcher, who went on writing alone, or with Massinger, until shortly before his death in 1625. The chronological sequence of these dramas, only about ten of which were printed during Fletcher's lifetime, remains the theme of bold and con-tradictory conjecture.

We have to observe in these glowing and redundant plays a body of lyrico-dramatic literature, proceeding directly from and parallel to the models instituted by Shakespeare, and continued for nearly ten years after his death. Nothing else in English is so like Shakespeare as a successful scene from a romantic comedy of Fletcher. Superficially, the language, the verse, the mental attitude often seem absolutely identical, and it is a singular tribute to the genius of the younger poet that he can endure the parallel for a moment. It is only for a moment; if we take Fletcher at his very best—in the ardent and melodious scenes of the *False One,* for in-stance, where, amid an array of the familiar Roman names, we find him desperately and directly challenging comparison with *Antony and Cleopatra*—we have only to turn from the shadow back to the substance to see how thin and unreal is this delicately tinted, hectic, and phantasmal picture of passion by the side of Shake-speare's solid humanity. Jonson has lost the stage because his personages are not human beings, but types of character, built up from without, and vitalised by no specific or personal springs of action. Beaumont and Fletcher are equally dead from the theatrical point of view, but from an opposite cause : their figures have not proved too hard and opaque for perennial interest, but too filmy and undulating; they possess not too much, but too little solidity. They are vague embodiments of instincts, faintly palpitating with desires and emulations and eccentricities, but not built up and set on firm feet by the practical genius of dramatic creation.

Yet no conception of English poetry is complete without a reference to these beautiful, sensuous, incoherent plays. The Alexandrine genius of Beaumont and Fletcher was steeped through and through in beauty; and so quickly did they follow the fresh morning of Elizabethan poetry that their premature sunset was tinged with dewy and "fresh-quilted" hues of dawn. In the short span of their labours they seem to take hold of the entire field of the drama, from birth to death, and Fletcher's quarter of a century helps us to see how rapid and direct was the decline. If the talent of Jonson had been more flexible, if the taste of Fletcher had not been radically so relaxed and luxurious, these two great writers should have carried English drama on after the death of Shakespeare—with less splendour, of course, yet with its character unimpaired. Unfortunately, neither of these excellent men, though all compact with talent, had the peculiar gift opportune to the moment's need, and ten years undid what it had taken ten years to create and ten more to sustain.

Around these leading figures there are grouped an infinite number of dramatists, some almost as deserving as Fletcher and Jonson of detailed notice, others scarcely lifted visibly out of the bewildering crowd of playwrights. Before the close of the reign of James I. it is believed that more than a thousand plays had been produced in London, and but few of these were without some spark of psychological audacity or lyrical beauty. This is the

serried mountain-mass which, on a hasty glance, seems
no more than the shoulders and bastions out of which
the huge peak of Shakespeare rises. Most of the more
salient of these secondary and tertiary dramatists are
exceedingly unequal, and assert the fame they possess on the score of one or two brilliant fragments
exalted by Lamb or by later critics, by whom the cult of
these writers has been pushed to some extravagance. It
must suffice here to pass rapidly over the claims of these
playwrights. Among pure Elizabethans, fellow-workers
with the young Shakespeare, THOMAS DEKKER claims
respect for a certain pitiful compassionateness, a tender
lyric sweetness, which occasionally finds very delicate
expression in brief passages which may atone for pages
upon pages of flabby incoherence. JOHN MARSTON,
whose versification owes much to Marlowe, was a harsh
and strident satirist, a screech-owl among the singing-
birds; in the first decade of the seventeenth century
he produced a series of vigorous rude tragedies and
comedies which possess a character of their own, not
sympathetic at all, but unique in its consistent note of
caustic misanthropy, and often brilliantly written.

The ponderous GEORGE CHAPMAN, who has other and
better claims upon us than his dramas offer—since he was
the admirable translator of Homer—issued between 1598
and 1608 a series of bombastic historical tragedies and
loosely articulated romantic comedies which have been
admired by thorough-going fanatics of the Elizabethan
drama, but in which, to a common observer, the faults
seem vastly to outweigh the rare and partial merits.
The errors of the school, its extravagance of sentiment,
its brutal insensibility, its turgid diction, its mean and
cruel estimate of women, its neglect of dramatic struc-

ture, its incoherence, are nowhere seen in greater relief than in the laborious dramas of Chapman.

Of these men we can form a more or less distinct personal impression. Others, of higher merit as writers for the stage, are absolutely shrouded voices. In the centre of the choir, but quite invisible, stands the figure of THOMAS HEYWOOD, a voluble secondary writer in the class of Shakespeare and Fletcher, claiming "an entire hand, or at least a main finger," in no fewer than 220 plays. He is remarkable chiefly for a pleasing mediocrity in picturesqueness, a prosaic, even spirit of flowing romance. Heywood rises once to real force of emotion in the naked, sombre atonement of *A Woman Killed with Kindness*. To THOMAS MIDDLETON the sweet uniformity of Heywood seemed insipid, and he strove after constant effect in violent complexity of plot and the vicissitudes of piratical adventure. He attempted every species of drama, and his reputation is weakened by his careless comedies, of which too many have survived. Had none but those fantastic imbroglios the *Changeling* and the *Spanish Gipsy* come down to us, Middleton would rank higher among the English poets than he does. Although a great many of his plays are lost, he is still weighed down by his abundance. For many years he was associated with William Rowley, an actor-author of whom little definite is known.

Much greater than these, greater in some respects than any but Shakespeare, is JOHN WEBSTER, who requires but a closer grasp of style and a happier architecture to rank among the leading English poets. The *Duchess of Malfy*, which is believed to have been produced in 1612, has finer elements of tragedy than exist elsewhere outside the works of Shakespeare. In a ruder form, we find

the same distinguished intensity of passion in the earlier
White Devil. Webster has so splendid a sense of the
majesty of death, of the mutability of human pleasures,
and of the velocity and weight of destiny, that he rises to
conceptions which have an Æschylean dignity ; but, unhappily, he grows weary of sustaining them, his ideas of
stage-craft are rudimentary and spectacular, and his
single well-constructed play, *Appius and Virginia*, has a
certain disappointing tameness.   Most of the Elizabethan
and Jacobean dramatists are now read only in extracts,
and this test is highly favourable to Webster, who strikes
us as a very noble poet driven by the exigencies of fashion
to write for a stage, the business of which he had not
studied and in which he took no great interest.   Of
CYRIL TOURNEUR, in whom the qualities of Webster are
discovered driven to a grotesque excess, the same may
be said.   His two lurid tragedies surpass in horror of
iniquity and profusion of ghastly innuendo all other
compositions of their time.   Cyril Tourneur is prince
of those whose design is "to make our flesh creep," and
occasionally he still succeeds.   This list of playwrights
might be indefinitely lengthened.   Nothing has been
said of Day, of Chettle, of Field, of Tailor ; but our
general survey would be merely confused by an attempt
to distinguish too clearly the vanishing points in the
crowded panorama.

In this glowing spring-tide of Elizabeth, all human
speech so naturally turned to verse that men of high
talent became poets when nature perhaps intended
them to be historians or philosophers.   In the laureate,
SAMUEL DANIEL, we meet with the first example of poetry
beginning to wither on the bough.   Daniel's grace,
smoothness, and purity seem to belong to a much later

period, and to a time when the imagination had lost its early fervour. He wrote lengthy historical poems, besides numerous sonnets, masques, and epistles. These last, which have the merit of brevity, are Daniel's most attractive contribution to English literature, and are singularly elegant in their stately, limpid flow of moral reflection. In prose, Daniel showed himself one of the most instructed of our early critics of poetry. Another philosophical writer, on whose style the turbulent passion of the age has left but little mark, is the great Irish jurist, Sir JOHN DAVYS, who, in his youth, composed several poems of the highest merit in their limited field. In his *Nosce Teipsum*, a treatise of considerable length and perspicuous dignity, dealing with the immortality of the soul, Davys was the first to employ on a long flight the solemn four-line stanza of which the type is supplied by the *Elegy in a Country Churchyard*. Three years earlier, in 1596, he had printed a most ingenious philosophical poem, *Orchestra*, in praise of dancing; but the delicacy of Davys's talent is best seen in a little work less known than either of these, the *Hymns of Astræa*. Both Daniel and Davys offer early and distinguished examples of the employment of imagination to illuminate elaborate mental processes.

Each of these men might easily have given their talent all to prose. Their friend and companion, MICHAEL DRAYTON, was not a better poet, but he was much more persistently devoted to the cultivation of the art of verse, and regarded himself as absolutely consecrated to the Muses. During a life more prolonged than that of most of his contemporaries, he never ceased to write—feverishly, crudely, copiously, very rarely giving to his work that polish which it needed to make it durable. Of his lyrical vocation there could be no doubt ; yet, if Daniel and Davys were prose-men who wrote poetry, Drayton was a prosaic poet. His masterpiece of topographical inge-nuity, the *Poly-Olbion*, a huge British gazetteer in broken-backed twelve-syllable verse, is a portent of misplaced energy. In his earlier historical pieces Drayton more closely resembles Daniel, whom, however, he exceeds in his lyrics as much as he limps behind him in his attempts at gnomic verse. Drayton writes like a man, and a few of his odes are still read with fervour ; but his general compositions, in spite of all their variety, abundance, and accomplishment, fail to interest us ; a prosy flatness spoils his most ambitious efforts. He helps us to com-prehend the change which was to come in sixty years, and through Cowley he prophesies of Dryden. Now, did space permit, we should speak of the coarse and fus-cous satirists of the Elizabethan time, and of such sym-bolists as the fantastic Lord Brooke. But these, interesting as in themselves they are, must hardly detain us here.

In the opening years of the seventeenth century the imitation of Spenser was cultivated by many disciples, among whom the most interesting were the Fletchers, cousins of the dramatist, and William Browne of Tavi-stock. In this group the predominant talent was that of GILES FLETCHER, to whom, indeed, the rarer quality can scarcely be denied. He was the author of the finest reli-gious poem produced in English literature between the *Vision of Piers Plowman* and *Paradise Lost*. In several passages of his fourfold *Christ's Victory and Triumph* (1610) Giles Fletcher solved the difficult problem of how to be at once gorgeous and yet simple, majestic and yet touching. At his apogee he surpasses his very master, for his imagination lifts him to a spiritual sublimity. In

9

the beatific vision in his fourth canto we are reminded
of no lesser poem than the *Paradiso*. It is right to say
that these splendours are not sustained, and that Giles
Fletcher is often florid and sometimes merely trivial.
The sonorous purity and elevation of Giles Fletcher at his
best give more than a hint of the approaching Milton, and
he represents the Spenserian tradition at its very highest.

But a poet was in the field who was to sweep the pleasant flowers of the disciples of Spenser before him as
ruthlessly as a mower cuts down the daisies with his
scythe.   In this age of mighty wits and luminous
imaginations, the most robust and the most elaborately
trained intellect was surely that of JOHN DONNE.   Born
as early as 1573, and associated with many of the purely
Elizabethan poets, we have yet the habit of thinking of
him as wholly Jacobean, and the instinct is not an
erroneous one, for he begins a new age.   His poems
were kept in manuscript until two years after his death
in 1631, but they were widely circulated, and they exercised an extraordinary effect.   Long before any edition
of Donne was published, the majority of living English
verse-writers were influenced by the main peculiarities
of his style.   He wrote satires, epistles, elegies, sonnets,
and lyrics, and although it is in the last mentioned that
his beauties are most frequent, the essence of Donne,
the strange personal characteristic which made him so
unlike every one else, is redolent in all.   He rejected
whatever had pleased the Elizabethan age ; he threw the
fashionable humanism to the winds ; he broke up the
accepted prosody ; he aimed at a totally new method in
diction, in illustration, in attitude.   He was a realist, who
studded his writings with images drawn from contemporary life.   For grace and mellifluous floridity he substi-

tuted audacity, intensity, a proud and fulgurant darkness, as of an intellectual thunder-cloud.

Unfortunately, the genius of Donne was not equal to his ambition and his force. He lacked the element needed to fuse his brilliant intuitions into a classical shape. He aimed at becoming a great creative reformer, but he succeeded only in disturbing and dislocating literature. He was the blind Samson in the Elizabethan gate, strong enough to pull the beautiful temple of Spenserian fancy about the ears of the worshippers, but powerless to offer them a substitute. What he gave to poetry in exchange for what he destroyed was almost wholly deplorable. For sixty years the evil taint of Donne rested on us, and our tradition is not free from it yet. To him—almost to him alone—we owe the tortured irregularities, the monstrous pedantries, the alembicated verbiage of the decline. " Rhyme's sturdy cripple," as Coleridge called him, Donne is the father of all that is exasperating, affected, and "metaphysical" in English poetry. He represented, with Marino in Italy, Gongora in Spain, and Bartas and D'Aubigné in France, that mania for an inflamed and eccentric extravagance of fancy which was racing over Europe like a hideous new disease ; and the ease and rapidity with which the infection was caught, shows how ready the world of letters was to succumb to such a plague. That Donne, in flashes, and especially in certain of his lyrics, is still able to afford us imaginative ecstasy of the very highest order —he has written a few single lines almost comparable with the best of Shakespeare's—must not blind us, in a general survey, to the maleficence of his genius. No one has injured English writing more than Donne, not even Carlyle.

Side by side with the magnificent efflorescence of poetical and particularly of dramatic talent in England, there was a certain development of prose also, but it was curiously inadequate to the needs of the race. With relative exceptions, prose remained, till the end of this period, either rude or else fantastic, and in either case encumbered. With Spenser and Marlowe and Shakespeare, there is but one master of prose worthy to be mentioned, and that is the "obscure, harmless" priest who wrote the *Ecclesiastical Polity*. RICHARD HOOKER was of the generation of Raleigh, Sidney, and Fulke Greville, those paladins of the English Renaissance, and where he sat with downcast eyes, henpecked, withdrawn into the "blessed bashfulness" of his little country study, he reflected in the intellectual order their splendid qualities. He had been for a few years Master of the Temple, where he "spake pure Canterbury," that is to say, proclaimed a conservative Anglicanism as opposed to the "Geneva" of the Calvinists. But his masterpiece was prepared for the press in the retreat of Boscombe, under the scourge of his terrible mother-in-law. The first four books of it appeared in 1594, another in 1597, and then in 1600 Hooker died prematurely, "worn out, not with age, but study and holy mortifications." The last three books of the *Polity* were ready for the press, but within a few days of his death they had disappeared, and what we now possess in their place is of doubtful authenticity.

Hooker is the first important philosophical and religious English writer. He is the earliest to perceive the importance of evolution, the propriety of preparing and conducting to a conclusion a great, consistent scheme. He sees things clearly and coolly in an age when controversial passion and political turmoil turned all other men's blood to fever. When he was at the Temple he had felt the pulse of life; he was profoundly aware of the demands and requirements of the age; but something infinitely serene in his intellectual nature lifted Hooker, even in the act of disputation, far above the wrangling of the sects. In his masterpiece, the *Laws of Ecclesiastical Polity*, we find no trace of that violent provinciality which is so tiresome in Elizabethan prose; the author spreads his wings broadly and gently, he dismisses all ideas which are not germane to humanity. This singular majesty of Hooker is aided by the fact that his First Book, in which the reader learns to become acquainted with him, particularly exemplifies his breadth. It deals with the general principle of law in the universe; it is a solemn eulogy of the diapason of discipline in nature.

The style of Hooker is distinguished by a sober and sustained eloquence. Certain of his contemporaries might equal him in purple passages, but not one of them approached his even flight. He was Latinised, not as his lumbering predecessors had been, but in the true humanistic spirit; and he had studied Aristotle and Plato with constant advantage to his expression. Hooker is, indeed, one of the earliest of our authors, in prose or verse, to show the influence of pure Hellenic culture. The limpidity and elegance of his periods are extraordinary. When all England was in bondage, Hooker alone freed himself from the clogged concatenation of phrases which makes early English prose so unwieldy; yet he gained his liberty at no such cost of grace and fulness as Bacon did in the snip-snap of his *Essays*. Hooker discovered, by the help of the ancients and the Bible, a middle way between long-drawn lusciousness and curt formality. He does not strive after effect; but when he is moved, his style is instinct with music. He never abuses quotation; he never forgets that he has an argument to conduct, and that life is short. In other words, he is the first great writer of practical English prose, and for a long time there is none other like unto him.

The vices of obscurity and uncouthness, indeed, weigh heavily upon most of the prose of this period. When prose wished to please, it was as stiff and florid as the gala-dress of Elizabeth's Court; when it merely wished to instruct, nothing could be more inelegant and humdrum. Some of the abundant literature of geographical adventure was spirited and forcible; it reached its highest point of merit in Raleigh's *Guiana* of 1596. The novel, or rather prose romance in its most rudimentary shape, had been essayed by Greene, Lodge, Nash, and others, in a form which displayed a pitiful poverty by the side of the vividly psychological drama of the next generation. Criticism made a variety of primitive essays, of which Daniel's *Defence of Rhyme* is perhaps the least imperfect. These pamphlets attempted to give a humanistic solution to the practical literary problems of the day, but seldom proceeded beyond a vague and learned trifling with the unessential. Finally, in the year 1597 sketches of ten of Bacon's sagacious *Essays* appeared. No work in the English language has been praised with more thoughtless extravagance. It has one great merit, it tended to break up the encumbered, sinuous Elizabethan sentence, and prepare for prose as Dryden and Halifax wrote it. But its ornament is largely borrowed from the school of Lyly and Lodge, its thoughts are commonplaces, and its arrangement of parts is desultory and confused; while Bacon's real mastery of English was a thing which came to him later, and will occupy our

attention in the following chapter. For superficial purposes, there are only two books of Elizabethan prose
in which we need to study the progress of that species
of literary expression, namely, the *Euphues* of Lyly, a
brilliant experiment, and the *Ecclesiastical Polity* of
Hooker, a permanent classic.

A literary enterprise of far-reaching importance was
set in motion by James I. when he called together at
Hampton Court, in 1604, a conference to discuss the
propriety of finally revising the English version of the
Scriptures. An adroit and practical scheme, drawn up
by the hand of the King himself, was laid before the
delegates for their consideration. It was accepted, and
in 1607 a committee of nearly fifty divines set to work to
produce an *Authorised Version* which should supersede
the not entirely satisfactory *Bishops' Bible*, issued by
Archbishop Parker in 1568. The general editorship of
the revision was placed in the hands of the most learned
personage in an erudite age, LANCELOT ANDREWES,
Bishop of Winchester, who was also responsible for
some parts of the work in detail. Andrewes was celebrated for his elegant and impassioned delivery, he was
stella prædicantium, and he seems to have had a positive
genius for the cadences of ecclesiastical language. It
must not be overlooked that the English of the version
of 1611, which is what was alone in use until the present
generation, was not truly Jacobean, or even Elizabethan,
but an archaic and eclectic arrangement of phrases, the
bulk of which had come down to Andrewes and his
colleagues from Parker, and so from Cranmer, and so
from Coverdale and Tyndale, and so from Wycliffe and
Purvey, and represented, in fact, a modification of a
mediæval impression of the Vulgate. The Authorised

English Bible represents the tongue of no historical period, but is an artificial product, selected with exquisite care, from the sacred felicities of two centuries and a half. Its effect upon later authorship has been constant, and of infinite benefit to style. Not a native author but owes something of his melody and his charm to the echo of those Biblical accents, which were the first fragments of purely classical English to attract his admiration in childhood.

IV

THE DECLINE

1620–1660

THE decline of letters in England began almost as soon as Shakespeare was in his grave, and by the death of James I. had become obvious. The period which we have now to consider was illuminated by several names of very high genius both in prose and verse, and by isolated works of extraordinary value and beauty. In spite, however, of the lustre which these give to it, no progress was made for forty years in the general structure of literature; at best, things remained where they were, and, in literary history, to stop still is to go back. It is possible that we should have a different tale to tell if the most brilliant Englishman who survived Shakespeare had realised what it was possible to do with the tongue of his country. At the close of James's reign FRANCIS BACON stood, as Ben Jonson put it, "the mark and acme of our language," but he gave its proficients little encouragement. He failed, for all his intuition, to recognise the turn of the tide; he thought that books written in English would never be citizens of the world. Anxious to address Europe, the universe, he felt no interest in his English contemporaries, and passed through the sublime age of Elizabethan poetry without conceding the fact of its existence.

But after his fall, in May 1621, Bacon wakened afresh to the importance of his native language. In a poignant letter to the King, who was to "plough him up and sow him with anything," he promised a harvest of writings in the vernacular. In 1605 he had already made a splendid contribution to criticism in his *Advancement of Learning;* otherwise, he had mainly issued his works in Ciceronian Latin. But in 1621 he finished his *History of Henry VII.;* in 1624 he was writing the *New Atlantis;* in 1625 the *Essays* (first issued in nucleus in 1597, and meagrely enlarged in 1612) were published in full, and the *Sylva Sylvarum* was completed. These works, with his public and private letters, combine to form the English writings of Bacon. They constitute a noble mass of work, but there is no question that the reputation of Bacon dwindles if we are forced to cut away his Latin books; he no longer seems to have taken the whole world of knowledge into his province. And in his English works, considered alone, we have to confess a certain poverty. He who thought it the first distemper of learning, that men should study words and not matter, is now in the singular condition of having outlived his matter, or, at least, a great part of it, while his words are as vivid as ever. We could now wish that he could have been persuaded to "hunt more after choiceness of the phrase, and the round and clear composition of the sentence, and the sweet falling of the clauses," qualities which he had the temerity to profess to despise.

Bacon described himself as "a bell-ringer, who is up first to call others to church." The *Advancement of Learning* was dictated by this enthusiasm. He would rise at cock-crowing to bid the whole world welcome to the intellectual feast. This is the first book in the English language which discusses the attitude of a mind seeking to consolidate and to arrange the stores of human knowledge. It was planned in two parts, the first to be a eulogy of the excellence of learning—its "proficience"—and the second to be a survey of the condition of the theme—its "advancement." Bacon had little leisure and less patience, and his zeal often outran his judgment in the act of composition. The *Advancement* is written, or finished at least, obviously in too great haste ; the Second Book is sometimes almost slovenly, and the close of it leaves us nowhere. But the opening part, in which Bacon sums up first the discredits and then the dignity of learning, defending wisdom, and justifying it to its sons, remains one of the great performances of the seventeenth century. The matter of it is obsolete, human knowledge having progressed so far forwards and backwards since 1605 ; and something dry and unripe in Bacon's manner—which mellowed in later life—diminishes our pleasure in reading what is none the less a very noble work, and one intended to be the prologue to the author's vast edifice of philosophical inquiry. At this point, however, he unluckily determined to abandon English brick for Latin stone.

This futile disregard of his own language robs English literature of the greater part of its heritage in Bacon. He desired an immortality of readers, and fancied that to write in English would "play the bankrupt with books." Hence, even in his *Essays* we are conscious of a certain disdain. The man is not a serious composer so much as a collector of maxims and observations ; he keeps his note-book and a pencil ever at his side, and jots down what occurs to him. If it should prove valuable, he will turn it out of this ragged and parochial English into the statelier and more lasting vehicle of Latin. He has no time to think about style; he will scribble for you a whole book of apophthegms in a morning. The *Essays* themselves — his "recreations," as he carelessly called them—are often mere notations or headings for chapters imperfectly enlarged, in many cases merely to receive the impressions of a Machiavellian ingenuity. They are almost all too short; the longest, those on "Friendship" and "Gardens," being really the only ones in which the author gives himself space to turn round. As a constructor of the essay considered as a department of literary art, Bacon is not to be named within hail of Montaigne.

Bacon desired that prose should be clear, masculine, and apt, and these adjectives may generally be applied to what he wrote with any care in English. He was so picturesque a genius, and so abounding in intellectual vitality, that he secured the graces without aiming at them. His *Essays* hold a certain perennial charm, artless as they are in arrangement and construction; but the student of literature will find greater instruction in examining the more sustained and uplifted paragraphs of the *Advancement*, where he can conveniently parallel Bacon with Hooker, the only earlier prose-writer who can be compared with him. He will observe with interest that the diction of Bacon is somewhat more archaic than that of Hooker.

When Bacon died, in 1626, he left English literature painfully impoverished. For the next fifteen years it may be said that prose of the higher kind scarcely existed, and that there threatened to be something like a return to barbarism. But two works which belong to a slightly earlier period must first of all be discussed. No book is more characteristic of the age, of its merits alike and of its faults, than that extraordinary emporium, the *Anatomy of Melancholy*, first issued in 1621. ROBERT BURTON, a clergyman, mainly resident at Christchurch, Oxford, was the author of this vast monograph on what we should now call neuresthènia. The text of Burton has been unkindly styled a collection of clause-heaps, and he is a typical example of that extreme sinuosity, one of the detestable tricks of the schools, to which the study of the ancients betrayed our early seventeenth-century prose-writers. Of the width of reading of such men as Bacon and Burton and Hales there have been no later specimens, and these writers, but Burton above all others, burden their folio pages with a gorgeous spoil of "proofs" and "illustrations" from the Greek and Latin authors. The *Anatomy of Melancholy*, though started as a plain medical dissertation, grew to be, practically, a huge canto of excerpts from all the known (and unknown) authors of Athens and Rome. All Burton's treasure was in Minerva's Tower, and the chamber that he fitted up there has been the favourite haunt of scholars in every generation. In his own his one book enjoyed a prodigious success, for it exactly suited and richly indulged the temper of the time. But Burton, delightful as he is, added nothing to the evolution of English prose in this its dangerous hour of crisis. The vogue of his entertaining neurotic compendium really tended to retard the purification of the language.

In 1623 was published a volume of prose so beautiful and unique that it must be mentioned here in spite of its comparative obscurity, *A Cypress Grove*, by the ornate Scotch poet, WILLIAM DRUMMOND of Hawthornden. This

was in substance nothing but a chain of philosophical
arguments against the fear of death ; but in manner it was
of a delicate fulness and harmony, a deliberate and studied
mellifluousness, which reminds the reader of nothing so
much as of the more elaborate passages of De Quincey.
Never before in English, and not again for a generation,
was prose written with so obvious an attention to the
balance of clauses and the euphony of phrases as is to be
discovered in this curious little treatise of Drummond's,
who deserves to be remembered, therefore, among the
constructors of melodious style.

With these exceptions, prose between Bacon and the
school of 1640 is mainly of a trivial importance—the
work of such fiery divines as Hall and Donne being excepted.   Under Charles I. the growth of English prose
was arrested, save where it blossomed forth in the
fashionable imitations of the clear and lively sketches of
Theophrastus, the pupil of Aristotle.   In 1598, Casaubon,
to whom and to Scaliger the modern literatures of Europe
owe so great a debt, had edited Theophrastus with a luminous commentary. JOSEPH HALL, by his *Characterisms*
(1608), and Sir THOMAS OVERBURY, by his *Characters*
(1614), had made the composition of similar short essays in
humorous philosophy the rage. Theophrastus had confined himself to studies of the intrinsic behaviour of representative men.   Bishop Hall, in his dignified little book,
had added the qualifications for holding certain special
offices.   In the generation of which we are speaking, the
example of Theophrastus, as seen through Hall and
Overbury, combined with the imitation of Bacon to produce a curious school of comic or ironic portraiture,
partly ethical and partly dramatic, typical examples of
which are the *Microcosmogony* of Earle, Owen Feltham's

Resolves, the *Country Parson* of George Herbert, and even, we may say, the later pamphlets of Dekker. No small addition to the charm of these light essays-in-little was the hope of discovering in the philosophical portrait the face of a known contemporary. This sort of literature culminated in Europe in the work of La Bruyère, but not until 1688, and was afterwards elaborated by Addison.

Meanwhile, it is true, the divines, and the great Dean of St. Paul's at their head, were preaching their obscure and disquieting sermons. JOHN DONNE died in 1631, but it was not until nine years later that an imperfect collection of his addresses was published. He is the noblest of the religious writers of England between Hooker and Jeremy Taylor; and the qualities which mark his astonishing poems, their occasional majesty, their tossing and foaming imagination, their lapses into bad taste and unintelligibility, the sinister impression of a strange perversity of passion carefully suppressed in them—all these, though to a less marked degree, distinguish the prose of Donne. Its beauties are of the savage order, and they display not only no consciousness of any rules which govern prose composition, but none of that chastening of rhetoric which had been achieved under Elizabeth by Hooker. Such books of Donne's as his paradox of suicide, the *Biathanatos*, unquestionably exhibit sympathy with what was morbid in the temper of the time; they are to theology what the tragedies of Ford are to drama. Probably the strongest prose work produced in England during the dead time of which we have spoken is WILLIAM CHILLINGWORTH'S *Religion of Protestants* (1637). This divine was somewhat slighted in his own age, as giving little show of learning in his discourses; but the perspicuity of his style and the force of his reasoning commended him to the Anglican divines of the Restoration. It is characteristic that Tillotson had a great admiration for this humane latitudinarian, and that Locke wrote, " If you would have your son reason well, let him read Chillingworth."

The masterpiece of Chillingworth stands almost alone, in a sort of underwood of Theophrastian character-sketches. The fashion for these studies was greatly encouraged by the decay of the drama, and particularly by that of comedy. To understand the causes and symptoms of that decay, we have to reconsider the position of Ben Jonson. By 1625 the deaths of all the Predecessors, followed by those of Shakespeare, of Beaumont, and finally of Fletcher, left Jonson in a condition of undisputed prestige. He had always been the most academic and dictatorial of the group, and now there was no one to challenge his supremacy. With health and a competency, it is probable that Ben Jonson would now have begun to exercise a wide authority, and he might have seriously modified the course of our literary history; but he was cramped by poverty, and in 1626 he was struck down, at the age at which Shakespeare had died, by paralysis. Jonson lived eleven years longer, but the spirit had evaporated from his genius, and he was but the sulky shadow of himself. The worst of it was that in some melancholy way he seems to have dragged English drama down with him, a blind Samson in his despair. The confused self-consciousness of those last comedies which Dryden cruelly styled his " dotages" is reflected in the work of the young men who clustered round him, who comforted his gloomy hours of public failure, and who were proud to accept the title of his poetic sons.

In temperament Jonson differed wholly from the other
leaders of Elizabethan drama. They, without exception,
were romantic; he, by native bias, purely classical. It
is not difficult to perceive that the essential quality of
his mind had far more in common with Corneille and
with Dryden than with Shakespeare. He was so full of
intelligence that he was able to adopt, and to cultivate
with some degree of zest, the outward forms of romanticism, but his heart was always with the Latins, and his
favourite works, though not indeed his best, were his
stiff and solid Roman tragedies. He brought labour to
the construction of his poetry, and he found himself
surrounded by facile pens, to whom he seemed, or
fancied that he seemed, "barren, dull, lean, a poor
writer." He did not admire much of that florid ornament in which they delighted, and which we also have
been taught to admire. He grew to hate the kind of
drama which Marlowe had inaugurated. No doubt,
sitting in the Apollo room of the Old Devil Tavern, with
his faithful Cartwright, Brome, and Randolph round
him, he would truculently point to the inscription above
the chimney, *Insipida poemata nulla recitantor*, and not
spare the masters of that lovely age which he had outlived. He would speak "to the capacity of his hearers,"
as he tells us that the true artificer should do, and they
would encourage him, doubtless, to tell of doctrines and
precepts, of the dignity of the ancients, of Aristotle,
"first accurate critic and truest judge" of poetry. They
would listen, nor be aware that, for all his wisdom, and
all the lofty distinction of his intellect, the palmy hour
of English drama—that hour in which it had sung out
like a child, ignorant of rules and precepts—had passed
for ever.

10

If the learning and enthusiasm of Jonson could not save it, it received little sustenance from other hands. One blow after another weakened and distracted it; almost year by year, and with a sinister rapidity, it sank into desuetude. The deaths of Shakespeare and Beaumont placed tragedy and romantic comedy mainly in the lax hands of Fletcher, who for some eight years more poured forth his magnanimous and sunshiny plays, so musical, so dissolute, so fantastic. Already, in this beautiful dramatic literature of Fletcher's, we have sunken below the serene elevation of Shakespeare. PHILIP MASSINGER joins Fletcher, and about 1624 is found taking his place as the most active and popular dramatic poet of the hour. By this time the flood of unequal, hurried plays, poured forth by Heywood and Middleton, is beginning to slacken, and soon these belated Elizabethans are dead or silent. Massinger holds the field, with an impetus that never equals that of Fletcher, and a tamer versification, a prosier, less coherent construction. More serious and solid than his predecessors, he has less fire and colour than they, and less of the tumultuous ecstasy that carried them on its wings. He dies in 1638.

Meanwhile, in JAMES SHIRLEY a placid and elegant talent makes its appearance, recurring, without vehemence or thrill, to the purely ornamental tradition of Shakespeare and Fletcher, and continuing, with a mild monotony, to repeat the commonplaces of the school until they are hopelessly out of fashion. Then, last of all, in a final brief blaze of the sinking embers, we encounter JOHN FORD, perhaps as genuine a tragic poet as any one of his forerunners, Shakespeare alone excepted, reverting for a moment to the old splendid diction, the haughty disregard of convention, the contempt for ethical restrictions. And so the brief and magnificent school of English drama, begun by Marlowe scarcely more than a generation before, having blazed and crackled like a forest fire fed with resinous branches, sinks almost in a moment, and lingers only as a heap of white ash and glowing charcoal.

The causes of the rapid decline of the drama have been sought in the religious and political disturbances of the country ; but, if we examine closely, we find that stage-poetry had begun to be reduced in merit before those disturbances had taken definite shape. It will probably be safer to recognise that the opening out of national interests took attention more and more away from what had always been an exotic entertainment, a pleasure mainly destined for the nobles and their re-tainers. There was a general growth of enthusiasm, of public feeling, throughout England, and this was not favourable to the cultivation of a species of entertain-ment such as the drama had been under Elizabeth, a cloistered art destined exclusively for pleasure, without a didactic or a moral aim. For many years there con-tinued to persist an interest in the stage wide enough to fill the theatres, in spite of the growing suspicion of such amusements ; but the audiences rapidly grew less select and less refined, less able to appreciate the good, and more tolerant of the rude and bad. In technique there was a falling off so abrupt as to be quite astonish-ing, and not easily to be accounted for. The "sons" of Ben Jonson, trained as they had been at his feet, sank into forms that were primitive in their rudeness. The curious reader may pursue the vanishing genius of poetic drama down through the writings of Randolph, of Jasper Mayne, of Cartwright, till he finds himself a bewildered spectator of the last gibberings and contortions of the spectre in the inconceivable "tragedies" of Suckling. If the wits of the universities, highly trained, scholarly young men, sometimes brilliantly efficient in other branches of poetry, could do no better than this, what wonder that in ruder hands the very primitive notions with regard to dramatic construction and propriety were forgotten. Before Shakespeare had been a quarter of a century in his grave, Shirley was the only person left writing in England who could give to fiction in dialogue the very semblance of a work of art.

We must pause for a moment to observe a highly interesting phenomenon. At the very moment when English drama was crumbling to dust, the drama of France was springing into vigorous existence. The conjectured year of the performance of our last great play, the *Broken Heart*, of Ford, is that of the appearance of the earliest of Corneille's tragedies. So rapidly did events follow one another, that when that great man produced *Le Cid*, English drama was moribund ; when his *Rodogune* was acted, it was dead ; and the appearance of his *Agésilas* saw it re-arisen under Dryden in totally different forms, and as though from a different hemisphere. It is impossible not to reflect that if the dramatic instinct had been strong in Milton, the profoundest of all religious tragedies might happen to be not that *Polyeucte* which we English have enviously to admire in the literature of France, but a play in which the noblest ideas of Puritanism might have been posed against worldly philosophy and sensual error. Yet even for a Milton in 1643 the ground would not have been clear as it was for Corneille. He had but to gather together and lift into splendid distinction elements whose main fault had been their imperfection.

For him, French tragedy, long preparing to blossom, was reaching its spring at last; for us, our too brief summer was at an end, and, cloyed with fruit, the drama was hurrying through its inevitable autumn. If Ben Jonson, tired and old, had felt any curiosity in glancing across the Channel, he might have heard of the success of a goodly number of pieces by a poet destined, more exactly than any Englishman, to carry out Jonson's own ideal of a tragic poet. He had desired that a great tragedian should specially excel in "civil prudence and eloquence," and to whom can these qualities be attributed if not to Corneille? The incoherent and scarce intelligible English dramatists of the decline were as blankly ignorant of the one as of the other.

The laxity of versification which our poetic drama permitted itself had much to answer for in the degradation of style. Ben Jonson had been too stiff; Shakespeare, with a divine instinct, hung balanced across the point which divides hardness of versification from looseness; but in the soft hands of Fletcher, the borders were already overpast, his followers became looser and more sinuous still, and the comparative exactitude of Massinger and Shirley was compromised by their languor. The verse of Ford, it is true, is correct and elegant, with a slight rigidity that seems pre-Shakespearian. But among the names which follow these we find not one that understood what dramatic blank verse should be. If there be an exception, it is WILLIAM CARTWRIGHT, whose plays, although they smell too much of the lamp, and possess no aptitude for the theatre, pour a good deal of waxen beauty into moulds of stately metre. It was of this typical Oxford poet, who died, still very young, in 1643, that Ben Jonson said, " My son Cartwright writes all like a man."

In one department of poetry, however, there is something else to chronicle than decline. The reign of Charles I., so unillustrious in most branches of literature, produced a very fine school of lyric poets. Among these JOHN MILTON was easily the greatest, and between the years 1631 and 1637 he contributed to English literature about two thousand of the most exquisite, the most perfect, the most consummately executed verses which are to be discovered in the language. This apparition of Milton at Horton, without associates, without external stimulus, Virtue seeing "to do what Virtue would, by his own radiant light," this is one of the most extraordinary phenomena which we encounter in our history. Milton was born in 1608, and proceeded to Cambridge in 1625, where he remained until 1632. During these seven years the eastern University was one of the main centres of poetical animation in the country; several true poets and a host of poetasters were receiving their education there. The poems of Dr. Donne, handed about in MS., were universally admired, and were the objects of incessant emulation.

Of all this environment, happily but surprisingly, not a trace is to be found on Milton. We find, indeed, the evidences of a loving study of Shakespeare and of the ancients, and in his earliest work a distinct following of those scholars of Spenser, Giles and Phineas Fletcher, who had been prominent figures at Cambridge just before Milton came into residence. What drew the young Milton to Giles Fletcher it is not difficult to divine. That writer's *Christ's Victory and Triumph* had been a really important religious poem, unequal in texture, but rising at its highest to something of that pure magnificence of imagination which was to be Milton's aim and glory.

Phineas Fletcher had composed a Scriptural poem, the *Apollyonists*, which was published in 1627. This was a fragment on the fall of the rebel angels, and Milton must have been greatly struck with it, for he paid it the compliment of borrowing considerably from it when he came to write *Paradise Lost*. When, at the close of 1629, Milton began his *Ode on the Morning of Christ's Nativity*, he was still closely imitating the form of these favourites of his, the Fletchers, until the fifth stanza was reached, and then he burst away in a magnificent measure of his own, pouring forth that hymn which carried elaborate lyrical writing higher than it had ever been taken before in England.

But, gorgeous as was the *Nativity Ode*, it could not satisfy the scrupulous instinct of Milton. Here were fire, melody, colour ; what, then, was lacking ? Well, purity of style and that "doric delicacy" of which Milton was to be the prototype—these were lacking. We read the *Nativity Ode* with rapture, but sometimes with a smile. Its language is occasionally turbid, incongruous, even absurd. We should be sorry that "the chill marble seems to sweat," and that "the sun in bed . . . pillows his chin upon an orient wave," if these were not like the tricks of a dear and valued friend, oddities that seem part of his whole exquisite identity. Such excrescences as these we have to condone in almost all that we find delightful in seventeenth-century literature. We may easily slip into believing these conceits and flatnesses to be in themselves beautiful ; but this is a complacency which is to be avoided, and we should rather dwell on such stanzas of the *Nativity Ode* as xix. and xxiv., in which not a word, not a syllable, mars the distinguished perfection of the poem, but in which every element combines to produce a solemn, harmonious, and imposing effect.

The evolution of Milton continued, though in 1630 we find him (in the *Passion*) returning to the mannerisms of the Fletchers. But, in the "Sonnet on his Twenty-Third Birthday" he is adult at last, finally dedicated, as a priest, to the sacred tasks of the poetic life, and ready to abandon all "the earthly grossness" which dragged down the literature of his age. And next we hear him put the golden trumpet to his lips and blow the melodies of "At a Solemn Music," in which no longer a trace of the "metaphysical" style mars the lucid perfection of utterance, but in which words arranged with consummate art summon before us a vision not less beatific than is depicted by Dante in his *Paradiso* or by Fra Angelico in his burning frescoes. Beyond these eight-and-twenty lines, no poet, and not Milton himself, has proceeded. Human language, at all events in English, has never surpassed, in ecstasy of spiritual elevation or in pure passion of melody, this little canzonet, which was, in all probability, the first-fruits of Milton's retirement to Horton.

In the sylvan Buckinghamshire village, "far from the noise of town, and shut up in deep retreats," Milton abandoned himself to study and reflection. He was weighed upon, even thus early, by a conviction of his sublime calling; he waited for the seraphim of the Eternal Spirit to touch his lips with the hallowed fire of inspiration, and he was neither idle nor restless, neither ambitious nor indifferent. He read with extreme eagerness, rising early and retiring late; he made himself master of all that could help him towards his mysterious vocation in Greek, Latin, French, Italian, and English.

To mark the five years of his stay at Horton, he produced five immortal poems, *L'Allegro*, *Il Penseroso*, *Arcades*, *Comus*, *Lycidas*, all essentially lyrical, though two of them assume the semi-dramatic form of the pageant or masque, a species of highly artificial poetry to which Ben Jonson and Campion had lent their prestige in the preceding age.

The ineffable refinement and dignity of these poems found a modest publicity in 1645. But the early poetry of Milton captured little general favour, and one small edition of it sufficed for nearly thirty years. No one imitated or was influenced by Milton's lyrics, and until the eighteenth century was well advanced they were scarcely read. Then their celebrity began, and from Gray and Collins onward, every English poet of eminence has paid his tribute to *Il Penseroso* or to *Lycidas*. If we examine closely the diction of these Horton poems, we shall find that in almost all of them (in *Comus* least) a mannerism which belonged to the age faintly dims their purity of style. Certain little tricks we notice are Italianisms, and the vogue of the famous Marino, author of the *Adone*, who had died while Milton was at Cambridge, was responsible, perhaps, for something. But, on the whole, lyrical poetry in this country has not reached a higher point, in the reflective and impersonal order, than is reached in the central part of *L'Allegro* and in the Spirit's epilogue to *Comus*.

Other lyrics there were less imperishable than these, yet excellent in their way, and vastly more popular than Milton's. Almost without exception these were the work of non-professional authors —soldiers, clergymen, or college wits—thrown off in the heat of youth, and given first to the world posthumously, by the piety of some friend. Of the leading lyrists of the earlier Cavalier group of the reign of Charles I., WILLIAM HABINGTON was the only one who published his poems in his lifetime. The forerunner of them all, and potentially the greatest, was THOMAS CAREW, who as early as 1620 was probably writing those radiant songs and "raptures" which were not printed until twenty years later. To an amalgam of Carew and Donne (whose poems, also, were first published posthumously, in 1633) most of the fashionable poetry written in England between 1630 and 1660 may be attributed. Carew invented a species of love-poetry which exactly suited the temper of the time. It was a continuation of the old Elizabethan pastoral, but more personal, more ardent, more coarse, and more virile. He was the frankest of hedonists, and his glowing praise of woman has genuine erotic force. In technical respects, the flexibility and solidity of his verse was remarkable, and, though he greatly admired Donne, he was able to avoid many of Donne's worst faults. Carew cultivated the graces of a courtier ; he was a Catullus holding the post of sewer-in-ordinary to King Charles I. His sensuality, therefore, is always sophisticated and well bred, and he is the father of the whole family of gallant gentlemen, a little the worse for wine, who chirruped under Celia's window down to the very close of the century. Indeed, to tell the truth, what began with Carew may be said to have closed with Congreve.

Of the same class are Sir JOHN SUCKLING, who wrote some fifteen years later, and RICHARD LOVELACE, who indited the typical song of aristocratic insubordination, as late as 1642 and onwards. The courtly race re-emerged after the Restoration in Sedley and Dorset, and was very melodiously revived in Rochester. Like his latest scholar, Carew made a very pious end ; but the lives of all these men had been riotous and sensuous, and their songs were struck from their wild lives like the sparks from their rapiers. Of a different class, superficially, were the lyrics of Habington and of GEORGE HERBERT, a devout Catholic gentleman and a mystical Anglican priest. Here there was more artifice than in Carew, and less fire. Herbert, in particular, is the type of the maker of conceits. Full of delicate ingenuity, he applies the tortured methods of Donne to spiritual experience, gaining more lucidity than his master at the expense of a good deal of intensity. But Herbert also, in his own field, was a courtier, like the lyrists of the Flesh, and he is close to Suckling and the other Royalists in the essential temper of his style. He was himself a leader to certain religious writers of the next generation, whose place is at the close of this chapter.

The *Temple* is by far the best-known book of verses of the whole school, and it deserves, if hardly that pre-eminence, yet all its popularity. Herbert has an extraordinary tenderness, and it is his singular privilege to have been able to clothe the common aspirations, fears, and needs of the religious mind in language more truly poetical than any other Englishman. He is often extravagant, but rarely dull or flat ; his greatest fault lay in an excessive pseudo-psychological ingenuity, which was a snare to all these lyrists, and in a tasteless delight in metrical innovations, often as ugly as they were unprecedented. He sank to writing in the shape of wings and pillars and altars. On this side, in spite of the beauty of their isolated songs and passages, the general decadence of the age was apparent in the lyrical writers. There was no principle of poetic style recognised, and when the spasm of creative passion was over, the dullest mechanism seemed good enough to be adopted. There are whole pages of Suckling and Lovelace which the commonest poetaster would now blush to print, and though it may be said that few of these writers lived to see their poems through the press, and had therefore no opportunity for selection, the mere preservation of so much crabbed rubbish cannot be justified.

A word must be spared for THOMAS RANDOLPH, a "son" of Ben Jonson, whose early death seems to have robbed us of a poet of much solidity and intellectual weight. He came nearer, perhaps, than any other man of his time to the sort of work that the immediate successors of Malherbe were just then doing in France; he may, for purposes of parallelism, be not inaptly styled an English Racan. His verse, stately and hard, full of thought rather than of charm, is closely modelled on the ancients, and inspires respect rather than affection. Randolph is a poet for students, and not for the general reader; but he marks a distinct step in the transition towards classicism.

About 1640 there was an almost simultaneous revival of interest in prose throughout the country, and a dozen writers of ability adopted this neglected instrument. It is not easy to describe comprehensively a class of literature which included the suavity of Walton, the rich rhetoric of Browne, the arid intelligence of Hobbes, the roughness of Milton, and the easy gaiety of Howell. But we may feel that the reign of Charles I. lacked a Pascal, as that of Elizabeth would have been greatly the better for a Calvin. What the prose of England under the Commonwealth wanted was clearness, a nervous limpidity; it needed brevity of phrase, simplicity and facility of diction. The very best of our prose-authors of that great and uneasy period were apt, the moment they descended from their rare heights of eloquence, to sink into prolixity and verbiage. In escaping monotony, they became capricious; there was an ignorance of law, an insensibility to control. The more serious writers of an earlier period had connived at faults encouraged by the pedantry of James I. This second race, of 1640, were less pedantic, but still languid in invention, too ready to rest upon the ideas of the ancients, and to think all was done when these ideas were re-clothed in brocaded language. But as we descend we find the earnestness and passion of the great struggle for freedom reflected more and more on the prose of the best writers. The divines became something more than preachers; they became Protestant tribunes. The evolution of such events as Clarendon encountered was bound to create a scientific tendency in the writing of history—a tendency diametrically opposed to the "sweet raptures and researching conceits" which Wotton thought praiseworthy in the long-popular *Chronicle* of Sir Richard Baker (1641). Even style showed a marked tendency towards modern forms. At his best Walton was as light as Addison, Browne as brilliantly modulated as Dr. Johnson, while the rude and naked periods of Hobbes directly prepared our language for the Restoration.

Milton as a prose-writer fills us with astonishment. The poet who, in *Comus*, had known how to obtain effects so pure, so delicate, and so graceful that verse in England has never achieved a more polished amenity, deliberately dropped the lyre for twenty years, and came forward as a persistent prose pamphleteer of so rude and fierce a kind that it requires all our ingenuity to see a relation between what he was in 1635 and was, again, in 1641.

Critics have vied with one another in pretending that they enjoy the invective tracts of Milton ; they would persuade us, as parents persuade children to relish their medicine, that the *Apology for Smectymnuus* is eloquent, and *Eikonoklastes* humorous.   But, if we are candid, we must admit that these tracts are detestable, whether for the crabbed sinuosity of their style, their awkward and unseemly heat in controversy, or for their flat negation of all the parts of imagination.   If they were not Milton's, we should not read one of them.   As they are his, we are constrained to search for beauties, and we find them in the *Areopagitica*, more than half of which is singularly noble, and in certain enthusiastic pages, usually autobiographical, which form oases in the desert, the howling desert, of Milton's other pamphlets.

CLARENDON was by a few months Milton's senior, yet in reading him we seem to have descended to a later age. That he owed not a little to the Theophrastian fashion of his youth is certain ; but the real portraits which he draws with such picturesque precision are vastly superior to any fantastical abstractions of Overbury or Earle. Clarendon writes, in Wordsworth's phrase, with his eye upon the object, and the graces of his style are the result of the necessity he finds of describing what he wishes to communicate in the simplest and most convincing manner.   The *History of the Great Rebellion* is not the work of a student, but of a soldier, an administrator, a practical politician in stirring times.   To have acted a great part publicly and spiritedly is not enough, as we are often reminded, to make a man the fit chronicler of what he has seen and done ; but in the case of Clarendon these advantages were bestowed upon a man who, though not a rare artist in words, had a marked capacity for expression and considerable literary training. It is his great distinction that, living in an age of pedants, he had the courage to write history—a species of literature which, until his salutary example, was specially over-weighted with ornamental learning—in a spirit of complete simplicity. The diction of Clarendon is curiously modern ; we may read pages of his great book without lighting upon a single word now no longer in use. The claims of the great Chancellor to be counted among the classics of his country were not put forward in the seventeenth century, the first instalment of his history remaining unprinted until 1752, and the rest of it until 1759.

In JEREMY TAYLOR we reach one of those delightful figures, all compact of charm and fascination, which tempt the rapid historian to pause for their contemplation. No better words can be used to describe him than were found by his friend, George Rust, when he said, "This great prelate had the good humour of a gentleman, the eloquence of an orator, the fancy of a poet, the acuteness of a schoolman, the profoundness of a philosopher, the wisdom of a chancellor, the reason of an angel, and the piety of a saint. He had devotion enough for a cloister, learning enough for a university, and wit enough for a college of virtuosi." Fancy was the great quality of Taylor, and it covers, as with brocade, all parts of the raiment of his voluminous writings. His was a mind of rare amenity and sweetness ; he was an eclectic, and the earliest great divine to free himself completely from the subtleties and "spinosities" of the schools. So graceful are his illustrations and pathetic turns of divinity, that his prose lives in its loftier parts as no other religious literature of the age does, except, per-

haps, the verse of George Herbert. Yet even Jeremy
Taylor suffers from the imperfections of contemporary
taste. His unction is too long-drawn, his graces too
elaborate and gorgeous, and modern readers turn from
the sermons which his own age thought so consummate
in their beauty to those more colloquial treatises of
Christian exposition and exhortation of which the *Holy
Living* and the *Holy Dying* are the types.

We note with particular interest those prose-writers of
the pre-Restoration period who cultivated the easier and
more graceful parts of speech and made the transition
more facile. As a rule, these were not the writers most
admired in their own age, and IZAAK WALTON, in particular, holds a position now far higher than any which
he enjoyed in his long lifetime. Yet modern biography
may almost be said to have begun in those easy,
garrulous lives of Donne and Wotton which he printed
in 1640, while in the immortal *Complete Angler* (1653) we
still possess the best-written technical treatise in the
language. Familiar correspóndence, too—a delightful
department of literature—owes much of its freedom and
its prestige to the extremely entertaining *Epistolæ Ho-
Elianæ* (1645), in which JAMES HOWELL surpassed all
previous letter-writers in the ease and liveliness of his
letters. And among these agreeable purveyors of amusement, civilisers of that over-serious age, must not be
omitted THOMAS FULLER, indignant as he might have
been at being classed with persons so frivolous. His
activity between 1639, when he published the *Holy
War*, and 1661, when he died, was prodigious. Without endorsing the extravagant praise of Coleridge, we
must acknowledge that the wit of Fuller was amazing,
if he produced too many examples of it in forms a

little too desultory for modern taste. He was all compact of intellectual vivacity, and his active fancy helped him to a thousand images as his pen rattled along. In such writers we see the age of the journalist approaching, although as yet the newspaper, as we understand it, was not invented. Fuller would have made a superb leader-writer, and Howell an ideal special correspondent. There was little in either of them of the solemnity of the age they lived in, except the longwindedness of their sentences. In them we see English literature eager to be freed from the last fetters of the Renaissance.

But Sir THOMAS BROWNE hugged those fetters closer to himself, and turned them into chased and fretted ornaments of gold. He was one of those rare prose-writers whom we meet at intervals in the history of literature, who leave nothing to improvisation, but balance and burnish their sentences until they reach a perfection analogous to that of very fine verse. Supported by his exquisite ear, Browne permits himself audacities, neologisms, abrupt transitions, which positively take away our breath. But while we watch him thus dancing on the tight-rope of style, we never see him fall; if he lets go his footing in one place, it is but to amaze us by his agility in leaping to another. His scheme has been supposed to be founded on that of Burton, and certainly Browne is no less captivated by the humours of melancholy. But if Burton is the greater favourite among students, Browne is the better artist and the more imaginative writer. There is, moreover, much more that is his own, in relation to parts adapted from the ancients, than in Burton. We find nothing of progress to chronicle in Browne, but so much of high, positive beauty that we do not class him in the procession of the writers of his time, but award him a place apart, as an author of solitary and intrinsic charm.

On the other hand, a writer far less charming than Browne, and now completely obsolete, did serviceable work in clarifying and simplifying prose expression, and in preparing for the lucidity of the Restoration. THOMAS HOBBES was the most brilliant pure intelligence between Bacon and Locke ; but his metaphysical system is now known to have been independent of the former, and derived from French sources. His views are embodied in his *Leviathan* (1651), a work of formidable extent, not now often referred to except by students, but attractive still from the resolute simplicity of the writer's style. In the next age, and especially when deism began to develop, Hobbes exercised a great influence, but this ceased when Locke gained the public ear.

As the century slipped away, English poetry came more and more under the spell of a corrupted Petrarchism. The imitation of Petrarch, seen through Marino and Tasso, penetrated all the poetic systems of Western Europe. It involved us, in English, in a composite style, exquisite and pretentious, simple, at once, and affected. A complicated symbolism, such as Donne had inaugurated, came into almost universal fashion, and verse was decomposed by an excess of antithesis, of forced comparisons, of fantastic metaphors. We have seen that, in the hands of the dramatists, blank verse, no longer understood, offered a temptation to loose and languid writing. In lyric poetry the rhyme presented some resistance, but everything tended to be too fluid and lengthy. The poets indulged themselves in a luxurious vocabulary ; like the Pléiade, a hundred years earlier, they yearned after

such words as "ocymore, dyspotme, oligochronian."
Similar defects had been seen in the Alexandrian poets
of Greece, in Ausonius, in the followers of Tasso; they
were at that moment rife in the French of the latest
Ronsardists and in the Spanish of Gongora. These
dolphin colours are constantly met with in dying literatures, and the English Renaissance was now at its last
gasp.

In the midst of these extravagancies, like Meleager
winding his pure white violets into the gaudy garland
of the late Greek euphuism, we find ROBERT HERRICK
quietly depositing his *Hesperides* (1648), a volume which
contained some of the most delicious lyrics in the language. This strange book, so obscure in its own age,
so lately rediscovered, is a vast confused collection of
odes, songs, epithalamia, hymns, and epigrams tossed
together into a superficial likeness to the collected poems
of Martial, with whom (and not at all with Catullus)
Herrick had a certain kinship. He was an isolated
Devonshire clergyman, exiled, now that his youth was
over, from all association with other men of letters,
grumbling at his destiny, and disdaining his surround-
ings, while never negligent in observing them with the
most exquisite fidelity. The level of Herrick's performance is very high when we consider the bulk of it.
He contrives, almost more than any other poet, to fill
his lyrics with the warmth of sunlight, the odour of
flowers, the fecundity of orchard and harvest-field.
This Christian cleric was a pagan in grain, and in his
petulant, lascivious love-poems he brings the old rituals
to the very lych-gate of his church and swings the
thyrsus under the roof-tree of his parsonage. He
writes of rustic ceremonies and rural sights with infinite

gusto and freshness, bringing up before our eyes at every turn little brilliant pictures of the country-life around him in Devonshire. Herrick is almost guiltless of the complicated extravagance which was rife when his single book appeared.

Crashaw and Vaughan, on the contrary, were full of it, and yet they demand mention, even in a superficial sketch of our poetry, for certain spiritual and literary qualities. RICHARD CRASHAW, a convert to Catholicism, who closed a hectic life prematurely in the service of the Holy House at Loretto in 1650, was a student of the Spanish and Italian mystics, and, in particular, we cannot doubt, of St. John of the Cross. His religious ecstasy and anguish take the most bewildering forms, sometimes plunging him into Gongorism of the worst description (he translated Marino and eclipsed him), but sometimes lifting him to transcendental heights of audacious, fiery lyricism not approached elsewhere in English. HENRY VAUGHAN was an Anglican mystic of quite another type, delicate, meditative, usually a little humdrum, but every now and then flashing out for a line or two into radiant intuitions admirably worded. In both there is much obscurity to be deplored; but while we cultivate Crashaw for the flame below the smoke, we wait in Vaughan for the light within the cloud.

Among the poets we have mentioned, and among the great majority of Commonwealth versifiers, there is to be traced no attempt to modify any further than Donne had essayed to do the prosody which had come into use with Spenser and Sidney. But it is now necessary to dwell on a phenomenon of paramount importance, the rise of a definite revolt against the current system of versification. Side by side with the general satisfaction in the loosely sinuous verse of the day, there was growing up a desire that prosody should be more serried, strenuous, neat, and "correct." Excess of licence led naturally to a reaction in favour of precision. It was felt desirable to pay more attention to the interior harmony of verse, to avoid cacophony and what had been considered legitimate poetic licences, to preserve grammatical purity —in short, to sacrifice common sense and sound judgment a little less to fancy. Most obvious reform of all, it was determined to resist the languid flow of syllables from line to line, but to complete the sense as much as possible in a nervous couplet. It has been customary to consider this reform as needless and impertinent. I am of opinion, on the other hand, that it was not merely wholesome but inevitable, if English versification was to be preserved from final ruin. It was not until more than a century of severe and rigid verse-writing by rule had rehabilitated the worn-out instrument of metre that it became once more fitted to produce harmonies such as those of Coleridge and Shelley.

From high up in the seventeenth century careful students have detected a tendency towards the smoother and correcter, but tamer prosody. I do not think that the beginnings of the classical heroic couplet in England can be explored with advantage earlier than in the works of Sir John Beaumont, who, dying in 1627, left behind him a very carefully written historical poem of *Bosworth Field*. George Sandys, the translator, in the course of his extensive travels, seemed to have gained French ideas of what the stopped couplet should be. But when all claims and candidates have been considered, it is really to EDMUND WALLER that is due the "negative inspiration" (the phrase is borrowed from

Sainte-Beuve) of closing up within bands of smoothness and neatness the wild locks of the British muse. He was the English Malherbe, and wrote with the same constitutional contempt for his predecessors. Dryden accepted him as the forerunner of the classic school, and calls him "the first that made writing [verse] easily an art; first showed us how to conclude the sense most commonly in distichs." Waller appears to have accepted this reform definitely about 1627 (Malherbe's strictly parallel reform dates from 1599), and he persisted in it long without gaining a single scholar. But in 1642 Sir John Denham joined him with his smooth, arid, and prosaic *Cooper's Hill*, and Cowley and Davenant were presently converted. These four, then, poets of limited inspiration, are those who re-emerge in the next age as the harbingers of vigorous prosody and the forerunners of Dryden and Pope.

It is in verse that we can study, far more easily than in prose, the crisis in English literature which we have now reached. That there is a distinction between the manner of Wilkins and of Tillotson, for instance, can be maintained and proved, yet to insist upon it might easily lead to exaggeration. But no one with an ear or an eye can fail to see the difference between Herrick and Denham; it cannot be too strongly affirmed; it is external as well as intrinsic, it is a distinction of form as well as essence. Denham, to put it otherwise, does not very essentially differ as a versifier from such a poet as Falconer, who lived one hundred and twenty years later. But between him and his exact contemporary Crashaw a great gulf is fixed; they stand on opposite platforms of form, of sentiment, of aim. In the years immediately preceding the Commonwealth, literature fell very low in

England. But we must not forget that it was a composite age, an age of variegated experiments and highly coloured attempts. One of these deserves a certain prominence, more for what it led to than what it was.

So long as the drama reigned amongst us, prose fiction was not likely to flourish, for the novel is a play, with all the scenery and the scene-shifting added, written for people who do not go to the theatre. But Sidney's example was still occasionally followed, and in the middle of the seventeenth century the huge romances of the French began to be imported into England and imitated. The size of the originals may be gathered when it is said that one of the most popular, the *Cléopâtre* of Calprenède, is in twenty-three tomes, each containing as much as a volume of a Mudie novel. The English translations began to be very numerous after 1650, a version of the *Grand Cyrus*, in nearly 7000 pages, enjoying an immense success in 1653. It is difficult to speak of these pompous, chivalric romances without ridiculing them. A sketch of the plot of one reads like a burlesque. The original works of the English imitators of these colossal novels are of inferior merit to the original products of the Rambouillet school ; the unfinished *Parthenissa*, composed in "handsome language" by Lord Orrery in 1654, is the best known of the former. The great vogue of these romances of chivalry was from 1650 to 1670, after which they were more or less merged in the "heroic" plays in rhymed verse which Dryden made popular. Their principal addition to literature was an attempt to analyse and reproduce the rapid emotional changes in the temperament of men and women, thus vaguely and blindly preparing the way for the modern realistic novel of psychology, and, more directly, for the works of Richardson. They were the main secular readings of Englishwomen during the final decade preceding the Restoration, and in their lumbering diffuseness and slackness they exemplify, to an almost distressing degree, the main errors into which, notwithstanding the genius of one or two individuals, and the high ambition of many others, English literature had sunken.

Between 1645 and 1660 the practice of literature laboured under extraordinary disabilities. First among these was the concentration of public interest on political and religious questions ; secondly, there was the suspicion and enmity fostered between men, who would otherwise have been *confrères*, by these difficulties in religion and politics ; thirdly, there was the languor consequent on the too-prolonged cultivation of one field with the same methods. It seems paradoxical to say of an age that produced the early verse of Milton and the prose of Browne and Jeremy Taylor, that it was far gone in decadence ; but these splendid and illuminating exceptions do not prevent the statement from being a correct one. England needed, not a few beacons over a waste of the waters of ineptitude, but a firm basis of dry land on which to build a practicable style for daily service ; and to get this the waters had to be drained away, and the beautiful beacons extinguished, by the cataclysm of the Restoration.

V

THE AGE OF DRYDEN

1660–1700

THE year 1660 provides us with a landmark which is perhaps more salient than any other in the history of English literature. In most instances the dates with which we divide our chronicle are merely approximations, points empirically taken to mark the vague transition from one age to another. But when Monk went down to Dover to welcome the agitated and astonished Charles, it was not monarchy only that he received into England, but a fresh era in literature and the arts. With that act of his, the old English Renaissance, which had long been dying, ceased to breathe, and a new departure of intellectual civilisation began. Henceforth the ideals of the leading minds of England were diametrically changed. If they had looked westwards, they now looked towards the east. Instantly those men who still remained loyal to the Jacobean habit passed out of fashion, and even out of notice, while those who had foreseen the new order of things, or had been constitutionally prepared for it, stood out on a sudden as pioneers and leaders of the new army of intelligence.

Before we consider, however, whither that army was to march, we must deal with a figure which belonged neither to the bankrupt past nor to the flushed and animated future. During twenty years Milton, but for an occasional sonnet, had said farewell to poetry. Not that the power had left him, not that the desire and intention of excelling in verse had passed away, but because other aspects of life interested him more, and because the exact form his great song should ultimately take had not impressed itself upon him. Milton permitted youth and middle age to pass, and remained obstinately silent. The Restoration caught him at his studies, and exposed him suddenly to acute personal danger. Towards merely political opponents Charles II. could afford to show himself lenient, and in politics there is no evidence that Milton had ever been influential. It is customary to think that Milton's official position laid him open to resentment, but in the day of its triumph the Monarchy could disdain an old paid servant of the Parliament, an emeritus-Secretary for Foreign Tongues to the Council. What it could less easily overlook was the author of *Eikonoklastes*, that rabid pamphlet in which not only the tenure of kings was savagely railed at, but the now sacred image of the martyred Charles I. was covered with ignominious ridicule. Milton's position was not that of Dryden or of Waller, who had eulogised Cromwell, and could now bow lower still to praise the King. He stood openly confessed as one of the most violent of spiritual regicides.

We might easily have lost our epic supremacy on the scaffold in August 1660, when the poet was placed so ominously in the custody of the Serjeant-at-Arms. It seems probable that, to combine two legends, Davenant interceded with Morice on his behalf, and so helpless a rebel was contemptuously forgiven. We find him discharged in December 1660; and when the physical agitations of these first months had passed away, we conceive the blind man settling down in peace to his majestic task. His vein, he tells us, flowed only from the vernal to the autumnal equinox, and in the spring of 1661 the noblest single monument of English poetry doubtless began to take definite form. " Blind, old, and lonely," as in Shelley's vision of him, he was driven from prosperity and ease by the triumph of the liberticide, only that he might in that crisis become, what else he might have failed to be, " the sire of an immortal strain," " the third among the sons of light."

There is reason to believe that Milton had already determined what should be the form and character of his *Paradise Lost* when Cromwell died. In 1663 he completed the poem. Two years later, at Elwood's suggestion, " What hast thou to say of Paradise found ?" he began the second and the shorter work, which he finished in 1665. The choral tragedy of *Samson Agonistes* followed, perhaps in 1667, which was the year of the publication of *Paradise Lost ; Paradise Regained* and *Samson* were printed together in 1671. Three years later Milton died, having, so far as is known, refrained from the exercise of verse during the last seven years of his life. It was, we may believe, practically between 1661 and 1667 that he built up the gorgeous triple structure on which his fame as that of the first among modern heroic poets is perennially sustained. The performances of Milton are surprising, yet his reticences are almost more amazing still. He sang, when the inspiration was on him, "with impetus and *æstro,*' and when the fit was off, could remain absolutely silent for years and years.

The Milton of the Restoration has little affinity with

the lyrical Milton whose work detained us in the last chapter. He appears before us now solely in the aspect of an epic poet (for the very choruses in *Samson* are scarcely lyrical). He is discovered in these austere and magnificent productions, but particularly in *Paradise Lost*, as the foremost, and even in a broad sense the only epic poet of England. The true epos of the ancient literatures had detailed in heroic sequence the achievements of the national hero, supported and roused and regulated by the immediate intervention of the national deities. It had been notable for its elevation, its simplicity, its oneness of purpose. The various attempts to write literary epics in England before Milton's time had failed, as they have failed since, and his only models were the *Iliad* and the *Æneid;* although it is not to be questioned that his conscious design was to do for his own country what Tasso, Ariosto, and Camoens, glories of the Latin race in the sixteenth century, had done for theirs. Those poets had forced the sentiments and aspirations of a modern age into the archaic shape of the epos, and had produced works which did not much resemble, indeed, the *Iliad* or the *Odyssey*, but which glorified Italian or Portuguese prowess, flattered the national idiosyncrasy, and preserved the traditional extent and something of the traditional form of the ancient epic.

There was, however, another great predecessor to whom, in the general tenor of his epic, Milton stood in closer relation than to the ancients or to the secular moderns. The one human production which we occasionally think of in reading *Paradise Lost* is the *Divine Comedy*. In Milton, as in Dante, it is not the prowess of any national hero which gives the poem its central interest, but the sovereign providence of God. Dante, however, was emboldened, by the circumstances of his epoch and career, to centre the interest of his great trilogy in present times, giving, indeed, to a theme in essence highly imaginative, and as we should say fabulous, an air of actuality and realism. Milton touches modern existence nowhere, but is sustained throughout on a vision of stupendous supernatural action far away in the past, before and during the very dawn of humanity. Such a story as *Paradise Lost* communicates to us could be credible and fascinating only to persons who had taken in the mysteries of the Hebrew Bible with their mother's milk, and who were as familiar with Genesis as with the chronicles of their own country. The poem presupposes a homely knowledge of and confidence in the scheme of the Old Testament, and in this sense, though perhaps in this sense only, those are right who see in *Paradise Lost* a characteristically " puritan " poem. If we take a Puritan to be a man steeped in Bible lore, then we may say that only " puritans " can properly appreciate the later poems of Milton, although there is much in the texture of these works which few Puritans, in the exacter sense, would, if they understood it, tolerate. It is a very notable fact that the only English epic is also the only epic taken from Biblical sources. So great has been the force of Milton that he has stamped on English eyes the picture he himself created of the scenes of Genesis, and Huxley complained that it was the seventh book of *Paradise Lost*, and not any misreading of Moses, which had imprinted indelibly on the English public mind its system of a false cosmogony.

The Fall and the Redemption of Man were themes of surpassing interest and importance, but at the first blush they might seem highly improper for lengthy treatment in blank verse. We shudder to think how they would have been dealt with by some of Milton's sterner co-religionists — how in Milton's youth they had been treated, for instance, by Sylvester and by Quarles. But it is necessary to insist that Milton stood not closer, intellectually, to such a divine as Baxter than he did to, let us say, such a seriously minded lay-churchman as Cowley. He was totally separated from either, and in all æsthetic questions was, happily for us, a law unto himself. Hence he allowed himself a full exercise of the ornaments with which his humanistic studies had enriched him. His brain was not an empty conventicle, stored with none but the necessities of devotion : it was hung round with the spoils of paganism and garlanded with Dionysiac ivy. Within the walls of his protesting contemporaries no music had been permitted but that of the staidest psalmody. In the chapel of Milton's brain, entirely devoted though it was to a Biblical form of worship, there were flutes and trumpets to accompany one vast commanding organ. The peculiarity of Milton's position was that among Puritans he was an artist, and yet among artists a Puritan.

Commentaries abound on the scheme, the theology, the dogmatic ideas of *Paradise Lost* and *Regained*. These, it may boldly be suggested, would scarcely in these days be sufficient to keep these epics alive, were it not for the subsidiary enchantments of the very ornament which to grave minds may at first have seemed out of place. Dryden, with his admirable perspicuity, early perceived that it was precisely where the language of the Authorised Version trammelled him too much that Milton failed, inserting what Dryden calls " a track of scripture " into the text. It is where he escapes from

Scriptural tradition that the grandiose or voluptuous images throng his fancy, and the melody passes from stop to stop, from the reed-tone of the bowers of Paradise to the open diapason of the council of the rebel angels. As he grew older the taste of Milton grew more austere. The change in the character of his ornament is deeply marked when we ascend from the alpine meadows of *Paradise Lost* to the peaks of *Paradise Regained,* where the imaginative air is so highly rarefied that many readers find it difficult to breathe. Internal evidence may lead us to suppose *Samson Agonistes* to be an even later manifestation of a genius that was rapidly rising into an atmosphere too thin for human enjoyment. Milton had declared, in a sublime utterance of his early life, that the highest poetry was not "to be obtained by the invocation of Dame Memory and her siren daughters," but by the direct purification of divine fire placed on the lips of the elect by the hallowed fingers of the seraphim. That inspiration, he did not question, ultimately came to him, and in its light he wrote. But we do him no dishonour after these years if we confess that he owed more of his charm than he acknowledged to the aid of those siren daughters. He was blind, and could not refresh the sources of memory, and by-and-by the sirens, like his own earthly daughters, forsook him, leaving him in the dry and scarce-tolerable isolation of his own integral dignity. Without his ineffable charm the Milton of these later poems would scarcely be readable, and that charm consists largely in two elements—his exquisite use of pagan or secular imagery, and the unequalled variety and harmony of his versification.

The blank verse of the epics has been at once the model and the despair of all who have attempted that easiest and hardest of measures since the end of the seventeenth century. On his manipulation of this form Milton founds his claim to be acknowledged the greatest artist or artificer in verse that the English race has produced. The typical blank iambic line has five full and uniform stresses, such as we find in correct but timid versifiers throughout our literature. All brilliant writers from Shakespeare downwards have shown their mastery of the form by the harmonious variation of the number and value of these stresses; but Milton goes much further in this respect than any other poet, and, without ever losing his hold upon the norm, plays with it as a great pianist plays with an air. His variations of stress, his inversions of rhythm, what have been called his " dactylic" and "trochaic" effects, add immeasurably to the freshness and beauty of the poem. When we read *Paradise Lost* aloud, we are surprised at the absence of that monotony which mars our pleasure in reading most other works of a like length and sedateness. No one with an ear can ever have found Milton dull, and the prime cause of this perennial freshness is the amazing art with which the blank verse is varied. It leaps like water from a spring, always in the same direction and volume, yet never for two consecutive moments in exactly the same form.

To us the post-Restoration writings of Milton possess a greater value than all else that was produced in verse for more than a hundred years; but in taking an historical survey we must endeavour to realise that his influence on the age he lived in was nil, and that to unprejudiced persons of education living in London about 1665, the author of *Paradise Lost* was something less than Flecknoe or Flatman. Nor to us, who see beneath the surface, does he present any features which bring him into the general movement of literature. He was a species in himself—a vast, unrelated Phœnix. In his youth, as we have seen, Milton had been slightly subjected to influences from Shakespeare, Spenser, and even the disciples of Spenser ; but after his long silence he emerges with a style absolutely formed, derived from no earlier poet, and destined for half a century to influence no later one. Critics amuse themselves by detecting in *Paradise Lost* relics of Du Bartas, of Vondel, of Cowley, even of lesser men ; but these were mere fragments of ornament disdainfully transferred to Milton's magnificent edifice as material, not as modifying by a jot the character of its architecture. It is very strange to think of the aged Milton, in stately patience, waiting for death to come to him in his relative obscurity, yet not doubting for a moment that he had succeeded in that " accomplishment of greatest things " to which his heart had been set at Cambridge more than forty years before.

We turn from Milton, then, wrapped like Moses in a cloud, and the contrast is great when we concentrate our attention on the state of letters in England around the foot of his mountain ; for here, at least, there was no isolation, but a combined unison of effort in a single direction was the central feature of the moment. During the strenuous political agitation of the Commonwealth, literature had practically come to an end in England. There were still, of course, men of talent, but they were weak, discouraged, unilluminated. Some were trying to keep alive, in its utter decrepitude, the Jacobean method of writing ; others were looking ahead, and were ready, at the cost of what capricious beauty remained in English verse, to inaugurate a new school of reason and correct-

12

ness. When 1660 brought back the Court, with its Latin
sympathies, the first of these two classes faded like ghosts
at cockcrow. Herrick, Shirley, Vaughan long survived
the Restoration, but no notice of them or of their writings
is to be found in any of the criticisms of the age. On
the other hand, the second class came forth at once
into prominence, and four small poets—Waller, with his
precise grace ; Denham, with his dry vigour ; Davenant,
who restored the drama ; Cowley, who glorified intellect
and exact speculation—were hailed at once as the masters
of a new school and the martyrs to a conquered barbarism. It was felt, in a vague way, that they had been
holding the fort, and theirs were the honours of a relieved
and gallant garrison.

The Commonwealth, contemplating more serious
matters, had neglected and discouraged literature. The
monarchy, under a king who desired to be known as a
patron of wit, should instantly have caused it to flourish ;
but for several years after 1660—why, we can hardly tell
—scarcely anything of the least value was composed. The
four poets just enumerated, in spite of the fame they had
inherited, wrote none but a few occasional pieces down to
the deaths of Cowley (1667) and Davenant (1668). There
was a general consciousness that taste had suffered a revolution, but what direction it was now to take remained
doubtful. The returning cavaliers had brought the
message back from France that the savagery of English
letters was to cease, but something better than Davenant's
plays or even Cowley's odes must surely take its place.
The country was eager for guidance, yet without a guide.
No one felt this more perspicuously than the youthful
Dryden, who described his own position long afterwards
by saying that in those days he "was drawing the out-

lines of an art without any living master to instruct" him in it.

The guidance had to come from France, and the moment of the Restoration was not a fortunate one. The first great generation after Malherbe was drawing to a close, and the second had not quite begun. The development of English literature might have been steadier and purer, if the exiled English courtiers had been kept in Paris ten years longer, to witness the death of Mazarin, the decay of the old Academic coterie, and the rise of Boileau and Racine. They left Chapelain behind them, and returned home to find Cowley—poets so strangely similar in their merits and in their faults, in their ambitions and in their failures, that it is hard to believe the resemblance wholly accidental. They had left poetry in France dry, harsh, positive, and they found it so in England. The only difference was that on this side of the Channel there was less of it, and that it was conducted here with infinitely less vigour, resource, and abundance. There was no Corneille in London, no Rotrou; the authority of Waller was late and feeble in comparison with that bequeathed by Malherbe.

It was, nevertheless, important to perceive, and the acutest Englishmen of letters did at once perceive, that what had been done in France about thirty years before was now just being begun in England; that is to say, the old loose romantic manner, say of Spenser or of Ronsard, was being totally abandoned in favour of "the rules," the unities, a closer prosody, a drier, exacter system of reasoning. Unfortunately, up to 1660 there was little real criticism of poetic style in France, and little effort to be dexterously complete all through a composition. Happy lines, a brilliant passage, had to excuse pages of flatness and

ineptitude. So it was in England. A few single lines of
Cowley are among the most beautiful of the century, and
he has short jets of enchanting poetry, but these lie scattered in flat wildernesses of what is intolerably grotesque.
The idea of uniform excellence was to be introduced,
directly in France and then incidentally here, by Boileau,
who was writing his first great satires when Charles II.
was in the act of taking possession of his throne.

Even in these first stumbling days, however, the new
school saw its goal before it. The old madness, the old
quaint frenzy of fancy, the old symbolism and impres-
sionism had utterly gone out. In their place, in the place
of this liberty which had turned to licence, came the
rigid following of "the ancients." The only guides for
English verse in future were to be the pole-star of the
Latin poets, and the rules of the French critics who
sought to adapt Aristotle to modern life. What such a
poet as Dryden tried to do was regulated by what, reading in the light of Scaliger and Casaubon, he found the
Latins had done. This excluded prettiness altogether,
excluded the extravagances and violent antics of the
natural school, but admitted, if the poet was skilful
enough to develop them, such qualities as nobility of
expression, lucidity of language, justice of thought, and
closeness of reasoning, and these are the very qualities
which we are presently to discern in Dryden.

Meanwhile, although poetry, in the criticism of poetry,
was the subject uppermost in the minds of the men of
wit and pleasure who clustered around the Court of
Charles, attention was paid, and with no little serious-
ness, to the deplorable state of prose. Here the distinction between old and new could not be drawn with as
much sharpness as it could in verse, yet here also there

was a crisis imminent. The florid, involved, and often very charming prose of such writers as Jeremy Taylor, Fuller, and Henry More, was naturally destined to become obsolete. Its long-windedness, its exuberance, its caprices of style, marked it out for speedy decay; its beauties, and they have been already dwelt upon, were dolphin colours. A time had come when what people craved in prose was something simpler and terser in form, less ornate, less orotund, more supple in dealing with logical sequences of ideas. England had produced several divines, essayists, and historians of great distinction, but she had hitherto failed to bring forth a Pascal.

The returning Royalists had left behind them in Paris an Academy which, with many faults, had yet for a quarter of a century been a great power for good in France. It had held up a standard of literature, had enforced rules, had driven the stray sheep of letters into something resembling a flock. The first important step taken in intellectual life after the Restoration was the foundation in England of a body which at its initiation seemed more or less closely to resemble the French Academy. In 1661 Cowley had issued his *Proposition for the Advancement of Learning*, the direct result of which was the institution of the Royal Society in 1662, with the King as patron, and Lord Brouncker, the mathematician, as first president. Cowley's tract was merely the match which set fire to a scheme which had long been preparing for the encouragement of experimental knowledge. As every one is aware, the Royal Society soon turned its attention exclusively to the exacter sciences, but most of the leading English poets and prose-writers were among its earlier members, and it does not seem to have been observed by the historians of our literature that the original scope of the assembly included the renovation of English prose. According to the official definition of the infant Royal Society, they "exacted from all their members a close, naked, natural way of speaking, positive expressions, clear senses, a native easiness, bringing all things as near the mathematical plainness as they can," and passed " a resolution to reject all the amplifications, digressions, and swellings of style." No literary Academy could have done more; and although the Royal Society soon dropped all pretensions to jurisdiction over prose-writing, this early action, coming when it did, can but have been of immense service to the new school. Nor must it be forgotten that among these savants who bound themselves to the exercise of lucidity and brevity in composition were Boyle, Clarendon, Barrow, Evelyn, Pearson, Pepys, Stanley, Burnet, the very representatives of all that was most vivid in the prose of the age. Of these not all survived to learn the lesson that they taught, but it is therefore, perhaps, the more significant that they should have accepted it in principle.

In all this movement JOHN DRYDEN's place was still insignificant. In his thirtieth year he was, as a later Laureate put it, faintly distinguished. But he was presently to find his opportunity in the resuscitation of dramatic poetry. From before the death of Ben Jonson the stage had begun to languish, and its decline cannot in fairness be attributed entirely to the zeal of the Puritans. But in 1641 Parliament had issued an ordinance ordaining that public stage-plays should cease, those who had been in the habit of indulging in these spectacles of lascivious pleasure being sternly recommended to consider repentance, reconciliation, and peace with God. This charge being found insufficient, an Act was passed in 1648 ordering that all theatres should be dismantled, all convicted actors publicly whipped, and all spectators fined. An attempt to perform the *Bloody Brother* of Fletcher merely proved that the authorities were in deadly earnest, for the actors were carried off to prison in their stage clothes. The drama is a form of art which cannot exist in a vacuum; starved of all opportunities of exercise, English play-writing died of inanition. Nothing could be more abjectly incompetent and illiterate than the closet-dramas printed during the Commonwealth. Men who had not seen a play for twenty years had completely forgotten what a play should be. It is scarcely credible that an art which had been raised to perfection by Shakespeare, should in half a century sink into such an abysm of feebleness as we find, for example, in the unacted dramas of the Killigrews. Nor did a spark of poetry, however wild and vague, survive in these degenerate successors of the school of Fletcher.

In the midst of this extremity of decay the theatres were once more opened. In 1656 Sir WILLIAM DAVENANT ventured to invite the public to "an entertainment by declamation and music, after the manner of the ancients," at Rutland House, in the City. This was the thin end of the wedge indeed ; but it has been wrongly described as a play, or even an opera. There was no dialogue, but extremely long rhapsodies in prose (which must surely have been read) were broken by songs and instrumental music. As no harm came of this experiment, in 1658 Davenant dared to open the old dismantled Cockpit in Drury Lane, and there produced his English opera, the *Siege of Rhodes*, which had been already seen at Rutland House. This dramatic production, afterwards greatly enlarged, was prodigiously admired in the Court of Charles II., and was looked upon as the starting-point of the new drama. The critics of the Restoration are never tired of applauding this "perfect opera," the versification of which was smooth and ingeniously varied indeed, yet without a touch of even rhetorical poetry. As nothing befell the daring Davenant, he was emboldened to bring out five-act plays, tragedies and comedies of his own, at Drury Lane, and, almost immediately after the King's return, patents were granted both to him and to Killigrew. In Betterton, Harris, and Mrs. Sanderson (for women now first began to take women's parts) a school of young actors was presently discovered, and the stage flourished again as if Puritanism had never existed.

But it was one thing to have clever actors and a protected stage, and quite another to create a dramatic literature. It might be very well for enthusiastic contemporaries to say that in his plays Davenant "does outdo both ancients and the moderns too," but these were simply execrable as pieces of writing. The long silence of the Commonwealth weighed upon the playwrights. Only one man in this first period wrote decently, a robust, vigorous imitator of Ben Jonson, JOHN WILSON, whose comedies and tragedies reproduced the manner of that master with remarkable skill. This, however, proved to be a false start. The new drama was no more to spring from the study of Ben Jonson than from a dim reminiscence of Shakespeare and Fletcher. It was to come from France, and mainly from Corneille. The old, almost simultaneous translation of the *Cid*, by Joseph Rutter, was forgotten; but in the years just preceding

the Restoration Sir William Lower had published a
series of versions of Corneille's tragedies, and these had
been widely admired. In his attempts at lyrical drama,
Davenant was undoubtedly imitating not Corneille only,
but Quinault. Early in his critical career, Dryden
announced that the four great models were Aristotle,
Horace, Ben Jonson, and Corneille ; and though he
refers vaguely and largely to the dramatists of Italy
and Spain, fearing by too great praise of a Frenchman to wound English susceptibilities, it is plain that
Dryden in his early tragedies is always eagerly watching
Corneille.

In that valuable and admirable treatise, *An Essay of
Dramatic Poesy*, 1668, published when he had already
produced five of his dramatic experiments, Dryden very
clearly and unflinchingly lays down the law about theatrical composition. Plays are for the future to be "regular"—that is to say, they are to respect the unities of time,
place, and action ; "no theatre in the world has anything
so absurd as the English tragi-comedy," and this is to be
rigorously abandoned ; a great simplicity of plot, a broad
and definite catastrophe, an observation of the laws of
stage decorum, these are to mark the English theatre in
future, as they already are the ornament of the French.
After all this, we are startled to discover Dryden turning
against his new allies, praising the English irregularity,
finding fault with Corneille, and finally unravelling his
whole critical web with a charming admission : "I admire the pattern of elaborate writing, but—I love Shakespeare." The fact is that the great spirit of Dryden, here
at the practical outset of his career, was torn between
two aims. He saw that English poetry was exhausted,
disillusioned, bankrupt, and that nothing short of a com-

·plete revolution would revive it; he saw that the Latin civilisation was opening its arms, and that England was falling into them, fascinated like a bird by a snake (and Dryden also was fascinated and could not resist); yet, all the time, he was hankering after the lost poetry, and wishing that a compromise could be made between Shakespeare and Aristotle, Fletcher and Molière. So, with all his effort to create "heroic drama" in England, no really well-constructed piece, no closely wrought and highly polished *Cinna* was to reward Dryden for his cultivation of the unities.

He could not, of course, foresee this, and the success which followed his suggestion, made in 1664, that "the excellence and dignity of rhyme" should be added to serious drama, must have ·made him look upon himself as a great and happy innovator. Etheredge, in the graver scenes of his *Comical Revenge*, instantly adopted the rhyming couplet, Dryden's own tragedies followed, and blank verse was completely abandoned until 1678. During these fourteen years, Sedley, Crowne, Settle, Otway, and Lee, in succession between 1668 and 1675, came to the front as industrious contributors to the tragic stage, each, with a touching docility, accepting the burden of rhyme; we therefore possess a solid mass of dramatic literature, much of it quite skilful in its own way, produced in a form closely analogous to that of the French. These are what were known as the "heroic plays," of which Dryden's *Conquest of Granada* is the type. This strange experiment has received from the critics of more recent times little but ridicule, and it may be admitted that it is not easy to approach it with sympathy. Still, certain facts should make it important to the literary historian. The taste for heroic drama showed a singularly literary preoccupation on the part of the public. To listen to the "cat and puss" dialogue, the στιχομυθία, required a cultivated attention, and the ear which delighted in the richness of the rhyme could hardly be a vulgar one.

The advantages of the system lay in the elegance and nobility of the impression of life, the melody of the versification ; its disadvantages were that it encouraged bombast and foppery, and was essentially monotonous. All was magnificent in those plays ; the main personages were royal, or on the steps of the throne. The heroic plays demanded a fuller stage presentment than the age might supply. If the *Indian Emperor* could now be acted under the management of Mr. Imré Karalfy, we should probably be charmed with the sonorous splendour of its couplets and the gorgeous ritual of its scenes. The *Rehearsal* (1672), with its delicious fooling, only added to the popular predilection for these royal tragedies. But Dryden, who had invented them, grew tired of them, and in *All for Love*, in 1678, he "disencumbered himself from rhyme." The whole flock of tragic poets immediately followed him, and heroic plays were an exploded fashion.

If we turn to these ponderous tragedies now, it is principally, however, to study the essays which are prefixed to them. In the general interest awakened concerning the *technique* of literature, these were frequent ; Lestrange, whose business it was to read them, complained that "a man had as good go to court without a cravat as appear in print without a preface." But Dryden's, composed, perhaps, in rivalry with the *Examens* of Corneille, are by far the most important, and form the first body of really serious and philosophical criticism to be discovered in English. We must not expect absolute consistency in these essays. They mark the growth of a mind, not the conditions of a mind settled in a fixed opinion. As fresh lights came up on his horizon, as he read Ben Jonson less and Shakespeare more, as Boileau and Bossu affected his taste, as Racine rose into his ken, and as he became more closely acquainted with the poets of antiquity, Dryden's views seem to vacillate, to be lacking in authority. But we err if this remains our final opinion; we mistake the movement of growth for the instability of weakness. To the last Dryden was a living force in letters, spreading, progressing, stimulating others by the ceaseless stimulus which he himself received from literature.

And while we study these noble critical prefaces we perceive that English prose has taken fresh forms and a new coherency. Among the many candidates for the praise of having reformed our wild and loose methods in prose, JOHN EVELYN seems to be the one who best deserves it. He was much the oldest of the new writers, and he was, perhaps, the very earliest to go deliberately to French models of brevity and grace. Early in the Commonwealth he was as familiar with La Motte le Vayer as with Aristotle; he looked both ways and embraced all culture. Yet Evelyn is not a great writer; he aims at more than he reaches; there is notable in his prose, as in the verse of Cowley, constant irregularity of workmanship, and a score of faults have to be atoned for by one startling beauty. Evelyn, therefore, is a pioneer; but the true artificers of modern English prose are a group of younger men of divers fortunes, all, strangely enough, born between 1628 and 1633. In genealogical order the names of the makers of modern style may be given thus—Temple, Barrow, Tillotson, Halifax, Dryden, Locke, and South.

Among these, the tradition of the eighteenth century gave the first place to JOHN TILLOTSON, Archbishop of Canterbury, whose influence on his contemporaries, and particularly on Dryden, was supposed to be extreme. Later criticism has questioned the possibility of this, and, indeed, it can be demonstrated that until after he was raised to the primacy in 1691 the publications of Tillotson were scattered and few; he seemed to withdraw from notice behind the fame of such friends as Barrow and Wilkins. But it must not be forgotten that all this time Tillotson was preaching, and that as early as 1665 his sermons were accepted as the most popular of the age. The clergy, we are told, came to his Tuesday lectures "to form their minds," and if so, young writers may well have attended them to form their style. The celebrated sweetness of Tillotson's character is reflected in his works, where the storms and passions of his career seem to have totally subsided. Urbanity and a balanced decorum are found throughout the serene and insinuating periods of this elegant latitudinarian. It was said of him that "there never was a son of absurdity that did not dislike, nor a sensible reader who did not approve his writings." He was a typical child of the Restoration, in that, not having very much to say, he was assiduous in saying what he had in the most graceful and intelligible manner possible.

By the side of Tillotson, ISAAC BARROW appears ponderous and even long-winded. He belongs to the new school more by what he avoids than by what he attains. He was a man of great intellectual force, who, born into an age which was beginning to stigmatise certain faults

in its predecessor, was able to escape those particular
errors of false ornament and studied quaintness, but
could not train his somewhat elephantine feet to dance on
the tight-rope of delicate ease. The matter of Barrow is
always solid and virile, and he has phrases of a delightful
potency. In considering the place of the great divines
in the movement of literature, it is to be borne in mind
that sermons were now to a vast majority of auditors
their principal intellectual pabulum. In days when
there were no newspapers, no magazines, no public
libraries, and no popular lectures, when knowledge was
but sparsely distributed in large and costly books, all
who were too decent to encounter the rough speech and
lax morality of the theatre had no source of literary
entertainment open to them except the churches. We
groan nowadays under the infliction of a long sermon,
but in the seventeenth century the preacher who stopped
within the hour defrauded an eager audience of a pleasure. It is not necessary to suppose that with the decay
of puritanical enthusiasm the appetite for listening to
sermons came to an end. On the contrary, public taste
became more eclectic, and a truly popular divine was
more than ever besieged in his pulpit. To these conditions the preachers lent themselves, and those who had
literary skill revelled in opportunities which were soon
to quit them for the essayist and the journalist. Nor
was the orthodoxy of the hour so strenuous that it
excluded a great deal of political and social allusion.
Sermons and books of divinity were expected to enter-
tain. There are few treatises of the age so lively as
the religious pamphlets of the unidentified author of
the *Whole Duty of Man*, and it was an appreciator
of the wicked wit of South who protested that his

addresses should be called, not Sunday, but week-day sermons.

From the rapid and luminous compositions of the divines, it was but a step to the masters of elegant mundane prose. Cruel commentators have conspired to prove that there was no subject on which Sir WILLIAM TEMPLE was so competent as to excuse the fluency with which he wrote about it. That the matter contained in the broad volumes of his *Works* is not of great extent or value must be conceded; but style does not live by matter only, and it is the bright modern note, the ease and grace, the rapidity and lucidity, that give to Temple his faint but perennial charm. He is the author, too, of one famous sentence, which may be quoted here, although our scope forbids quotation, because it marks in a very clear way the movement of English prose. Let us listen to the cadence of these words :

" *When all is done, human life is, at the greatest and the best, but like a froward child, that must be played with and humoured a little to keep it quiet till it falls asleep, and then the care is over.*"

This is the modern manner of using English. It is divided by an abysm from the prose of the Commonwealth, and in writing such a sentence Temple showed himself nearer to the best authors of our living age than he was to such contemporaries of his own as Hobbes or Browne.

Of all those, however, who contrived to clarify and civilise the prose of the Restoration, and to make it a vehicle for gentle irony and sparkling humour, the most notable was " Jotham, of piercing wit and pregnant thought." There exists some tiresome doubt about the bibliography of the Marquis of HALIFAX, for his anonymous miscellanies were not collected until 1704, when he had been nine years dead. But no one questions the authenticity of *Advice to a Daughter*; and if internal evidence, proof by style and temper, are worth anything at all, they must confirm the tradition that it is to the same pen we owe the *Character of a Trimmer* and the *Anatomy of an Equivalent*. In these ironic tracts, so adroit, so grave, so graceful, we find ourselves far indeed from the storm and turmoil of the Commonwealth. In Halifax we see the best and the most sympathetic side of the Restoration, its conservative scepticism, its reserve, its urbane and moderate virtue. In a letter to Cotton, Halifax confesses that his favourite reading had always been Montaigne, and he is a link between that delicious essayist and the *Spectators* and *Tatlers* of a later age.

It was characteristic of the new age, anxious to fix the grounds of opinion and base thought in each province exactly, that it should turn to the phenomena of the human mind and inquire into the sources of knowledge. This work fell particularly to the share of that candid and independent philosopher JOHN LOCKE, and the celebrated *Essay on the Human Understanding* (1690), in which he elaborates the thesis that all knowledge is derived from experience, marks a crisis in psychological literature. Locke derived all our ideas from sensation and reflection, believing the mind to be a passive recipient of simple ideas, which it cannot in the first instance create, but can retain, and can so modify and multiply as to form that infinity of complex ideas which we call the Understanding. In short, he protested against the empirical doctrine of "innate notions" being brought into the world by the soul. Where Locke's method and teaching, however, were peculiarly useful were in their admirable challenge to those pedantic assumptions and baseless propositions which had up to his time disturbed philosophy. Locke refuses to parley with the obscurities of the schools, and he sits bravely in the dry and searching light of science.

Locke's contributions to theology are marked by the same intense determination to arrive at truth, and he was accused of having been the unconscious father of the deists. But, in fact, in religion, as in philosophy, his attitude is not so much sceptical as scrupulous. He ardently desires to get rid of the dubious and the non-essential. His candour is not less displayed in his tractates on education and government. Everywhere Locke is the embodiment of enlightened common-sense, toleration, and clairvoyance. He laid his hand on the jarring chords of the seventeenth century, and sought to calm and tune them, and in temperament, as in influence, he was the inaugurator of a new age of thought and feeling. He was the most liberally-minded man of his time, and in his modesty, candour, and charity, no less than in the astounding reverberations caused by his quiet philosophical utterances, Locke reminds us of Charles Darwin. As a writer he is not favourably represented by the *Essay*, which is arid in form, and at no time was he in possession of an attractive style; but in some of his more familiar treatises we see how lucid and simple he could be at his best, and how completely he had exchanged the ornate manner of the Commonwealth for a prose that was competent to deal with plain matters of fact.

We dwell, more or less lovingly, on these names of the precursors of a modern prose, yet not one of them, not Halifax, not Tillotson, not Temple, survives as the

13

author of any book now generally read by the larger
public. Even the *Prefaces* of Dryden, it must regretfully
be admitted, are no longer familiar to any but literary
readers. The Restoration prose most effectively appreciated by the masses, and still alive on the shelves of the
booksellers, is that of writers never recognised at all by
the polite criticism of their own day. In a country book-
shop you shall no longer happen upon the *Sacred Theory
of the Earth* or upon *Public Employment preferred to
Solitude*, but you shall upon Pepys' *Diary* and the
Pilgrim's Progress and *A Call to the Unconverted*.

These works do not stand on the same or even on
neighbouring levels of literary merit; but they have this
in common, that neither Baxter nor Bunyan nor Pepys
set any value on literature, or concerned himself at all with
the form under which he transmitted his ideas. There was
this difference, however, that while Bunyan was unconsciously a consummate artist and a man instinct with
imagination, the other two impress us solely by the striking quality of the narrative, or the exhortations which
they impart in the first words that occur to them. It is
to JOHN BUNYAN, therefore, that our attention must here
for a moment be given. Like Milton, he was an ana-
chronism in the age of Charles II., and we observe with
surprise that it was in an epoch of criticism, of reason,
of combined experimental eclecticism, that two isolated
men of genius put forth, the one an epic poem, the other
a couple of religious allegories, steeped in the purest and
most ideal romance, and each unrivalled in its own class
throughout other and more propitious ages of English
literature. Nor, though the simple, racy compositions
of Bunyan may not seem to have had any very direct
influence on literature of the more academic kind, has

the stimulus of his best books on humble minds ceased ever since, but has kept the language of the poor always hardy and picturesque, with scarcely less instant benefit than the Bible itself. Whether these narratives, and, most of all, the *Life and Death of Mr. Badman*, had not a direct influence on the realistic novel of the middle of the following century, is a question which criticism has scarcely decided ; but that they prepared the minds of the readers of those novels is beyond all doubt.

During the first twenty years after the Restoration, poetry was very little cultivated in England outside the limits of the heroic drama. That new instrument, the couplet, was acknowledged to be an admirable one, and to have excluded all competitors. But very little advance had been made in the exercise of it during the forty years which had followed the publication of Denham's *Cooper's Hill*. Dryden, for all his evidence of force, was disappointing his admirers. He had shown himself a supple prose-writer, indeed ; but his achievements in verse up to his fiftieth year were not such as could claim for him any pre-eminence among poets. He was at last to discover his true field ; he was about to become the greatest English satirist, and in doing so to reveal qualities of magnificent metrical power such as his warmest. followers had not dreamed of. Since the Elizabethans had cultivated a rough and obscure species of satire moulded upon Persius, serious work of this class had gone out of fashion. But in the reign of Charles I. a rattling kind of burlesque rhyming, used for similar purposes in most of the countries of Europe, came into service for parodies, extravagant fables, and satirical attacks. In France, Scarron raised it to the level of literature, but it was known in England before the days of Scarron. Cleveland had used it, and Sir John Mennis, in whose *Musarum Deliciæ* we find—

> " *He that fights and runs away*
> *May live to fight another day;* "

and later on it was brought into great popularity by Cotton and SAMUEL BUTLER. The famous *Hudibras* of the latter, "written in the time of the Late Wars," was kept in MS. till 1663, when the publication of so gross a lampoon on the Presbyterians became possible. It was greatly relished, and though it is a barbarous and ribald production of small literary value, it is still praised, and perhaps occasionally read. It affords rare opportunities for quotation, every few pages containing a line or couplet of considerable facetiousness. *Hudibras* was incessantly imitated, and the generic term Hudibrastics was invented for this kind of daring doggerel.

Butler, however, is a mere episode. Genuine satire was reintroduced by Marvell, and ten years later revived by Oldham. The example of that very gifted, if sinister, young man, seems to have finally directed Dryden's attention to a species of poetry which must already have occupied his thoughts in the criticism of Casaubon as well as in the marvellous verse of Boileau. Dryden did not, however, at first directly imitate the ancients or strike an intrepid blow at contemporary bad taste. His *Absalom and Achitophel* (1681–82) is political in character, a gallery of satirical portraits of public men, so painted as to excite to madness the passions of a faction at a critical moment. No poem was ever better timed. Under the thin and acceptable disguise of a Biblical narrative, the Tory poet gibbeted without mercy the heads and notables of the rival party. The two poems which closely followed it bore the same stamp. In *MacFlecknoe* the manner is more closely that of Boileau, whom Dryden here exceeds in force of bludgeon as far as he lags behind him in skill of rapier practice. But these four satires hold together, and should always be read in unison. In them Dryden suddenly rises to the height of his genius. Everything about him has expanded—the daring eloquence, the gusto of triumphant wit, and above all the majestic crash of the couplet, have for the first time been forged into a war-trumpet, through which the trumpeter can peal what notes he wishes.

For the next twenty years, in spite of his congenital irregularity of performance, Dryden continued to be incomparably the greatest poet of his age. Although he wrote personal satire no more, he never lost that resonance, that voluminous note which the anger of 1681 had ripened in him. In *The Hind and the Panther* he softened the music a little, and embroidered a harsh garment with beautiful ornament of episode. In his successive odes and elegies, his copious verse-translations, his songs and his fables, he enlarged his ground, and even in his tragedies and comedies fell no longer below an average of merit which would have sufficed to make another man famous. This may be a proper moment for a consideration of Dryden's place in English poetry. It is certain that of those who are undeniably the leaders of our song he is far from being the most beloved. The fault is not all his, nor all that of the flat and uninspiring epoch in which he lived. A taste for poetry at the present day often involves no intellectual consideration whatever. Charm alone is made the criterium of excellence, and we often praise nothing but that which startles us by the temerity of fancy or the *morbidezza* of artistic detail. But

Dryden, like Horace and Dante, judged otherwise. In his own words, "They cannot be good poets who are not accustomed to argue well." When he congratulated the age of which he was the greatest ornament on its poetical superiority, he was thinking mainly of intelligence and of workmanship. We value these qualities less, perhaps too little ; but, at all events, we shall do no justice to Dryden if we exclude them from our main conception of his aims. What he wished to do, and what he did, was to follow the great Latin poets with a close, yet easy reverence, and to observe, more obliquely, what the consummate Frenchmen of his own time were achieving. To all this he added a noble roughness and virility of speech which was part of his English birthright, a last legacy from the Chaucer and Shakespeare whom he still had the width of vision to admire. Dryden's exuberant vivacity, his solidity of judgment, his extraordinary command of all the rhetorical artifices of poetry, pointed him out as a leader of men, and should prepare us to find his influence the dominant one in all verse-writing in England for a hundred years after his death. It was Dryden who gave impetus and direction to the oratorical and anti-lyrical movement which continued to rule English poetry until, in its final decay, it was displaced by the romantic naturalism of Wordsworth.

The foundation and development of modern English comedy on the pure Terentian basis is, from a technical point of view, one of the most remarkable features of the epoch which we are examining. The romantic comedy, in which Shakespeare had excelled, and in which even Shirley might be considered respectable, had vanished entirely with the closing of the theatres. What passed for comedy at the Restoration was of the Jonsonian type, the comedy of humours—we have already spoken of Wilson's efforts in this direction. But the true modern comedy, of which Corneille's *Le Menteur* (1642) is the first finished example, comedy as Molière understood it, was imported into England by Etheredge, in the *Man of Mode*. Sedley, too, less elegantly, was also an innovator; and a few years later WILLIAM WYCHERLEY, who had written a couple of farces or imbroglios in the Spanish style, produced in the *Country Wife* a vigorous and sparkling imitation of *L'Ecole des Femmes*, and followed it up with the *Plain Dealer*, one of the most brutally cynical, but none the less one of the best-constructed pieces which have ever held the stage. With his magnificent gaiety and buoyancy, Wycherley exaggerated and disfigured the qualities which should rule the comic stage, but they were there; he was a ruffian, but a ruffian of genius. Wycherley and Etheredge represented comedy under Charles II. At the very close of the century there came the young wits whom I have elsewhere attempted to distinguish by calling them the Orange School. Of these WILLIAM CONGREVE was the greatest; his reign was short, from 1693 to 1700, but it was extremely brilliant. No one, perhaps, in any country, has written prose for the stage with so assiduous a solicitude for style. Congreve balances, polishes, sharpens his sentences till they seem like a set of instruments prepared for an electrical experiment; the current is his unequalled wit, and it flashes and leaps without intermission from the first scene to the last. The result is one of singular artificiality; and almost from the outset—from the moment, at all events, that Congreve's manner ceased to dazzle with its novelty—something was felt, even by his contemporaries, to be wanting.   The something, no doubt, was humanity, sympathy, nature.

Sir John Vanbrugh has none of Congreve's pre-eminence in style.   He has no style at all : he simply throws his characters at one another's heads, and leaves them to fight it out as they will.   But he has great fire and vigour of redundant fancy.   After him came Farquhar, with his mess-room tone, and what Pope called his " pert, low dialogue," but also with a manly tenderness that excused his faults.   Steele followed, with his lachrymose comedies of sentiment; and in Susannah Centlivre the music that Etheredge had begun to so sprightly a tune, came to an ignominious finale.   Of all the brilliant body of literature so produced in some forty years, not one piece has held the stage.   There were moral reasons for this inevitable exclusion.   If merit of a purely literary or even theatrical kind were alone to be considered, revivals of Wycherley and Congreve ought to be frequent.   But the fact is that Restoration comedy is of a universal profligate coarseness which enters into the very essence of the plot and is irradicable.   It is only by dint of the most delicate pilotage that one or other of these admirably written comedies is now and again, in an extremely modified form, safely steered across the footlights.   In 1698 the non-juror Jeremy Collier made an attack on the immorality and profaneness of the English stage. The public was on Collier's side, and his blows were so efficient that they practically killed, not indecency only, but the practice of comedy itself.

No general survey of the close of the seventeenth century could be complete without a reference to the celebrated dispute as to what was called the Old and the New Philosophy.   It occupied all the countries of Europe,

but chiefly France, where the private sessions of the
French Academy were torn with disputes about the relative importance of the ancient and the modern writers.
It was raised very definitely by Fontenelle in 1688, and
by Perrault, each of whom was on the side of the
moderns. In this country, in 1692, Temple, with voluminous elegance and pomp, printed a solemn defence of
the Greeks and Latins, and took occasion to praise, in
terms of the most exaggerated hyperbole, certain *Epistles
of Phalaris*, supposed to be written in Attic Greek by a
Sicilian tyrant of the sixth century before Christ. Nobody possessed Phalaris, and to meet a sudden demand,
a publisher issued an edition of his text. Charles Boyle,
the editor, though a young man of slight erudition,
doubted the authenticity of the *Letters;* but they were
proved to be spurious in the immortal dissertation by
RICHARD BENTLEY, a publication which marks an era
in the development of European scholarship. It is
the most brilliant piece of destructive commentary that,
perhaps, was ever published, and it revealed in Bentley
a critic of an entirely new order. But even more extraordinary was the textual and verbal work of Bentley,
whose discovery, as Bunsen has pointed out, is the science of historical philology. Into the controversy which
raged around the phantom of Phalaris, Swift presently
descended ; but he added nothing to scholarship, and
what he gave to literature must be treated in the next
chapter. Meanwhile it is not uninstructive to find
Bentley closing these forty years of mainly critical movement with such an exact criticism of the ancients as no
one since the days of Scaliger had approached.

Throughout the period from 1660 to 1700 the word
"criticism" has had incessantly to invade our narrative.

Looked upon broadly, this was the least creative and the most critical of all the main divisions of our literary history. The Renaissance had finally departed; after a lingering illness, marked at first by fantastic conceits, then by utter insipidity, it had died. It was necessary to get hold of something quite living to take its place, and what France originally, and then England from 1660 onwards, chose, was the *imitatio veterum*, the literature, in prose and verse, which seemed most closely to copy the models of Latin style. Aristotle and Horace were taken not merely as patterns, but as arbiters. No feature was permitted unless classical authority for it could be produced, and it was needful at every step to test an innovation by the rules and the unities. Hence the temper of the age became essentially critical, and to discuss the machinery of the musical box more important than to listen to the music. Instead of the licentious use of any stanzaic form that might suit the whim of the poet, serious verse was practically tied down to the heroic couplet of two rhyming lines of five beats each. This had been mainly the creation of Waller in England, as the regular pendulous alexandrine was of Malherbe in France. Rhyme of this exact and balanced kind had been defended, even for plays, by Dryden, on the ground that it is that "which most regulates the fancy, and gives the judgment its busiest employment."

All this is much out of fashion nowadays, and to our impressionist critics, eager for sensations—for the " new note," for an "individual manner"—must seem preposterous and ridiculous. But a writer like Dryden, responsible for the movement of literature in the years immediately succeeding the Restoration, had a grave task before

him. He was face to face with a bankruptcy ; he had
to float a new concern on the spot where the old had
sunken.   That uniformity of manner, that lack of salient
and picturesque individuality, which annoy the hasty
reader, were really unavoidable.   Dryden and Tillotson,
Locke and Otway, with their solicitude for lucidity of
language, rigidity of form, and closeness of reasoning,
were laying anew the foundations upon which literature
might once more be built.   It is better to build on
Malherbe and Dryden, even if we think the ground-
plan a little dull, than upon Marino and Gongora.

Unfortunately, in an age so closely set upon externals
and the manipulation of language, it was likely that the
inward part of literature might be neglected. Accordingly, while the subjects of the latest Stuarts were polishing their couplets and clarifying their sentences, they
neglected the natural instincts of the heart.   It was an
age of active intellectual curiosity, but not of pathos
or of passion.   The stage was for ever protesting the
nobility of its sentiments, yet, save in *Venice Preserved*,
it is difficult to find a single Restoration play where
there is any tenderness in the elevation, any real tears
behind the pomp of the rhetoric.   The theatre was so
coarse that its printed relics remain a scandal to European civilisation, and that the comedies of Otway and
Southerne (for the tragedians were the greatest sinners
when they stooped to farce) could ever have been acted
to mixed audiences, or to any audience at all, can hardly
be conceived.   It would, of course, be very narrow-
minded to judge the whole age by its plays.   It had its
pure divines, its refined essayists and scholars, its austere
philosophers.   But we cannot go far wrong in taking
that redoubtable gossip Pepys as a type of the whole.

It was not an enthusiastic, nor a delicate, nor an impassioned age, and we must not look for intensity in its productions. What we should admire and should be grateful for are its good sense, its solidity of judgment, and its close attention to thoroughness and simplicity in workmanship.

VI

THE AGE OF ANNE

1700–1740

DURING the final years of the reign of William III. literature in England was in a stagnant condition. Almost the only department in which any vitality was visible was comic drama, represented by Congreve, Cibber, Vanbrugh, and Farquhar. A vast quantity of verse was poured forth, mainly elegiac and occasional, but most of it of an appalling badness. At the death of Dryden, in 1700, only two noticeable non-dramatic poets survived. Garth, who had just published a polished burlesque, the *Dispensary*, under the influence of Boileau's *Le Lutrin*, and Addison, whose hyperbolic compliments addressed to "godlike Nassau" were written in verse which took up the prosody of Waller as if Dryden had never existed. In criticism the wholesome precepts of Dryden seemed to have been utterly forgotten, and Rymer, a pedagogue upon Parnassus, was pushing the rules of the French Jesuits to an extreme which excluded Shakespeare, Fletcher, and Spenser from all consideration, and threatened the prestige of Dryden himself. In prose Bishop Burnet was writing, but he properly belongs to an earlier and again to a later age, Samuel Clarke was preaching, Steele was beginning to feel his way, Shaftesbury was privately printing one short tract. On the whole, it was the lowest point reached by English literature during the last three hundred years. The cause of such sterility and languor can scarcely be determined. The forces which had been introduced in the first decade after the Restoration were exhausted, and it was necessary to rest a little while before taking another start.

But in 1702 Queen Anne ascended the throne, and her brief reign is identified with a brilliant revival in English letters, in the hands of a group of men of the highest accomplishment and originality. It must be noted, however, that this revival did not take place until the Queen was near her end, and that of the writers of the age of Anne but few had published anything considerable until within three years of her death. It would be historically more exact to distinguish this period in literature as the age of George I., the years from 1714 to 1727 being those in which some of the most characteristic works of the school were published ; but the other name has become hallowed by long practice, and George I. certainly deserves as little as any monarch who ever reigned the credit of being a judicious patron of letters. It is interesting, indeed, to note that by 1714 almost all the characteristic forces of the age were started. Pope had reached his *Homer;* Swift was pouring forth tracts ; Shaftesbury, Arbuthnot, Mandeville, and even Berkeley had published some of their most typical writings ; while the *Tatler* and the *Spectator* had actually run their course. All this activity, however, dates from the very close of Queen Anne's life. Between 1711 and 1714 a perfect galaxy of important works in prose and verse burst almost simultaneously from the London presses. It was as though a cloud which had long obscured the heavens had been swept away by a wind, which, in so doing, had revealed a splendid constellation. In 1702 no country in civilised Europe was in a more melancholy condition of intellectual emptiness than England ; in 1712 not France itself could compare with us for copious and vivid production.

Meanwhile, almost unperceived, the critic had begun to make his appearance, for the first time, in the form with which we have since been familiar. The French asserted that it was Castelvetro and Piccolomini, Italian writers of the end of the sixteenth century, who first taught that just comprehension of the *Poetics* of Aristotle in which modern criticism began. These scholars, however, were unknown in England, where it was the French critics, and, in particular, Rapin and Le Bossu, who introduced to us the Aristotelian criticism of imaginative literature. René Rapin, in particular, exercised an immense authority in this country, and was the practical law-giver from the last quarter of the seventeenth century onward. Rymer and Dennis founded their dogmas entirely on his *Reflections*, merely modifying to English convenience his code of rules. Rapin has been strangely forgotten ; when he died in 1687, he was the leading critic of Europe, and he is the writer to whom more than to any other is due the line taken by English poetry for the next hundred years. The peculiarity of his *Reflections*, which were promptly translated into English, was, that they aimed at adapting the laws and theories of Aristotle to modern practice. As is often the case, Rapin was less rigid than his disciples ; he frequently develops a surprisingly just conception of what the qualities of the highest literature should be.

The school of Rapin, who moulded the taste and practice of the young men who were to be the pioneers of the age of Anne, claimed for Aristotle the unbounded allegiance of all who entered the domain of verse. Every man of judgment was blindly to resign his own opinions to the dictates of Aristotle, and to do this because the reasons given for these rules are as convincing and as lucid as any demonstration in mathematics. But Aristotle had approached literature only as a philosopher; for Rapin they claimed the merit of having been the first to apply the Aristotelian principles to modern practice. The English disciples of Rapin accepted his formulas, and used them to give literature a new start, and thus Rapin came to be the father of eighteenth-century criticism. The first review of a book in the modern sense may be said to have been JOHN DENNIS's tract on a fashionable epic of the moment, published in 1696; here was a plea for sober judgment, something that should be neither gross praise nor wild abuse. The subject of this tract was negligible, but Dennis presently came forward with dissertations on more serious forms of literature. Dennis has been resolutely misjudged, in consequence of his foolish attitude towards his younger contemporaries in old age, but in his prime he was a writer of excellent judgment. He was the first English critic to do unstinted justice to Milton and to Molière, and he was a powerful factor in preparing public opinion for the literary verdicts of Addison.

It is not to be supposed that critics of the prestige of Dennis or Rymer would address the public from a less dignified stage than that of a book, or, at worst, a sixpenny pamphlet. But at the close of the reign of William III. we meet with the earliest apparition of literary criticism in periodical publications. In other words, the newspaper was now beginning to take literary form, and the introduction of such a factor must not be left unmentioned here. The first reviews printed in an English newspaper were those appended by Dunton to the *Athenian Gazette* in 1691 ; but these were not original, they were simply translated out of the *Journal des Savans*. Notices of books, in the modern sense, began to be introduced very timidly into some of the news-sheets about the year 1701. Nor was this the only direction in which literary journalism was started ; men of real importance began to take part in newspaper-writing, and the English press may name among the earliest of its distinguished servants such personages as Atterbury, Kennet, Hoadley, and Defoe.

While, therefore, we cannot claim for the opening years of the century the production of any master-pieces, and while its appearance, from an intellectual point of view, is to us quiescent, yet without doubt the seeds of genius were swelling in the darkness. In all departments of thought and art, Englishmen were throwing off the last rags of the worn-out garments of the Renaissance, and were accustoming themselves to wear with comfort their new suit of classical formulas. In poetry, philosophy, history, religion, the age was learning the great lesson that the imagination was no longer to be a law unto itself, but was to follow closely a code dictated by reason and the tradition of the ancients. Enthusiasm was condemned as an irregularity, the daring use of imagery as an error against manners. The divines were careful to restrain their raptures, and to talk and write like lawyers. Philosophical writers gladly modelled themselves on Hobbes and Locke, the nakedness of whose unenthusiastic style was eminently sympathetic to them, although they conceived a greater

14

elegance of delivery necessary. Their speculations became mainly ethical, and the elements of mystery and
romance almost entirely died out. Neither the pursuit
of pleasure nor the assuaging of conscience, no active
force of any kind, became supreme with the larger class
of readers ; but the new bourgeois rank of educated
persons, which the age of Queen Anne created, occupied itself in a passive analysis of human nature. It
loved to sit still and watch the world go by ; an appetite
for realistic description, bounded by a decent code, and
slipping neither up into enthusiasm nor down into scepticism, became the ruling passion of the age. During
the sixteenth and seventeenth centuries, common-sense
had been by no means characteristic of the English race,
which had struggled, flaunted, or aspired. It now went
back to something like its earlier serenity, and in an age
of comparatively feeble emotion and slight intensity took
things as they were. In Shaftesbury, a writer of provi-
sional but extraordinary influence, we see this common-
sense taking the form of a mild and exuberant optimism ;
and perhaps what makes the dark figure of Swift stand
out so vividly against the rose-grey background of the
age is the incongruity of his violence and misanthropy in
a world so easy-going.

In chronological sequence, it should, perhaps, be the
theology of the early part of the reign of Anne which
should first attract us, but it need not detain us long.
The golden age of Anglican theology had long passed
away, and in the progress of latitudinarianism, culminating, through Locke, in the pronounced deists, literature
as an art has little interest. A tolerant rationalism was
not likely to encourage brilliant writing, the orthodox
churchmen wrote like wrangling lawyers, and the non-

jurors and dissenters, who produced some vigorous scholars later on, were now as dreary as their opponents. Of the early deists, Shaftesbury alone was a man of style, and him we shall presently meet with in another capacity. Among the theologians, the most eminent writer was SAMUEL CLARKE, "the greatest English representative of the *a priori* method of constructing a system of theology." His once famous collection of *Boyle Lectures* (1704-5) long seemed a classic to admiring readers, and still affects our conventional notions of theology. Clarke, however, has few readers to-day, and his manner of statement, which resembles that of a mathematician propounding a theorem, is as tedious to us now as it was fascinating to the group of young controversialists who clustered round Clarke during his brief career at Cambridge. In the hands of Clarke and his school, theological writing followed the lines laid down for it by Tillotson, but with a greatly accentuated aridity and neatness. In the search for symmetry these authors neglected almost every other excellence and ornament of literary expression.

If philosophy at the opening of the eighteenth century could give a better account of itself, it was mainly because the leading philosopher was a born writer. The third Earl of SHAFTESBURY has been strangely neglected by the historians of our literature, partly because his scheme of thought has long been rejected, and partly because his style, in which some of the prolixity of the seventeenth century still lingered, was presently obliterated by the technical smartness of Addison and Swift. With the meaning of Shaftesbury's doctrine of virtue, and with the value of his optimism and plea for harmony, we have nothing here to do, but his influence on writing in his own age and down the entire eighteenth century is highly important to us. Commonly as the fact is overlooked, Shaftesbury was one of the literary forces of the time— he was, perhaps, the greatest between Dryden and Swift. He died in 1713, two years after his miscellaneous treatises, written at intervals during the fifteen years preceding, had been published in those handsome volumes of the *Characteristics.* Shaftesbury's long residences in Holland gave him the opportunity of becoming thoroughly acquainted with the movement of Continental thought to an extent doubtless beyond any previous writer of English prose. The effect is seen on his style and temper, which are less insular than those of any of the men with whom it is natural to compare him. It is to be noted also that Shaftesbury was the earliest English author whose works in the vernacular were promptly admired abroad, and he deserves remembrance as the first who really broke down the barrier which excluded England from taking her proper place in the civilisation of literary Europe.

The writers who were to shine in prose immediately after the death of Shaftesbury were distinguished for the limpid fluency and grace of their manner. In this Shaftesbury did not resemble them, but rather set an example for the kind of prose which was to mark the central years of the century. There is nothing about him which reminds us of the nobleman that writes with ease: he is elaborate and self-conscious to the highest degree, embroidered with ornament of dainty phraseology, anxious to secure harmony and yet to surprise the fancy. The style of Shaftesbury glitters and rings, proceeding along in a capricious, almost mincing effort to secure elegance, with a sort of colourless euphuism, which is desultory and a little irritating indeed, yet so curious that one marvels that it should have fallen completely into neglect. He is the father of æstheticism, the first Englishman who developed theories of formal virtue, who attempted to harmonise the beautiful with the true and the good. His delicate, Palladian style, in which a certain external stiffness and frigidity seem to be holding down a spirit eager to express the passion of beauty, is a very interesting feature of the period to which we have now arrived. The modern attitude of mind seems to meet us first in the graceful, cosmopolitan writings of Shaftesbury, and his genius, like a faint perfume, pervades the contemplation of the arts down to our own day. Without a Shaftesbury there would hardly have been a Ruskin or a Pater.

Be this as it may, it is quite certain that the brilliant school of poets who began to make their appearance just as Shaftesbury was dying, owed to him the optimism of their religious and philosophical system. But it was mainly to the French that they were indebted for the impetus which started them; and if France had already made a deep mark on our literature between 1660 and 1674, it made another, not less indelible, in 1710. What the influence of Rapin, thirty-five years before, had done to regulate taste in England, and to enforce the rules laid down by the ancients, had not proved stimulating to poetic genius, and, with the death of Dryden, we have seen that poetry practically ceased to exist in England. When it returned it was mainly in consequence of the study of another Frenchman, but this time of a poet, Boileau, whose influence on the mind of Pope, carefully concealed by the latter, was really far greater than any critic has ventured to confess. There were certain qualities in Boileau which can but have appealed directly to the young Pope, who in 1710 was twenty-two years of age. Boileau had not been so closely wedded to pedantic rules as his friends the Jesuit critics were. He had insisted on inspiration, on the value of ceaseless variety, on obedience to the laws of language. The preface to the 1701 edition of his works is one of the landmarks of European criticism, and we can scarcely doubt that it awakened a high spirit of emulation in the youthful Pope. In it Boileau had urged that none should ever be presented to the public in verse but true thoughts and just expressions. He had declaimed against frigidity of conceit and tawdry extravagance, and had proclaimed the virtues of simplicity without carelessness, sublimity without presumption, a pleasing air without *fard*. He had boldly convicted his predecessors of bad taste, and had called his·lax contemporaries to account. He had blamed the sterile abundance of an earlier period, and the uniformity of dull writers. Such principles were more than all others likely to commend themselves to Pope, and his practice shows us that they did.

We cannot think of the poetry of the age of Anne and not of ALEXANDER POPE. As little ought we to analyse Pope and fail to admit what he owes to Boileau. The "Law-giver of Parnassus" gave laws, it is certain, to the hermit of Windsor Forest. The work of no other great English writer has coincided with that of a foreigner so closely as Pope's does with that of Boileau. The French satirist had recommended polish, and no one practised it more thoroughly than Pope did. Boileau discouraged love-poetry, and Pope did not seriously attempt it. Boileau paraphrased Horace, and in so doing formulated his own poetical code, in *L'Art Poetique;* Pope did the same in the *Essay on Criticism.* Boileau specially

urged the imitation of Homer on young poets, and
Pope presently devoted himself to the *Iliad*. In *Le
Lutrin* Boileau had written the best mock-heroic, till
Pope, in closely analogous form, surpassed him in the
Rape of the Lock. The *Satires* of Pope would not have
been written but for those of his French predecessor ;
and even Pope's *Elegy* and *Eloisa* can be accounted for
in the precepts of Boileau. The parallel goes very far
indeed : it is the French poet first, and not the English
one, who insists that the shepherds of pastoral must not
speak as they do in a country village. Pope's very
epitaphs recall Boileau's labours with the inscriptions of
the Petite Académie. That purity and decency of phrase
which the school of Pope so beneficially introduced into
the coarse field of English literature had been strenuously urged on Frenchmen by Boileau. It cannot be too
strongly emphasised that it is not so much to Dryden,
whose influence on Pope has certainly been exaggerated,
but to the author of *Le Lutrin*, that the poetry of the age
of Anne owed its general impulse, and its greatest poet
the general tendency of almost every branch of his production. It is true that Pope told Spence that " I learned
versification wholly from Dryden's works," his prosody
being a continuation and development of that of Dryden ;
but in the use to which he put his verse, it was certainly
the great Frenchman (who died two months before Pope's
earliest important poem was published) that was his
master. Walsh had told him, in 1706, that " the best of
the modern poets in all languages are those that have
the nearest copied the ancients " ; but we may not doubt
that it was through Boileau that Pope arrived at a comprehension of Horace, and so of Aristotle.

For more than thirty years Pope was so completely the

centre of poetical attention in England that he may almost be said to have comprised the poetry of his time. There is no second instance of an English poet preserving for so long a period a supremacy comparable to his. It is possible to defend the position that one or two other versemen of the age did some particular thing better than Pope, though even this requires argument; but it is quite certain that he alone excelled over a wide range of subjects. The fact of Pope's poetical ubiquity, however, is rendered much less miraculous by the consideration that if he triumphed over the entire field, the area of that field was extremely restricted. There was never a period, from the Middle Ages till to-day, when the practice of verse was limited to so few forms as it was under the reign of Pope. Lyrical writing, save in the mildest and most artificial species, was not cultivated; there was no poetical drama, tragic or comic ; there was no description of nature, save the merest convention ; there was scarcely any love-poetry ; no devotional verse of 'any importance ; no epic or elegy or ode that deserved the name. Poetry existed, practically, in but three forms—the critical or satirical, the narrative or didactic, and the occasional—these three, indeed, being so closely correlated that it is not always very easy to distinguish them.

It was Pope's aim to redeem verse from unholy uses, to present to the reader none but true thoughts and noble expressions, and to dedicate the gravest form to the highest purpose. His actual practice was not at first so exalted. The boyish *Pastorals* scarcely call for notice ; but in the *Essay on Criticism* he achieved at twenty-one a work of rare grace and authority. He began where other poets have left off, and it is not a little characteristic of Pope's temperament that he should not open with strong, irregular verse, and push on to the comparative stagnation of the critical attitude, but should make this latter the basis of his life-work. The *Essay* is in most respects inferior to its French prototype, more hastily and irregularly composed, and with far less ripeness of judgment; but it is graceful and eloquent, and for the eighteenth century it provided an almost unchallenged code of taste. MATTHEW PRIOR in the same year, though more than twice the age of Pope, ventured upon the earliest publication of his poems, bringing from the close of the seventeenth century a certain richness of style which we find not in the younger man. His ballads and songs, with their ineffable gaiety, his satires and epigrams, so lightly turned, enriched the meagre body of English verse with a gift, much of which should really be attributed to the age of Dryden. But Prior was not less closely related to the generation of Pope in his Horatian attitude and his brilliant Gallic grace. He was, however, but an occasional trifler with his charming muse, and had none of the younger master's undeviating ambition.

From 1711, to follow the career of Pope is to take part in a triumph in which the best of his contemporaries secures but a secondary part. The *Rape of the Lock* (1712–14) lifted Pope at once to the first rank of living European poets. In lightness of handling, in elegance of badinage, in exquisite amenity of style—that is to say, in the very qualities which Latin Europe had hitherto, and not without justice, denied us—the little British barbarian surpassed all foreign competitors. This is the turning-point of English subserviency to French taste. Pope and his school had closely studied their Boileau, and had learned their lesson well, so well that for the future England is no longer the ape of the French, but is competent, more and more confidently as the century descends, to give examples to the polite world.

A few years later all the countries of Europe were taking these examples, and the imitation of Pope grew to be the rage from Sweden to Italy. Meanwhile, the youth of four-and-twenty was gaining mastery in his art. The *Messiah* (of 1712) reached a pitch of polished, resonant rhetoric hitherto undreamed of, and was a " copy of verses" which became the model and the despair of five generations of poets. Each of these productions stamped more defi-nitely the type of "classical" versification, tone, and character, and all Pope had now to do was to enlarge his knowledge of human nature, and to cultivate that extreme delicacy of phrase and rapidity of intellectual movement which were his central peculiarities.

He had early learned to master the art of poetry ; but although he was already famous, none of those works in which he was to concentrate and illustrate the whole thought and fashion of his age were yet written. Pope was far more than the most skilful of versifiers : he was the microcosm of the reign of George I. There is scarcely a belief, a tradition, an ideal of that age which is not to be discovered lucidly set down in the poems of Pope, who was not vastly above his epoch, as some great poetical prophets have been, but exactly on a level with it, and from our distance its perfect mirror. But before he took up this work of his advanced years he gave the remainder of his youth to a task of high and fertile discipline. From 1713, when Swift was going about begging subscriptions for "the best poet in Eng-land, Mr. Pope, a Papist," till 1725, when the *Odyssey* appeared, he was mainly occupied in translating from the Greek, or in revising the translations of others. His individuality was so strong, or his realisation of Hellenic art so imperfect, that he conceived a Homer of his own, a Homer polished and restrained to polite uses, no longer an epic poet, but a *conteur* of the finest modern order, fluent, manly, and distinguished, yet essentially a writer of Pope's own day and generation. The old complaints of Pope's *Homer* are singularly futile. It was not an archaistic or a romantic version that England and her subscribers wanted ; they desired a fine, scholarly piece in the taste of their own times, and that was exactly what Pope was competent to give them.

But if they were the gainers by his twelve years' labour, so was he. The close study of the Homeric diction gave firmness and ease to his style, concentrated his powers, determined his selection of poetic material. What Pope wrote during the Homeric period was not considerable in extent, but it included his only incursions into the province of love, the beautiful *Elegy to the Memory of an Unfortunate Lady* and the *Eloisa to Abelard* (1717). These years, however, marked the solidification of the school of which he was the acknowledged leader, even though some of its members seemed his enemies. Addison, his great rival, had published in 1713 his tragedy of *Cato*, in which the rules of Horace were applied with stringent exactitude, the result being of an exquisite frigidity. In the same year Gay came forward, a skilful and fairly independent satellite of Pope ; between 1713 and 1726 contributing a copious and sprightly flow of short pastorals, songs, and epistles. The elegant Archdeacon of Clogher, too, Thomas Parnell, wrote with gravity and wit under the direct stimulus of Pope's friendship. He died in 1718, and the posthumous collec-

tion which his master issued four years later contained
some harmonious odes and narratives which have not
quite disappeared from living English literature. Tickell,
who loved Addison and hated Pope, was writing, between
1719 and 1722, poems which owed more to Pope than to
Addison, and in particular an elegy on the great essayist
which is one of the most dignified funeral pieces in the
language. Prior, who died in 1721, had finally collected
his writings in 1718, and Swift ever and anon put forth
an erratic fragment of vivid caustic verse. All this record
of poetical activity dates from those years during which
Pope was buried in Homer, but through it all his own
claim to the highest place was scarcely questioned,
although he was the youngest of the group.

Pope emerged from Homer in 1725, ready to take his
place again in militant literature. But the world was not
the same to him. Of his elders and compeers half passed
away while he was finishing the *Iliad*—Garth, Parnell,
Addison, Lady Winchelsea, and Prior. Congreve and
Gay grew languid and fatigued. The great quarrels of
Pope's life began, and the acrid edge was set on his
temper. But Atterbury had long ago assured him that
satire was his true forte, and Swift encouraged him to
turn from melancholy reflection on the great friends he
had lost, to bitter jesting with the little enemies that
remained to him. In 1728-29 the *Dunciad* lashed the
bad writers of the age in couplets that rang with the
crack of a whip. During the remainder of his life, Pope
was actively engaged in the composition and rapid publication of ethical and satirical poems, most of which
appeared in successive folio pamphlets between 1731 and
1738. It has been conjectured that all these pieces were
fragments of a great philosophical poem which he in-

tended one day to complete, with the addition of that
New Dunciad (1742) which was the latest of Pope's important writings. Among these scattered pieces the most
famous are the four parts of the *Essay on Man*, the
Epistle to Dr. Arbuthnot, and the successive *Imitations
of Horace*.

In these poems of the maturity of Pope there is no
longer any distinct trace of French influence. They
mark the full coming of age of the English classical
school. The lesson first taught by the Royalists who
came back from the Continent in 1660 was now completely learned; criticism had finished its destructive
work long before, and on the basis so swept clear of all
the ruins of the Renaissance a new kind of edifice was ·
erected. In the *Fables* of Dryden, in the tragedies of
Otway and Congreve (the *Mourning Bride*), something
was left of the sonorous irregularity of the earlier seventeenth century, a murmur, at least, of the retreating
wave. But in such a satire as of the *Use of Riches*
not the faintest echo of the old romantic style remains.
It is not fair, in such a conjunction, to take passages in
which the colloquial wit of Pope is prominent; but
here are verses which are entirely serious, and intended
to be thoroughly poetical :

> " *Consult the genius of the place in all ;*
> *That tells the waters or to rise or fall,*
> *Or helps the ambitious hill the heavens to scale,*
> *Or scoops in circling theatres the vale;*
> *Calls in the country, catches opening glades,*
> *Joins willing woods, and varies shades from shades;*
> *Now breaks, or now directs, the intending lines ;*
> *Paints as you plant, and, as you work, designs.*"

Is this poetry or not ? That is the question which
has troubled the critics for a hundred years, and seems

as little to be capable of solution as the crux of pre-destination and free-will. That it is not poetry of the same class as a chorus out of *Prometheus Unbound* or a tirade out of the *Duchess of Malfy* is obvious; but this is no answer to the query. Certain facts need to be observed. One is, that to several successive generations of highly intelligent men this did appear to be poetry, and of a very high order. Another is, that since the revolution compassed by Wordsworth we have been living under a prejudice in favour of the romantic manner which may or may not be destined to last much longer. If another revolution in taste should overwhelm us, *Adonais* and *Tintern Abbey* may easily grow to seem grotesquely unreadable. It is wise, therefore, not to moot a question which cannot be solved, as Matthew Arnold tried to solve it, by calling "Dryden and Pope not classics of our poetry, but classics of our prose." Pope was not a classic of prose; he wrote almost ex-clusively in a highly finished artistic verse, which may evade the romantic formulas, but is either poetry or nothing. The best plan is to admit that it is poetry, and to define it.

In their conception of that class of poetry, then, of which the later works of Pope supply the most brilliant example, the English classicists returned to what the French had taught them to believe to be a Latin manner. They found in the admirable poets of anti-quity, and particularly in Horace, a determination to deal with the average and universal interests and obser-vations of mankind, rather than with the exceptional, the startling, and the violent. They desired to express these common thoughts and emotions with exquisite exactitude, to make of their form and substance alike

an amalgam of intense solidity, capable of a high polish.
If we had asked Pope what quality he conceived that
he had achieved in the *Essay on Man*, he would have
answered, "Horatii curiosa felicitas," the consummate
skill in fixing normal ideas in such a way as to
turn common clay into perdurable bronze. By the
side of such a design as this it would have seemed to
him a poor thing to dig out rough ore of passion, like
Donne, or to spin gossamer-threads of rainbow-coloured
fancy, like Shelley. We may not agree with him, because we still live in a romantic age. It is hardly likely,
moreover, that, whatever change comes over English
taste, we shall ever return exactly to the Boileauesque-
Horatian polishing of commonplaces in couplets. But
to admire Ibsen and Tolstoi, and to accept them as
imaginative creators, is to come back a long way towards
the position held by Pope and Swift, towards the sup-
position that the poet is not a child dazzled by lovely
illusions and the mirage of the world, but a grown-up
person to whom the limits of experience are patent, who
desires above all things to see mankind steadily and
perspicuously. In its palmy days at least, that is to say
during the lifetime of Pope, "classical" English poetry
was, within its narrow range, an art exquisitely performed by at least one artist of the very first class.
That this height was not long sustained, and that decline
was rapid, will be our observation in a later chapter.

More durable has been the impress on our prose of the
great critical contemporaries of Pope. One of the landmarks in the history of literature is the date, April 12,
1709, when Mr. Isaac Bickerstaff began to circulate his
immortal lucubrations in the first gratis number of the
Tatler. Here, at last, the easy prose of everyday life

had found a medium in which, without a touch of pedantry, it could pass lightly and freely across the minds of men. The place which those newspapers hold in our memory is quite out of proportion with the duration of their issue. We hardly realise that the *Tatler* lasted only until January 1711, and that the *Spectator* itself, though started two months later, expired before the close of 1712. Three years and eight months sufficed to create the English essay, and lift it to an impregnable position as one of the principal forms of which literature should henceforth consist. In this great enterprise, the importance of which in the history of literature can hardly be exaggerated, popular opinion long gave the main, almost the exclusive credit to JOSEPH ADDISON. But the invention of the periodical essay we now know to have been RICHARD STEELE'S, and of the 271 *Tatlers* only 42 are certainly Addison's.

In the *Spectator* their respective shares were more exactly balanced, and the polished pen of Addison took precedence. We gather that, of these immortal friends, Steele was the more fertile in invention, Addison the more brilliant and captivating in execution. It was cruel in Swift, and only partly true, to say that politics had turned Steele from "an excellent droll" into "a very awkward pamphleteer"; yet Steele could be awkward. "The elegance, purity, and correctness" which delighted all readers of the essays were contributed by Addison, and were appreciated in his own age to a degree which appears to us slightly exaggerated, for we have learned to love no less the humour and pathos of Steele. Without the generous impulse of Steele the unfailing urbanity of Addison might have struck a note of frigidity. Contemporaries, who eagerly welcomed their daily sheet, in which Mr. Spectator re-tailed the reflections and actions of his club, did not pause to think how much of its unique charm depended on the fortunate interaction of two minds, each lucid, pure, and brilliant, yet each, in many essential quali-ties, widely distinguished from the other. "To enliven morality with wit, and to temper wit with morality," was indeed a charming design when practised by two moralists, each of whom was witty in a different direction from the other.

The presentation of the first number of the *Tatler* to the town marked nothing less than the creation of modern journalism. Here, as in so much else, France had been ahead of us, for since 1672 the *Mercure* and its successors had satisfied the curiosity of Parisians as to things in general. *Quicquid agunt homines,* said the motto, and it was Steele who made the discovery for Englishmen that the daily diversion of the newspaper was one which might be made so fascinating and so neces-sary that the race might presently be unable to dispense with it. The earliest English newspaper is usually said to be that leaf issued in 1622, under the pseudonym of *Mercurius Britannicus,* by Nathaniel Butter; but the sheets of this kind, generically known as *Mercuries,* had little of the aspect of a modern journal. The *Public In-telligencer* (1663), of Roger L'Estrange, had more of the true newspaper character, and began the epoch of the gazettes, "pamphlets of news," as they were called. The *Daily Courant* (1702) was the earliest daily journal. In all these precursors of the *Tatler* there had been scarcely a touch of literature. In his opening number Steele offered an unprecedented olio, combining social gossip,

15

poetry, learning, the news of the day, and miscellaneous entertainment ; and he appealed at once to a whole world of new readers.

The result was something of so startling and delightful a novelty that the town was revolutionised. At first the anonymity was well preserved; but in the fifth *Tatler* Addison recognised a remark he had made to Steele, and in the eighteenth he was dragged into the concern. As the periodical continued, and the taste of the public became gauged, the portion given to news was reduced, and the essay took a more and more prominent place. It is generally conjectured that this was due to Addison's influence, whose part in the whole transaction was the academic one of pruning and training the rough shoots that sprang from Steele's vigorous wilding. If Steele continued, however, to be predominant on the *Tatler*, Addison so completely imprinted his own image upon the later journal that to this day Mr. Spectator is an equivalent of Addison's name. The famous circle of typical figures, the Club, was broadly sketched by Steele, but it was Addison who worked the figures up to that minute perfection which we now admire in Will Honeycomb and Sir Roger de Coverley. So complete was the cooperation, however, that it would be rash to decide too sharply what in the conception of the immortal essays belongs to one friend and what to the other.

In examining the light literature of a hundred years earlier, we were confronted by the imitation of Theophrastus, and now, in the *Spectator*, we meet with it again. The best of the modern Theophrastians was La Bruyère, and it were idle to deny that the characters of Addison were originally modelled on French lines. It would be a serious error indeed to think of Addison as a mere imitator of the *Caractères*, as Marivaux was later of the *Spectator*, but English criticism has hardly been content to admit the closeness of the earlier resemblance. Addison and Steele did not consider it their duty to satirise particular persons, and they possessed a gift in the dramatic creation, as distinguished from the observation, of types such as La Bruyère did not possess, or, at all events, did not exercise ; but the invention of combining a moral essay with a portrait in a general, desultory piece of occasional literature was not theirs, but La Bruyère's. His field, however, was limited to the streets of cities, and he did nothing to expand the general interests of his contemporaries ; he was a delightful satirist and most malicious urban gossip. But Addison and Steele had their eye on England as well as on London ; their aim, though a genial, was an ethical and elevated one ; they developed, studied, gently ridiculed the country gentleman. In their shrewdly civil way they started a new kind of national sentiment, polite, easy, modern, in which woman took her civilising place ; they ruled the fashions in letters, in manners, even in costume. They were the first to exercise the generous emancipating influence of the free press, and an epoch in the history of journalism was marked when, the preface to Dr. Fleetwood's *Sermons* being suppressed by order of the House of Commons, fourteen thousand copies of it were next morning circulated in the columns of the *Spectator*.

In several ways, however, these marvellous journals were proved to be ahead of their age. When the *Spectator* ceased, at the close of 1712, there was a long obscuration of the light of the literary newspaper. Political heat disturbed the *Guardian*, and later ventures enjoyed even smaller success. To the regret of all true lovers of literature, Addison and Steele were presently at daggers drawn in opposed and quite inglorious news-sheets. But the experiment had been made, and the two famous journals may live all the more brilliantly in our memory because their actual existence was not too lengthy to permit them to come to life again in the more durable form of books.

We have hitherto said nothing of JONATHAN SWIFT, yet he flows right across the present field of our vision, from William III. to George II. His course is that of a fiery comet that dashes through the constellation of the wits of Anne, and falls in melancholy ashes long after the occultation of the last of them. The friend and companion of them for a season, he pursues his flaming course with little real relation to their milder orbits, and is one of the most singular and most original figures that our history has produced. Swift was a bundle of paradoxes—a great churchman who has left not a trace on our ecclesiastical system, an ardent politician who was never more than a fly on the wheel. He is immortal on the one side on which he believed his genius ephemeral; he survives solely, but splendidly, as a man of letters. His career was a failure: he began life as a gentleman's dependent, he quitted it "like a poisoned rat in a hole"; with matchless energy and ambition, he won neither place nor power; and in the brief heyday of his influence with the Ministry, he who helped others was impotent to endow himself. Swift is the typical instance of the powerlessness of pure intellect to secure any but intellectual triumphs. But even the victories of his brain were tainted; his genius left a taste of brass on his own palate. That Swift was ever happy, that his self-torturing nature was capable of contentment, is not certain; that for a long period of years he was wretched beyond the lot of man is evident, and those have not sounded the depths of human misery who have not followed in their mysterious obscurity the movements of the character of Swift.

His will was too despotic to yield to his misfortunes; his pride sustained him, and in middle life a fund of restless animal spirits. We know but little of his early years, yet enough to see that the *splendida bilis*, the *sæva indignatio*, which ill-health exacerbated, were his companions from the first. We cannot begin to comprehend his literary work without recognising this. His weapon was ink, and he loved to remember that gall and copperas went to the making of it. It was in that deadest period, at the very close of the seventeenth century, that his prodigious talent first made itself apparent. With no apprenticeship in style, no relation of discipleship to any previous French or English writer, but steeped in the Latin classics, he produced, at the age of thirty, two of the most extraordinary masterpieces of humour and satire which were ever written, the *Tale of a Tub* and the *Battle of the Books*. It was not until five or six years later (1704) that he gave them together, anonymously, to the press. In the *Tale of a Tub* every characteristic of Swift's style is revealed— the mordant wit, the vehement graceful ease, the stringent simplicity. To the end of his days he never wrote better things than the description of the goddess of Criticism drawn by geese in a chariot, the dedication to Prince Posterity with its splendid hilarity and irony, the doubly distilled allegorical apologue of the Spider and the Bee. In his poisonous attacks on the deists, in his gleams of sulky misanthropy, in the strange filthiness of his fancy, in the stranger exhilaration which seizes him whenever the idea of madness is introduced—in all these things Swift reveals his essential character in this his first and perhaps greatest book. Although every one admired it, the *Tale of a Tub* was doubtless fatal to his ambition, thus wrecked at the outset on the reef of his ungovernable satire. The book, to be plain, is a long gibe at theology, and it is not surprising that no bishopric could ever be given to the inventor of the Brown Loaf and the Universal Pickle. He might explain away his mockery, declare it to have been employed in the Anglican cause, emphasise the denial that his aim was irreligious; the damning evidence remained that when he had had the sacred garments in his hands he had torn away, like an infuriated ape, as much of the gold fringe as he could. The fact was that, without any design of impiety, he knew not how to be devout. He always, by instinct, saw the hollowness and the seamy side. His enthusiasms were negative, and his burning imagination, even when he applied it to religion, revealed not heaven but hell to him.

The power and vitality of such a nature could not be concealed; they drew every sincere intellect towards him. Already, in 1705, Addison was hailing Swift as " the most agreeable companion, the truest friend, and the greatest genius of the age." We take him up again in 1711, when the slender volume of *Miscellanies* reminds us of what he had been as a writer from the age of thirty-five to forty-five. The contents of this strange book name for us the three caustic religious treatises, the first of Swift's powerful political tracts (the *Sacramental Test*), various other waifs and rags from his culminating year, 1708, gibes and flouts of many kinds revealing the spirit of " a very positive young man," trifles in verse and prose to amuse

his friends the Whig Ministers or the ladies of Lord
Berkeley's family. Nothing could be more occasional
than all this ; nothing, at first sight, less imbued with
intensity or serious feeling. Swift's very compliments
are impertinent, his arguments in favour of Christianity
subversive. But under all this there is the passion of
an isolated intellect, and he was giving it play in the
frivolities of a compromising humour.

The published writings of Swift during the first forty-
four years of his life were comprised in two volumes of
very moderate dimensions. But if the purely literary
outcome of all this period had been exiguous, it was now
to grow scantier still. At the very moment when the
group of Anne wits, led by Pope and Addison, were entering with animation upon their best work, Swift, almost
ostentatiously, withdrew to the sphere of affairs, and for
ten years refrained entirely from all but political authorship. His unexampled *Journal to Stella*, it is true, belongs
to this time of obscuration, but it is hardly literature,
though of the most intense and pathetic interest. Swift
now stood "ten times better" with the new Tories than
ever he did with the old Whigs, and his pungent pen
poured forth lampoons and satirical projects. The
influence of Swift's work of this period upon the style of
successive English publicists is extremely curious ; he
began a new order of political warfare, demanding lighter
arms and swifter manoeuvres than the seventeenth century
had dreamed of. Even Halifax seems cold and slow
beside the lightning changes of mood, the inexorable
high spirits of Swift. That such a tract as the *Sentiments
of a Church of England Man*, with its gusts of irony, its
white heat of preposterous moderation, led on towards
Junius is obvious; but Swift is really the creator of the

whole school of eighteenth-century rhetorical diatribe on its better side, wherever it is not leaden and conventional. It may be said that he invented a vital polemical system, which was used through the remainder of the century by every one who dealt in that kind of literature, and who was at the same time strong enough to wield such thunderbolts.

That no one, until the time of Burke, who had other ammunition of his own, could throw these bolts about with anything of Swift's fierce momentum, it is scarcely necessary to say. His velocity as an antagonist was extraordinary. He was troubled by no doubt of his own opinion, nor by any mercy for that of his enemy. He was the first Englishman to realise, in the very nest of optimism, that the public institutions of a society could be, and probably were, corrupt. In the generation of Shaftesbury this discovery was really a momentous one. Mandeville made it soon after, but to his squalid moral nature the shock was not so great as it was to Swift's. That most things were evil and odious in the best of all possible worlds was a revelation to Swift that exhilarated him almost to ecstasy. He could hardly believe it to be true, and trembled lest he should be forced to admit that, after all, Pope and Shaftesbury were sound in their optimism. But his satire probed the insufficiency of mankind in place after place, and there gradually rose in Swift, like an intoxication, a certainty of the vileness of the race. When he was quite convinced, madness was close upon him, but in the interval he wrote that sinister and incomparable masterpiece, *Gulliver's Travels*, in which misanthropy reaches the pitch of a cardinal virtue, and the despicable race of man is grossly and finally humiliated.

Swift declared that if the world had contained a dozen Arbuthnots, *Gulliver's Travels* should have been burned. The charming physician was not only one of the very few persons whom Swift respected, but of his own generation the first to come completely under his literary influence.   If we take the lash out of the style of Swift, we have that of JOHN ARBUTHNOT, who can often hardly be distinguished from his friend and master.   Without personal ambition of any kind, no vanity deterred Arbuthnot from frankly adopting, as closely as he could, the manner of the man whom he admired the most.   As he was a perfectly sane and normal person, with plenty of wit and accomplishment, and without a touch of misanthropy, Arbuthnot served to popularise and to bring into general circulation the peculiar characteristics of Swift, and to reconcile him with his contemporaries.

Swift would have been well content to be named with Arbuthnot, but to find Mandeville's works bracketed with his own would have given him a paroxysm of indignation. Yet they were really so closely allied in some essentials of thought that it is natural to regard them together. BERNARD DE MANDEVILLE was a misanthropical Dutch doctor settled in London, who attacked the optimism of Shaftesbury in a coarse but highly effective and readable volume called the *Fable of the Bees*.   For twenty years after this he was a pariah of the English press, writing odious, vulgar, extremely intelligent books, in which he extended his paradoxical thesis that private vices are public benefits. Mandeville was a daring thinker, who permitted no traditional prejudice, no habit of decency, to interfere with the progression of his ideas.   He was by far the ablest of the English deists, and though all the respectability of his time drew away from him, and voted him, like the grand jury of Middlesex, a public nuisance, he was not without his very distinct influence on the progress of English literature. He was an emancipator of thought, a rude and contemptuous critic of the conventions. In himself base and ugly—for all his writings reveal a gross individuality—the brute courage of Mandeville helped English speculation to slip from its fetters. His style is without elegance, but, what is strange in a foreigner, of a remarkable homeliness and picturesque vigour.

Another writer who was kept outside the sacred ring of the Anne wits was DANIEL DEFOE, who comes in certain aspects close to Mandeville, but has a far wider range and variety. Several dissimilar writers are combined in Defoe, all, with one exception, of a pedestrian and commonplace character. He was in his earlier years the very type of what was called "a hackney author," that is to say, a man of more skill than principle, who let out his pen for hire, ready at his best to support the Ministry with a pamphlet, at his worst to copy documents for stationers or lawyers. In these multifarious exercises Defoe was as copious as any journalist of our own time, and from 1700 to 1720 had a very large share in the miscellaneous writing of the day. The literary character which these humdrum productions illustrate seems to have been far from fascinating. All that we can praise in this Defoe of the pamphlets and journals is industry and a sort of lucid versatility. He was a factor in the vulgarisation of English, and he helped, in no small measure, to create a correct, easy, not ungraceful style for common use in the eighteenth century.

But as he approached the age of sixty, Defoe suddenly appeared in a new light, as the inaugurator of a new school of English prose fiction. In 1719 he published the immortal romance of *Robinson Crusoe*. Everything which had been written earlier than this in the form of an English novel faded at once into insignificance before the admirable sincerity and reality of this relation. It is difficult to conjecture what it was that suggested to the veteran drudge this extraordinary departure, so perfectly fresh, spirited, and novel. The idea of the European sailor marooned on an oceanic island had been used in 1713 by Marivaux in his novel of *Les Effets Surprenants*, but there is no further similarity of treatment. In his later picaresque romances Defoe is manifestly influenced by Le Sage, but *Robinson Crusoe* can scarcely be traced to French or Spanish models. It was an invention, a great, unexpected stroke of British genius, and it was immediately hailed as such by the rest of Europe. It was one of the first English books which was widely imitated on the Continent, and it gave direction and impetus to the new romantico-realistic conception of fiction all over the world. The French, indeed, followed Defoe more directly than the English themselves, and his most obvious disciples are Prévost, Rousseau, and Bernardin de Saint-Pierre. It was in his *Émile*, where he prefers Defoe as an educator to Aristotle, Pliny, or Buffon, that Rousseau finally drew the full admiration of Europe upon *Robinson Crusoe*. In England, however, the bourgeois romances of Defoe long remained without influence and without prestige, widely read indeed, but almost furtively, as vulgar literature fit for the kitchen and the shop.

In Defoe and Mandeville we have strayed outside the inner circle of Queen Anne wits. We return to its centre in speaking of Bolingbroke and Berkeley. With the progress of criticism, however, the relative value of these two typical eighteenth-century names is being slowly

but decisively reversed.   The fame of BOLINGBROKE,
once so universal, has dwindled to a mere shadow.   He
lives as an individual, not any longer as a writer.   His
diffuse and pompous contributions to theistical philosophy are now of interest mainly as exemplifying several
of the faults of decaying classicism—its empty rhetoric,
its vapid diction, its slipshod, inconsistent reasoning.   In
fact, if Bolingbroke demands mention here, it is mainly
as a dreadful example, as the earliest author in which the
school which culminated in Pope, Addison, and Swift is
seen to have passed its meridian and to be declining.
The cardinal defect of classicism was to be its tendency
to hollowness, to intellectual insincerity and partisan-
ship, and this defect is so clearly exposed in Bolingbroke
that we read him no longer.

The opposite fate has rewarded the clear and starry
genius of GEORGE BERKELEY.   In his own day respected,
but not highly regarded as a writer, he has gradually so
strengthened his hold upon us by the purity of his taste,
that in an age of predominance in prose we regard him
as a master.   In spite of Shaftesbury, Berkeley is the
greatest English thinker between Locke and Hume, and
as a pure metaphysician he is perhaps without a rival.
His person and his character were as charming as his
genius, and when he came up to London for the first
time in 1713 he conquered all hearts.   Pope expressed
everybody's conviction when he declared that there had
been given " to Berkeley every virtue under heaven."
He had at that time already circulated his curious hypo-
thesis of phenomenalism, his theory that what we see
and touch is only a symbol of what is spiritual and
eternal—that nothing is, but only seems to be.   His
writings, long pondered and slowly produced, culminated

in 1744 in the brilliant and paradoxical treatise on the merits of tar-water, which was afterwards called *Siris*.

Locke had almost removed philosophy outside the confines of literature ; Shaftesbury had shown that the philosopher could be elegant, florid, and illustrative ; it remained for Berkeley to place it for a moment on the level of poetry itself. There had, perhaps, been written in English no prose so polished as that of Berkeley. Without languor or insipidity, with a species of quiet, unstrained majesty, Berkeley achieved the summit of a classic style. No student of the age of Anne should fail to study that little volume of dialogues which Berkeley issued under the title of *Hylas and Philonous*. It belongs to the *annus mirabilis* 1713, when Pope, Swift, Arbuthnot, Addison, Steele, were all at the brilliant apex of their genius, and when England had suddenly combined to present such a galaxy of literary talent as was to be matched, or even approached, nowhere on the continent of Europe.

Theology, which had taken so prominent a place in the literature of the seventeenth century, fell into insignificance after the year 1700. We have already spoken of Clarke, a stiff and tiresome writer, but the best of his class. To compare Hoadley with Massillon, or Sherlock with Saurin, is but to discover how great an advantage the French still preserved over us, who had never, even in the palmy days of our theology, enjoyed a Bossuet. Perhaps the most spirited contribution to religious literature published in the early years of the century was Law's *Serious Call* (1729), a book isolated from its compeers in all qualities of style and temper, the work of a Christian mystic who seemed to his contemporaries that hateful thing " an enthusiast."

The period of English literature which we have now roughly sketched is one of the most clearly defined and homogeneous in our history.   In its consideration we are not troubled by the variety and diversity of its aims, by the multitude of its proficients, or by the distribution of its parts.   All is definite, exiguous ; all, or almost all, is crystallised round a single point; that point is common-sense applied to the imagination, to the highest parts of man.   In all the expressions of this definite spirit, whether in Pope or Clarke, in Addison or Berkeley, we find a tendency to the algebraic formula, rather than to colour, fancy, or fire.   In other words, pure intelligence does the work of literature, intelligence applied alike to concrete forms and abstract ideas, actively and energetically applied, without sentimentality or enthusiasm.   The age of Anne succeeded in raising this literature of mathematical intelligence to the highest pitch of elegant refinement.   But before it closed there were manifest signs of the insufficiency of such a manner to support a complex artistic system.

What in the hands of Pope and Addison was so brilliant and novel that all the world was charmed, could but prove in those of their disciples cold, mechanical, and vapid.   There were very dangerous elements in the optimism of the time, in its profound confidence in the infallibility of its judgment, in the ease with which it had become accustomed to rigid rules of composition, in the dry light of formalism by which it was so prompt to observe art and nature.   These might satisfy for a moment, might produce a single crop of splendid literature, but they bore no fruit for the morrow.   Even the prevalent admiration of the authors of antiquity was a source of danger, for these great fountain-heads of imagination were regarded. not as they really wrote, but as seen distorted through the spectacles of the French Jesuit critics. The poets of antiquity were cultivated as incomparable masters of rhetoric, and on the basis of Horace, and even of Homer, there was founded a poetry totally foreign to antique habits of thought.

We have not, however, to consider what dangers lay ahead of the system, but what it produced in the first quarter of the eighteenth century, and for this, within limits, we can have little but praise.   England now joined, and even led, the movement of European nations from which she had hitherto been excluded as a barbarian. In a " polite" age the English writers became the most polite.   Pope and Addison had nothing more to learn from their Continental contemporaries ; they became teachers themselves.   In their hands the English language, which had been a byword for furious individuality and unbridled imaginative oddity, became a polished and brilliant instrument in the hands of an elegant and well-bred race.   So far, if we go no further, all was well. A little group of scholars and gentlemen, closely identified in their personal interests, had taken English literature under their care, and had taught it to express with exquisite exactitude their own limited and mundane sensations.   These were paving the way for a frigid formalism which would become intolerable in the hands of their followers ; but in their own day, in their brief Augustan age, the direct result was not merely brilliant in itself, but of an infinite benefit to English as a vehicle for an easy and rapid exercise of the intelligence.

VII

THE AGE OF JOHNSON

1740–1780

THE period which we have just quitted was one of effort concentrated in one middle-class coterie in London, an age of elegant persiflage and optimistic generalisation marshalled by a group of highly civilised and "clubable" wits. That at which we have now arrived was the exact opposite. Its leading exponents were not associates, or, in most cases, even acquaintances ; its labours were not in any large degree identified with London, but with places all over the English-speaking world. From 1712 to 1735 attention is riveted on the mutual intercourse of the men who are writing, and then upon their works. From 1740 to 1780 the movements of literature, rather than those of men of letters, are our theme. Solitary figures closely but unconsciously and accidentally related to other solitary figures, ships out of call of one another, but blown by the same wind—that is what the age of Johnson presents to us.

If the combination of personal communication, so interesting in the earlier age, is lacking now, it is made up for to us by the definition of the principal creative impulses, which prove, to our curiosity and surprise, independent of all personal bias. The similarity between Swift and Arbuthnot, between Pope and Parnell, is easily explained by their propinquity. But how are we to account for the close relation of Gray and Collins, who never met ; of Fielding and Richardson, who hated one another at a distance ; of Butler at Bristol, and Hume at Ninewells ? This central period of the eighteenth century took a wider and more democratic colouring ; its intellectual life was more general, we had almost said more imperial. Letters could no longer be governed by the dictatorship of a little group of sub-aristocratic wits met in a coffee-house to dazzle mankind. The love of literature had spread in all directions, and each province of the realm contributed its genius to the larger movement.

In poetry, which must occupy us first, the forces which now attract our almost undivided attention are not those which appealed to contemporary criticism. Pope and his school had given a perfect polish to the couplet, had revived a public interest in satire and philosophic specu-lation in verse, had canonised certain forms of smooth and optimistic convention, had, above all, rendered the *technique* of "heroic verse" a thing which could be studied like a language or a science. It was strictly in accordance with the traditions of literature that no sooner was the thing easy to do than the best poets lost interest in doing it. It was Thomson who made the first re-sistance to the new classical formula, and it is, in fact, Thomson who is the real pioneer of the whole romantic movement, with its return to nature and simplicity. This gift would be more widely recognised than it is if it had not been for the poet's timidity, his easy-going indolence. The *Winter* of Thomson, that epoch-making poem, was published earlier than the *Dunciad* and the *Essay on Man*, earlier than *Gulliver's Travels* and the *Political History of the Devil ;* it belongs in time to the

16

central period of Queen Anne.   But in spirit, in
temper, in style, it has nothing whatever to do with
that age, but inaugurates another, which, if we consider
exactly, culminated, after a slow but direct ascent, in
Wordsworth.

The positive interest which the poetry of the middle of
the eighteenth century now possesses for us may be
slight; its relative or historical interest is very great.   In
it we see English verse timidly reasserting its characteristic qualities and resuming forbidden powers.   The
change was gradual, without revolution, without violent
initiative.   Passion did not suddenly return in its bolder
forms, but an insidious melancholy shook the pensive
bosom.   For nearly eighty years the visual world, in its
broader forms, had scarcely existed for mankind; it was
not to be expected that shy and diffident poets, such as
were those of this new period, men in most cases of subdued vitality, should flash out into brilliant colourists and
high-priests of pantheism.   They did their work gingerly
and slowly; they introduced an obvious nature into
their writings; they painted, with a deprecating pencil,
familiar scenes and objects.   With Thomson they removed the fog that had obscured the forms of landscape,
with Gray they asserted the stately beauty of mountains,
with Young they proclaimed anew the magic of moonlight, with Walpole they groped after the principles of
Gothic architecture.   That their scenes were painted in
grey and greenish neutral-tint, that their ruined arches
were supported on modern brickwork, that falsity and
fustian, a hollow eloquence and a frigid sententiousness
spoiled many of their enterprises, is not to the point.
We must occupy ourselves, not with what they failed to
do, but with their faltering successes.   They were the

pioneers of romanticism, and that is what renders them attractive to the historian.

Nor was it in England only, but over all Europe, that the poets of the age of Johnson were the pioneers of romantic feeling and expression. In the two great movements which we have indicated—in a melancholy sensibility pointing to passion, in a picturesqueness of landscape leading to direct nature-study—the English were the foremost of a new intellectual race. As a child of the eighteenth century, Stendhal, reminded the French, " Le pittoresque—comme les bonnes diligences et les bateaux à vapeur—nous vient d'Angleterre." It came to France partly through Voltaire, who recorded its manifestations with wonder, but mainly through Rousseau, who took it to his heart. Not instantly was it accepted. The first translator of the *Seasons* into French dared not omit an apology for Thomson's " almost hideous imagery," and it took years for the religious melancholy of Young to sink into German bosoms. But when there appeared the *Nouvelle Heloïse,* a great and catastrophic work of passion avowedly built up on the teaching of the English poets of the funereal school, a book owing everything to English sensibility, then the influence of British verse began, and from 1760 to 1770 the vogue and imitation of it on the Continent was in full swing. To the European peoples of that time Young was at least as great an intellectual and moral portent as Ibsen has been to ours.

It was in a comparative return to a sombre species of romanticism, and in a revolt against the tyranny of the conventional couplet, that these poets mainly affected English literature. JAMES THOMSON is at the present hour but tamely admired. His extraordinary freshness, his new outlook into the whole world of imaginative life, deserve a very different recognition from what is commonly awarded to him. The *Hymn* which closes the *Seasons* was first published in 1730, when Pope was still rising towards the zenith of his fame. It recalled to English verse a melody, a rapture which had been entirely unknown since Milton's death, more than sixty years before. We may be told that the close observation of natural phenomena which made the four books of the *Seasons* so illustrious had never, although scouted or disregarded, been entirely lost. The names of Lady Winchelsea, of Gay, even of John Philips, may be quoted to prove to us that the poets still had eyes, and knew a hawk from a hernshaw. But these pedestrian studies of nature had no passion in them; they were but passages of an inventory or of a still-life painting. With Thomson, and mainly with his majestic *Hymn*, another quality came back to poetry, the ecstasy of worship awakened by the aspect of natural beauty. We can but wonder what lines such as

> " *Ye forests bend, ye harvests wave, to Him;*
> *Breathe your still song into the reaper's heart,*
> . *As home he goes beneath the joyous moon,*"

could have meant to readers such as Warburton and Hurd. We may answer—To them, as to Johnson, they could have meant nothing at all; and here began the great split between the two classes of eighteenth-century students of poetry—those who clung to the old forms, and exaggerated their aridity, down to the days of Hayley and Darwin; and those who falteringly and blindly felt their way towards better things, through Gray, and Percy's *Reliques,* and Warton's revelation of the Elizabethans.

Another powerful innovator was EDWARD YOUNG, but

his influence was not so pure as that of Thomson. The author of *Night Thoughts* was an artist of a force approaching that of genius, but his error was to build that upon rhetoric which he should have based on imagination. The history of Young is one of the most curious in the chronicles of literature. Born far back in the seventeenth century, before Pope or Gay, he wrote in the manner of the Anne wits, without special distinction, through all the years of his youth and middle life. At the age of sixty he collected his poetical works, and appeared to be a finished mediocrity. It was not until then, and after that time, that, taking advantage of a strange wind of funereal enthusiasm that swept over him, he composed the masterpiece by which the next generation knew him, his amazingly popular and often highly successful *Night Thoughts*. It was in the sonorous blank verse of this adroit poem that the vague æsthetic melancholy of the age found its most striking exposition. It was hardly completed (in 1744) before a prose rival and imitation, the *Meditations among the Tombs* of Harvey, deepened its effect and surpassed it in popularity, though never approaching it in real literary ability. These two books, so pompous, unctuous, and hollow — the one illuminated by passages of highly artistic execution, the other mere barren bombast — occupied the fancies of men for well-nigh one hundred years, surviving the great revival, and successfully competing with Wordsworth and Keats.

This sepulchral rhetoric in Miltonic verse, whether embodied in Young's rolling iambics or compressed into the homelier vigour of Blair's *Grave*, was what passed for poetry *par excellence* one hundred and fifty years ago. With this taste the style in grottoes, urns, and tombs closely corresponded, and to this much of the superficial character of what was most enjoyed in Gray, Collins, and even Goldsmith, may be traced. The great gift of the first two of this trio was the renewed elaboration of their verse-form. Thomson had revived the beautiful Spenserian measure ; in the *Odes* of THOMAS GRAY and of WILLIAM COLLINS a variety of stanzaic forms illustrated a return to pre-Drydenic variety and ease of prosody. To a world that scarcely appreciated the meaning of verse which was not either a succession of five-beat couplets or a mass of stiff blank verse, Gray introduced choral measures, richly and elaborately rhymed, full of complicated triumphal melody ; Collins, at the same moment, in a lower key, whispering rather than shouting, fashioned his delicate, cold, aerial music. Unhappily, in the middle of the eighteenth century everything conspired to drag the pioneers of free art back to the bondage of rhetoric, and the work of Gray and Collins was instantly retarded and parodied by the frosty talent of Akenside, in whose hands the newly found lyrical fire was turned to ice. The impact of Gray on Europe was delayed, but could not be suppressed. The *Elegy in a Country Churchyard* is the direct precursor, not only of Chateaubriand, but of Lamartine, and is the most characteristic single poem of the eighteenth century.

From 1740 to 1760 the Thomsonian and the Graian influences were predominant. About the latter date there was a relapse into something of the old Jesuit precision. In Churchill and his companions, regardless of the more solemn and Latin satire which Johnson had been cultivating, a return was made to the lighter and more primitive forms which Pope had used. For a moment the sombre romantic school seemed swept out of existence, but the popularity of the savage couplets of Churchill was brief. All that was left of the reaction was soon seen in the modified classicism of Goldsmith, with its didactic couplets as smooth and as lucid as Pope's, its humanity and grace, its simplicity and picturesque sweetness. In the *Deserted Village* (1770) we have the old kind of starched poetry at its very best, and at its latest, since after Goldsmith the movement which had begun with Pope ceased to possess any real vitality.

The close of this central period of the eighteenth century was stilted and inefficient in poetry. The rigidity of the classical system, now outworn after the exercise of one hundred years and more, strangled thought and expression, and forced those who desired to write to use mere centos of earlier and freer masters. The elegiac school had lasted but a very few years; its successes are dated almost exclusively between 1742 and 1760. The new poetic feeling, however, never fell into complete desuetude, for at the very moment when Gray and Young were becoming silent, several new forces asserted themselves, all moving in the direction of reform in taste. Of these the earliest was the revelation, between 1760 and 1763, of the mysterious paraphrases of Ossian; in 1765 Bishop Percy issued his *Reliques* of primitive English poetry; in 1770 the untimely death of Chatterton revealed an extraordinary genius of a novel kind; and from 1777 onwards Thomas Warton, in his *History of English Poetry*, was recalling readers to masterpieces of art and passion that were not bound down to the rules nor dwarfed by the classical tradition. Of all these elements the least genuine was undoubtedly the first mentioned, but it is equally certain that it was the strongest. The vogue of OSSIAN through all Europe became immense ; no real British writer, not Shakespeare himself, enjoyed so universally the respect of Europe as the shadowy Ossian did at the close of the eighteenth century.   Critics of high position gravely discussed the relative magnitude of Homer and of the author of *Fingal,* and by no means invariably gave the crown to the Greek.   The key to the extraordinary success of these Caledonian forgeries is that they boldly offered to release the spirit of Europe from its pedagogic bondage.   No one, not even Goethe, was anxious to inquire too closely concerning the authority of fragments which professed to come to us from an extreme antiquity, tinged with moonlight and melancholy, exempt from all attention to the strained rules and laws of composition, dimly primitive and pathetically vague, full of all kinds of plaintive and lyrical suggestiveness.   When Napoleon, in 1804, desired to give the highest possible praise to a new, modern, brilliantly emancipated, literary production, he could find no better epithet for it than "vraiement Ossianique."   And this suggests in what light we have to regard Macpherson's forgeries, so irritating to our cultivated taste in their bombastic pretentiousness. It was not what they were that fascinated Europe, it was what they suggested, and the product is what we read in Goethe, Byron, Chateaubriand.

The greatest literary discovery, however, of the middle of the eighteenth century was the novel.   In late years criticism has dwelt more and more seriously on the position of those who practically created the most entertaining and the most versatile of all the sections of modern literature.   With due respect to the writers of fiction from the sixteenth century down to Defoe and Marivaux, it was in the year 1740 that the European novel, as we understand it, began to exist. The final decay of the theatre led to the craving on the part of English readers for an amusement which should be to them what the seeing of comedies had been to their parents, and of tragedies to their grand-parents. The didactic plays of such writers as Lillo, who lived until 1739, were practically the latest amusements of the old school of play-goers, who were weary of drama, weary of the old pompous heroic story, of chronicles of pseud-Atalantic scandal, of the debased picaresque romance. Something entirely new was wanted to amuse the jaded mind of Europe, and that new thing was invented by the fat little printer of Salisbury Court. SAMUEL RICHARDSON conceived what Taine has called the " Roman anti-romanesque," the novel which dealt entirely with a realistic study of the human heart set in a frame of contemporary middle-class manners, not in any way touched up or heightened, but depending for the interest it excited solely on its appeal to man's interest in the mirrored face of man.

It was a particularly fortunate thing that in this far-spreading work of Richardson's he was accompanied by several writers who were almost his coevals, who were not subjugated by his prestige, but each of whom pushed on the same important reform in a province peculiarly favourable to himself. In considering the first great blossoming of the English novel, we find that a single quarter of a century included all the great novels of the age, and that Richardson was neither imitated nor over-shadowed, but supported by such wholly original fellow-labourers as Fielding, Smollett, Sterne, and Goldsmith. Each of our first five novelists presented a gift of his own to the new-born infant, prose fiction, and we must now consider what these gifts were.

What was Richardson's addition to literature may be described in a condensed form as a combination of art in the progress of a narrative, force in the evolution of pathos, and morality founded upon a profound study of conduct. Of the group, he was the one who wrote least correctly ; Richardson, as a pure man of letters, is the inferior, not merely of Fielding and Sterne, but of Smollett. He knows no form but the tedious and imperfect artifice of a series of letters. He is often without distinction, always without elegance and wit ; he is pedantic, careless, profuse ; he seems to write for hours and hours, his wig thrown over the back of a chair, his stockings down at heel. But the accidents of his life and temperament had inducted him into an extraordinary knowledge of the female heart ; while his imagination permitted him to clothe the commonplace reflections of very ordinary people in fascinating robes of simple fancy. He was slow of speech and lengthy, but he had a magic gift which obliged every one to listen to him.

The minuteness of Richardson's observations of common life added extremely to the pleasure which his novels gave to readers weary of the vagueness, the empty fustian of the heroic romances. His pages appealed to the instinct in the human mind which delights to be told over again, and told in scrupulous detail, that which it knows already. His readers, encouraged by his almost oily partiality for the moral conventions, gave themselves up to him without suspicion, and enjoyed each little triviality, each coarse touch of life, each prosaic circumstance, with perfect gusto, sure that, however vulgar they might be, they would lead up to the triumph of virtue. What these readers were really assisting at was the triumph of anti-romantic realism.

Very different in kind, though of equal value to literature, is the gift to his generation of HENRY FIELDING,
whose *Joseph Andrews* in 1742 succeeds so oddly to the
Pamela of 1740–41. He also set out to copy human
nature faithfully and minutely, but his view of life was
more eclectic than that of Richardson. A much greater
writer, in his own virile way one of the most skilful of all
manipulators of English, he is saved by his wider learning and experience from the banality of Richardson.
As Mr. Leslie Stephen has well said, Fielding, more than
any other writer, gives the very form and pressure of the
eighteenth century. He is without the sensibility of
Richardson, which he disdained ; his observation of the
movements of the heart is more superficial ; he cannot
probe so deeply into the fluctuating thoughts of woman.
He has the defects of too great physical health ; he is
impatient of the half-lights of character, of nervous im-
pressionability. He can spare few tears over Clarissa, and
none at all over Clementina ; he laughs in the sunshine
with Ariosto. He also is a moralist, but of quite another
class than Richardson ; he is pitiful of the frailties of instinct, sorry for those who fall from excess of strength.
Hence, while Richardson starts the cloistered novel of
psychology, of febrile analysis, Fielding takes a manlier
note, and deals with conduct from its more adventurous
side.

The various qualities of Fielding are seen to successive
advantage in *Joseph Andrews* (1742) with its profuse
humour, in *Jonathan Wild* (1743) with its cynical irony, in
Amelia (1751) with its tenderness and sentiment ; but it
is in *Tom Jones* (1749) that the full force of the novelist
is revealed. This was the first attempt made by any
writer to depict in its fulness the life of a normal man,

without help from extraordinary conditions or events, without any other appeal to the reader than that made simply to his interest in a mirror of his own affections, frailties, hopes, and passions. Fielding, in each of his works, but in *Tom Jones* pre-eminently, is above all things candid and good-humoured. He is a lover of morals, but he likes them to be sincere ; he has no palliation for their rancid varieties. He has his eye always on conduct ; he is keen to observe not what a man pretends or protests, but what he does, and this he records to us, sometimes with scant respect for our susceptibilities. But it has been a magnificent advantage for English fiction to have near the head of it a writer so vigorous, so virile, so devoid of every species of affectation and hypocrisy. In all the best of our later novelists there has been visible a strain of sincere manliness which comes down to them in direct descent from Fielding, and which it would be a thousand pities for English fiction to relinquish.

By LAURENCE STERNE the course of fiction was re- versed a little way towards Addison and Steele in the two incomparable books which are his legacy to English literature. We call *Tristram Shandy* (1760–67) and *A Sentimental Journey* (1768) novels, because we know not what else to call them ; nor is it easy to define their fugitive and rare originality. Sterne was not a moralist in the mode of Richardson or of Fielding ; it is to be feared that he was a complete ethical heretic ; but he brought to his country as gifts the strained laughter that breaks into tears, and the melancholy wit that saves itself by an outburst of buffoonery. He introduced into the coarse and heavy life of the eighteenth century elements of daintiness, of persiflage, of moral versatility ; he prided himself on the reader's powerlessness to conjecture what was coming next. A French critic compared Sterne, most felicitously, to one of the little bronze satyrs of antiquity in whose hollow bodies exquisite odours were stored. He was carried away by the tumult of his nerves, and it became a paradoxical habit with him to show himself exactly the opposite of what he was expected to be. You hàd to unscrew him for the aroma to escape. His unseemly, passionate, pathetic life burned itself away at the age of fifty-four, only the last eight of which had been concerned with literature. Sterne's influence on succeeding fiction has been durable but interrupted. Ever and anon his peculiar caprices, his selected elements, attract the imitation of some more or less analogous spirit. The extreme beauty of his writing has affected almost all who desire to use English prose as though it were an instrument not less delicate than English verse. Nor does the fact that a surprising number of his "best passages" were stolen by Sterne from older writers militate against his fame, because he always makes some little adaptation, some concession to harmony, which stamps him a master, although unquestionably a deliberate plagiarist. This fantastic sentimentalist and disingenuous idealist comes close, however, to Richardson in one faculty, the value which he extracts from the juxtaposition of a variety of trifling details artfully selected so as to awaken the sensibility of ordinary minds.

If in Sterne the qualities of imagination were heightened, and the susceptibilities permitted to become as feverish and neurotic as possible, the action of TOBIAS SMOLLETT was absolutely the reverse. This rough and strong writer was troubled with no superfluous refinements of instinct. He delighted in creating types of eccentric profligates and ruffians, and to do this was to withdraw from the novel as Richardson, Fielding, and Sterne conceived it, back into a form of the picaresque romance. He did not realise what his greatest compeers were doing, and when he wrote *Roderick Random* (1748) he avowedly modelled it on *Gil Blas*, coming, as critics have observed, even closer to the Spanish *picaros* spirit than did Le Sage himself. If Smollett had gone no further than this, and had merely woven out of his head one more romance of the picaresque class, we should never have heard of him. But his own life, unlike those of his three chief rivals, had been adventurous on land and under sail, and he described what he had seen and suffered. Three years later he published *Peregrine Pickle* (1751), and just before he died, in 1771, *Humphrey Clinker*. The abundant remainder of his work is negligible, these three books alone being worthy of note in a sketch of literature so summary as this.

In the work of the three greater novelists the element of veracity is very strong, even though in the case of Sterne it may seem concealed beneath a variegated affectation of manner. In each, however, the main aim, and the principal element of originality, is the observation of mankind as it really exists. But Smollett was not great enough to continue this admirable innovation; he went back to the older, easier, method of gibbeting a peculiarity and exaggerating an exception. He was also much inferior to his rivals in the power of constructing a story, and in his rude zeal to "subject folly to ridicule, and vice to indignation," he raced from one rough episode to another, bestowing very little attention upon that evolution of character which should be the essence of successful fiction. The proper way to regard Smollett is, doubtless, as a man of experience and energy, who was encouraged by the success of the realistic novel to revive the old romance of adventure, and to give it certain new features. The violence of Smollett is remarkable ; it was founded on a peculiarity of his own temper, but it gives his characters a sort of contortion of superhuman rage and set grimaces that seem mechanically horrible. When young Roderick Random's cousin wishes to tease him, he has no way of doing it short of hunting him with beagles, and when it is desired that Mrs. Pickle should be represented as ill tempered, a female like one of the Furies is evoked. But while it is easy to find fault with Smollett's barbarous books, it is not so easy to explain why we continue to read them with enjoyment, nor why their vigorous horse-play has left its mark on novelists so unlike their author as Lever, Dickens, and Charles Reade. Smollett's best book, moreover, is his latest, and its genial and brisk comicality has done much to redeem the memory of earlier errors of taste.

With the work of these four novelists, whose best thoughts were given to fiction, were associated two or three isolated contributions to the novel, among which the *Vicar of Wakefield* and *Rasselas* are the most celebrated. Neither Johnson nor Goldsmith, however, would have adopted this form, if a direct and highly successful appeal to the public had not already been made by Richardson and Fielding. These masterly books were episodic ; they have little importance in our general survey. We judge them as we judge the flood of novels which presently rushed forth in all the languages of Europe, as being the results of a novelty which the world owes to the great English pioneers. The novel, indeed, was the first gift of a prominent kind which the world owed to England. The French boudoir novel, as exemplified by Crébillon *fils*, faded out of existence when Richardson rose over the Continent. The lucidity, directness, and wholesomeness of this new species of fiction made a way for it at once ; within a marvellously short space of time all Europe was raving over *Pamela* and *Clarissa*. The anti-romantic novel swept heroic and picaresque fiction out of the field, and it was the uncommon good fortune of the humdrum old printer to prepare the way for Rousseau and Goethe, to be imitated by Voltaire, and to win the enthusiastic adulation of Diderot and of Marmontel, who preferred *Sir Charles Grandison* to all the masterpieces of antiquity. The type of novel invented in England about 1740–50 continued for sixty or seventy years to be the only model for Continental fiction ; and criticism has traced on every French novelist, in particular, the stamp of Richardson, if not of Sterne and Fielding, while the Anglomania of Rousseau is patent to the superficial reader.

The literature which exercised so wide an influence, and added so greatly to the prestige and vital force of English manners of thought, is not to be disregarded as trivial. The introduction of the novel, indeed, was to intellectual life as epoch-making as the invention of railways was to social life : it added a vast and inexhaustibly rich province to the domain of the imagination. The discovery that a chronicle of events which never happened to people who never existed, may be made, not merely as interesting and probable, but practically as *true* as any record of historical adventure, was one of most far-reaching importance. It was what Fielding called " the prosai-comi-epos " of the age, invented for the ceaseless delight of those who had tasted the new pleasure of seeing themselves as others saw them. The realistic novel was as popular as a bit of looking-glass is among savages. It enabled our delighted forefathers to see what manner of men they were, painted without dazzling or "sub-fusc" hues, in the natural colours of life. For us the pathos of Richardson, the sturdy, manly sense of Fielding, the sensibility of Sterne, the unaffected humanity of Goldsmith, possess a perennial charm, but they cannot be to us quite what they were to those most enviable readers who not merely perused them for the first time, but had never conceived the possibility of seeing anything like them. That fresh eagerness we never can recover.

The complex age illustrated by such poets as Young, and such novelists as Fielding, found its fullest personal exponent in Dr. SAMUEL JOHNSON, not the greatest writer, indeed, in English literature, but perhaps the most massive figure of a man of letters. The gradual tendency of the century had more and more come to be concentrated upon attention to common-sense, and in Johnson a character was developed, of noble intelligence, of true and tender heart, of lambent humour, in whose entire philosophy every impulse was subordinated to that negative virtue. Johnson became, therefore, the leading intellect of the country, because displaying in its quintessence the quality most characteristic of the majority of educated men and women. Common-sense gave point to his wit, balance to his morality, a Tory limitation to his intellectual sympathy. He keeps the central path ; he is as little indulgent to enthusiasm as to infidelity ; he finds as little place in his life for mysticism as for coarse frivolity. *Vita fumus,* and it is not for man to waste his years in trying to weigh the smoke or puff it away; bravely and simply he must labour and acquiesce, without revolt, without speculation, in "all that human hearts endure." This virile hold upon facts, this attitude to conduct as a plain garment from which the last shred of the Shaftesbury gold-lace optimism had been torn, explains the astounding influence Johnson wielded during his lifetime. His contemporaries knew him to be thoroughly honest, profoundly intelligent, and yet permeated by every prejudice of the age. They loved to deal with facts, and no man had so large a stock of them at his disposal as Johnson.

For nearly fifty years Johnson was occupied in literary composition. Yet his books are not so voluminous as such a statement would lead us to expect. It is doubtful whether, with a competency, Johnson would have written at all, for he was ponderously indolent, moving slowly, and easily persuaded to stop, loving much more to read, to ponder, and to talk than to write, and, indeed, during long periods of his career unable to put pen to paper. Of his principal productions the most famous may be called occasional, for they were written suddenly, under a pressing need for money, in a jet of violent energy which was succeeded by prolonged inertia. He essayed every species of composition, and it cannot be said that he was unsuccessful in any, according to the estimate of the age. His two poems, satires imitated from Juvenal, are less "poetical," perhaps, in the recent sense than any writings of their reputation in the language, but the solidity and sententiousness of their couplets kept them moderately popular for more than half a century. As an essayist, it is less fair to judge Johnson by his *Ramblers* than by his lighter and less pompous *Idlers ;* yet even the former were till lately habitually read. He lent his dignified and ponderous imagination to the task of producing fiction, and *Rasselas* takes its place among the minor classics of our tongue. Towards the end of his life, Johnson came forward four times with a weighty pamphlet as completely outside the range of practical politics as those of Carlyle. He is also the writer of two diaries of travel, of sermons, of a tragedy, of certain critical ana—all of them, in the strict sense, occasional, and almost unprofessional.

The only works on which Johnson can be said to have expended elaborate attention are his *Dictionary*, which scarcely belongs to literature, and his *Lives of the English Poets* (1779–81). The latter, indeed, is his *magnum opus;* on it, and on it alone, if we except his reported sayings, the reputation of Johnson as a critic rests. This extremely delightful compendium can never cease to please a certain class of readers, those, namely, who desire intellectual stimulus rather than information, and who can endure the dogmatic expression of an opinion with which they disagree. No one turns to Johnson's pages any longer to know what to think about Milton or Gray ; no one any longer considers that Cowley was the first correct English poet, or that Edmund Smith was a great man. Half Johnson's selected poets are read no longer, even by students; many of them never were read at all. What we seek in these delightful volumes is the entertainment to be obtained from the courageous exposition, the gay, bold decisiveness, the humour and humanity of the prodigious critic, self-revealed in his preferences and his prejudices. There are no "perhaps's" and "1 think's ;" all is peremptory and assertive; you take the judgment or you leave it, and if you venture to make a reservation, the big voice roars you down. This remarkable publication closes the criticism of the century; it is the final word of the movement which had been proceeding since 1660; it sums it up so brilliantly and authoritatively that immediate revolt from its principles was a matter of course. During the very same years Thomas Warton was publishing his *History of English Poetry*, in which all the features were found which Johnson lacked—broad and liberal study, an enthusiasm for romance, a sense of something above and beyond the rules of the Jesuits, a breadth of real poetry undreamed of by Johnson. Warton knew his subject; Johnson did not. Warton prophesied of a dawning age, and Johnson stiffly contented himself with the old. Warton was accurate, painstaking, copious; Johnson was careless, indolent, inaccurate; yet, unfair as it seems, to-day everybody still reads Johnson, and no one opens the pages of Warton.

The extraordinary vitality of Johnson is one of the most interesting phenomena in literary history. That the greater part of it did not exhale with the fading memory of his friends is due to the genius of his principal disciple. It has been customary to deny capacity of every kind to JAMES BOSWELL, who had, indeed, several of the characteristics of a fool; but the qualities which render the *Life of Johnson* one of the great books are not accidental, and it would be an equal injustice to consider them inherent in the subject. The life and letters of Gray, which Mason had published in 1775, gave Boswell a model for his form, but it was a model which he excelled in every feature. By Mason and Boswell a species of literature was introduced into England which was destined to enjoy a popularity that never stood higher than it does at this moment. Biographies had up to this time been perfunctory affairs, either trivial and unessential collections of anecdotes, or else pompous eulogies from which the breath of life was absent. But Mason and Boswell made their heroes paint their own portraits, by the skilful interpolation of letters, by the use of anecdotes, by the manipulation of the recollections of others; they adapted to biography the newly discovered formulas of the anti-romantic novelists, and aimed at the production of a figure that should be interesting, lifelike, and true.

It was a very happy accident which made Dr. Johnson the subject of the first great essay in this species of portraiture. Boswell was a consummate artist, but his sitter gave him a superb opportunity. For the first time, perhaps, in the history of literature, a great leader of intellectual society was able after his death to carry on unabated, and even heightened, the tyrannous ascendency of his living mind. The picturesqueness of his dictatorial personage, his odd freaks and pranks, his clearness of speech, his majestic independence of opinion, went on exercising their influence long after his death, and exercise it now. Still, in the matchless pages of Boswell we see a living Johnson, blowing out his breath like a whale, whistling and clucking under the arguments of an opponent, rolling victoriously in his chair, often "a good deal exhausted by violence and vociferation." Never before had the salient points in the character and habits of a man of genius been noted with anything approaching to this exactitude and copiousness, and we ought to be grateful to Boswell for a new species of enjoyment.

By the side of Johnson, like an antelope accompanying an elephant, we observe the beautiful figure of OLIVER GOLDSMITH. In spite of Johnson's ascendency, and in spite of a friendship that was touching in its nearness, scarcely a trace of the elder companion is to be discovered in the work of the younger. Johnson's style is massive, sonorous, ponderous ; enamoured of the pomp of language, he employs its heaviest artillery for trifles, and points his cannon at the partridge on the mountains. The word which Johnson uses is always the correct one so far as meaning goes, but it is often more weighty than the occasion demands, and more Latin. Hence it was, no doubt, that his spoken word, being more racy and more Saxon, was often more forcible than his printed word. · There is no ponderosity about Goldsmith, whose limpid and elegant simplicity of style defies analysis. In that mechanical and dusty age he did not set up to be an innovator. We search in vain, in Goldsmith's verse or prose, for any indication of a consciousness of the coming change. He was perfectly contented with the classical traditions, but his inborn grace and delicacy of temper made him select the sweeter and the more elegant among the elements of his time. As a writer, purely, he is far more enjoyable than Johnson ; he was a poet of great flexibility and sensitiveness; his single novel is much fuller of humour and nature than the stiff *Rasselas ;* as a dramatist he succeeded brilliantly in an age of failures ; he is one of the most perfect of essayists. Nevertheless, with all his perennial charm, Goldsmith, in his innocent simplicity, does not attract the historic eye as the good giant Johnson does, seated for forty years in the undisputed throne of letters.

Through the first half of the eighteenth century, those who speculated with any freedom on the principles of religion and on its relation to conduct were loosely classed together as deists. In its general denunciation of independent thought, the age made no distinction between the optimistic rationalists, who proceeded from

Shaftesbury, and philosophic scepticism of a critical or even destructive kind. Those who approach the subject from the purely literary standpoint, as we do in these pages, are in danger of underrating the intellectual importance of this undermining of faith, because it was conducted by men whose talent and whose command of style were insufficient to preserve their writings. On the other hand, all the most eminent and vital authors combine to deride and malign the deists and to persuade us of their insignificance. When we see Swift, in his magnificent irony, descend like an eagle upon such an intellectual shrewmouse as Collins, whose principal modern advocate describes him as "always slipshod in style and argument, and tedious in spite of his brevity," we think the contest too unequal to be interesting. Nor does a brief literary history afford us occasion to dilate on such very hackney writers as Toland and Tindal, Whiston and Leslie.

Towards the middle of the century, however, the habit of mind engendered by the humble, but sometimes entirely sincere, destructive deists, bore fruit in a species of literature which they had not dreamed of. There can be little question that the progress of critical speculation, the tendency to take obvious things for granted no longer, but to discuss their phenomena and distinguish their bases, led to the happiest results in the province of history. To the period which we have now reached, belong three histories of high rank—all three, as it was long believed, of the very highest rank—Hume, Robertson, Gibbon. If modern taste no longer places the first two of these in quite so exalted a position as the eighteenth century did, each, at any rate, so far surpassed any previous rival as to be considered in another class. In the trio we do not hesitate to recognise the pioneers of a new kind of literature, the earliest scientific historians of the English school. Till 1753, history in England had meant no more than the compilation of memoirs ; it was now to be a branch of creative literature, carefully constructed and subjected to wholesome criticism.

Born in 1711, DAVID HUME began in 1736 to publish philosophical treatises, and in 1741 to be an essayist in a broader and less technical field. His studies in the British constitution and his inquiries into political precedents led him gradually to attempt a History of Great Britain from the Union to his own day. The volume containing *James I. and Charles I.* appeared in 1754, and produced an extraordinary sensation. Hume's long practice in philosophy had prepared him to excel in the specious presentment of facts, and the point of view which he chose to adopt was novel, and calculated to excite a great deal of discussion. His book was read with as much avidity as a novel by Richardson or Fielding —a result which was aided by the simplicity and elegance of his style, which proceeds, limpid, manly, and serene, without a trace of effort. The *History* was concluded by a sixth volume in 1762, and Hume lived on for fourteen years more, dying in the enjoyment of an uncontested fame, as the greatest of modern historians.

This position it would be absurd to say that he has maintained. Hume had little of the more recently developed conscientiousness about the use of materials. If he found a statement quoted, he would indolently adopt it without troubling to refer to the original document. He was willing to make lavish use of the collections of Thomas Carte, a laborious and unfortunate predecessor of his, whose Jacobite prejudices had concealed his considerable pretensions as an historical compiler. Carte died just when Hume's first volume appeared, and this fact perhaps saved Hume from some unpleasant animadversions. Modern critics have shown that Hume's pages swarm with inaccuracies, and that, what is a worse fault, his predilections for Tory ideas lead him to do wilful injustice to the opponents of arbitrary power. All this, however, is little to the point; Hume is no longer appealed to as an authority. He is read for his lucid and beautiful English, for the skill with which he marshals vast trains of events before the mental eye, for his almost theatrical force in describing the evolution of a crisis. If we compare his work from this point of view with all that had preceded it in English literature, we shall see how eminent is the innovation we owe to Hume. He first made history readable.

Ten years younger than Hume, there can be no question that WILLIAM ROBERTSON owed his initiation as a writer to the more famous philosopher. In 1759, when still a minister in a parish in Edinburgh, he produced his *History of Scotland*, in which he dealt with the half-century preceding the point where Hume began. This was the first, and remained the most famous, of a series of historical works which achieved a success the incidents of which read to us now as almost fabulous. If the record can be believed, Robertson was the British author who, of all in the eighteenth century, was continuously the best paid for what he wrote. In Robertson the faults as well as the merits of Hume were exaggerated. His style, with a certain Gallic artificiality, was nevertheless extremely brilliant and graceful, and in the finish of its general summaries surpassed that of the elder historian. But Robertson was still more unwilling than Hume to turn to the original sources of knowledge, still more content to take his facts second-hand, and not less superficial in his estimate of the forces underlying the movements of political and social history.   It may be doubted whether the exercise of such research as we think inevitable for such a task, and as both Hume and Robertson disdained, might not have spoiled that brilliant, if always inadequate, evolution which so deeply fascinated their contemporaries, and may still, for a while, dazzle ourselves.   What they wrote was not so much history in the exact sense, as a philosophical survey of events, in which they thought it, not admissible only, but proper, to tincture the whole with the colour of their own convictions or political views. They were, in fact, empirics, who prepared the world of readers for genuine scientific history, and the founder of the latter was Gibbon.

To EDWARD GIBBON, who timidly deprecated comparison with Robertson and Hume, criticism is steadily awarding a place higher and higher above them.   He is, indeed, one of the great writers of the century, one of those who exemplify in the finest way the signal merits of the age in which he flourished.   The book by which he mainly survives, the vast *Decline and Fall of the Roman Empire*, began to appear in 1776, and was not completed until 1788.   It was at once discovered by all who were competent to judge, that here was a new thing introduced into the literature of the world.   Mézeray and Voltaire had written in French, Hume and Robertson in English, historical works which had charming qualities of the rhetorical order, but which did not pass beyond the rudimentary stage of history, in which the hasty compilation of documents, without close investigation of their value, took the place of genuine and independent research. At length in Gibbon, after a life of forty years mostly spent in study and reflection, a writer was found who united "all the broad spirit of comprehensive survey with the thorough and minute patience of a Benedictine." After long debate, Gibbon fixed upon the greatest historical subject which the chronicle of the world supplied; undaunted by its extreme obscurity and remoteness, he determined to persevere in investigating it, and to sacrifice all other interests and ambitions to its complete elucidation. The mysterious and elaborate story of the transition from the Pagan to the Christian world might well have daunted any mind, but Gibbon kept his thoughts detached from all other ideas, concentrating his splendid intellect on this vast and solitary theme, until his patience and his force moved the mountain, and "the encyclopædic history," as Freeman calls it, "the grandest of all historical designs," took form and shape in six magnificent volumes.

Some modern critics have found the attitude of Gibbon unsympathetic, his manner cold and superficial, his scepticism impervious to the passion of religious conviction. We may admit that these charges are well founded, and set them down to the credit of the age in which he lived, so averse to enthusiasm and ebullition. But to dwell too long on these defects is to miss a recognition of Gibbon's unique importance. His style possesses an extraordinary pomp and richness; ill adapted, perhaps, for the lighter parts of speech, it is unrivalled in the exercise of lofty and sustained heroic narrative. The language of Gibbon never flags; he walks for ever as to the clash of arms, under an imperial banner; a military music animates his magnificent descriptions of battles, of sieges, of panoramic scenes of antique civilisation. He understood, as few historical writers have done, how much the reader's enjoyment of a sustained narrative depends on the appeal to his visual sense. Perhaps he leaned on this strength of his style too much, and sacrificed the abstract to the concrete. But the book is so deeply grounded on personal accurate research, is the result of reflection at once so bold and so broad, with so extraordinary an intuition selects the correct aspect where several points of view were possible, that less than any other history of the eighteenth century does the *Decline and Fall* tend to become obsolete, and of it is still said, what the most scientific of historians said only a generation ago, "Whatever else is read, Gibbon must be read too."

History, fiction, poetry—these were the three departments in which the literature of the centre of the eighteenth century in England mainly excelled, so far as form was concerned, and of these we have now given a rapid survey. If we consider philosophy, we must revert again to Hume, the leading utilitarian of the age, and as a critic of thought without a rival. It is difficult, however, to give to the philosophical writings of Hume more prominence in such an outline as this than we give to those of Locke, although his merit as a writer on speculative subjects is never quite so negative as Locke's. The limpid grace of his style is apparent even in a production so technical as the *Treatise of Human Nature*. Still less must Hutcheson, Hartley, or Reid detain us, prominent as was the position taken by each of these in the development of philosophical speculation. Philosophy by this time had become detached from *belles lettres;* it was now quite indifferent to those who practised it whether their sentences were harmonious or no.

Their sole anxiety was to express what they had to say with the maximum of distinctness. Philosophy, in fact, quitted literature and became a part of science.

Nor was theology more amenable to the charms of style. The one great man of religious intellect, JOSEPH BUTLER, was wholly devoid of literary curiosity, and austerely disdainful of the manner in which his thoughts were expressed. When his thought is direct, Butler's style is lucid and simple ; but when, as is often the case, especially in the *Analogy*, he packs his sentences with labouring complexities of argument, he becomes exceedingly clumsy and hard. Butler stood in complete isolation, as utterly distinct from his contemporaries as Milton had been from his. But if we descend to the commoner ground of theology, we scarcely meet with features more appropriate to our present inquiry. The controversy of Lowth with Warburton was lively, but it was not literature ; the sceptics and the unitarians did not conduct their disquisitions with more elegance than the orthodox clergy ; while Paley, whose *Horæ Paulinæ* comes a little later than the close of our present period, seems to mark in its worst form the complete and fatal divorce of eighteenth-century theology from anything like passion or beauty of form. A complete aridity, or else a bombastic sentimentality, is the mark of the prose religious literature of the time. In the hands of Hurd or Hugh Blair we have come far, not merely from the gorgeous style of Fuller and Taylor, but from the academic grace of Tillotson and the noble fulness of Barrow. This decay of theological literature was even more strongly marked in France, where, after the death of Massillon, we meet with no other noticeable name until the nineteenth century opens. It was due, without doubt, to the suspicion of enthusiasm and highly strung religious feeling which was felt throughout Europe in the generations preceding the Revolution.

In one department of letters this period was very rich. Whether they owed it or no to their familiarity with Parisian society and social modes, those strangely assorted friends, Gray and HORACE WALPOLE, exceeded all their English contemporaries in the composition of charmingly picturesque familiar letters. Less spontaneous, but of an extreme elegance and distinction, were the letters addressed by the fourth Earl of Chesterfield to his natural son, a correspondence long considered to be the final protocol of good breeding in deportment. Of a totally different character were the caustic political invectives issued in the form of correspondence, and under the pseudonym of Junius, between 1769 and 1772 ; but these were letters which gave no pleasure to the recipients, and the form of which precluded all reply. It is, perhaps, not fair to include Junius among the letter-writers, but the correspondence of Chesterfield, Walpole, and Gray will certainly bear comparison with the best in the same class which was produced in France during the eighteenth century. Walpole, in particular, excels all the French in the peculiarly Gallic combination of wit, mundane observation, and picturesque, easy detail.

We have spoken of the dawn of a revived romanticism in poetry. The signs of it were not less obvious in the prose of this period. Gray, with his fervent love of mountain scenery and recognition of the true sublime, is at the head of the naturalists. But great praise is due to the topographical writers who more and more drew attention to the forms of natural landscape. The observations of Gilpin, Uvedale Price, and Gilbert White, although made towards the close of the period we are examining, were not published until much later. Gilpin, in particular, is a pathetic instance of a man full of appreciation of natural beauty, prevented by the tradition of his time from expressing it ; sensible of the charm of the visible world, yet tongue-tied and bound by sterile habits of repression. After the seal of a hundred years had been set on the eyes and mouths of men, it was not suddenly or without a struggle that they could welcome and respond to a revived consciousness of the loveliness of wild scenery.

The central portion of the eighteenth century marks a progress in the democratisation of literature. The love of books and the habit of reading spread rapidly and widely through all parts of the country and all ranks of society. The world of letters was no longer, as it had been in the age of Anne, a small circle of sub-aristocratic bourgeois who wrote for one another and for the polite toilets of London. The capital was no longer remarkable for the importance of its literary representatives ; the life of letters was in the provinces, was almost cosmopolitan. English literature now, for the first time, became European, and in order to obtain that distinction it was forced more and more to cast aside its original characteristics and to relinquish its insularity. That it did so with effect is proved by the very interesting fact that while up to this date we have seen England either solitary or affected by Italy or France without the knowledge of those powers, we find it now suddenly producing the most powerfully radiating literature in Europe, and forming the taste of Germany, France, and the world. The final actor in the work of fusing the

Saxon and the Latin literatures in one general style was
Rousseau, who combined, as Mme. de Staël noted, the
taste and habits of France with the ideas and sentiments
of the North.

The freedom and rough simplicity of English life,
its energy, its cultivation of truth and sincerity—
qualities, no doubt, viewed by the Continental Anglo-
maniacs under too rosy a light, but still, in outline, re-
cognisably national—these were what fascinated, in their
different ways, Voltaire, Prévost, Diderot, and above all
Rousseau. Conducted by these enthusiasts, the literature of barbarous England was received with open arms
in all the academies and salons of Europe, and a new
literature was everywhere stimulated into existence by the
rivalry of such Englishmen as Young, Richardson, and
Hume. On the other hand, it is impossible to overlook
the influence of Montesquieu on such English minds as
those of Gray, Gibbon, and Adam Ferguson ; and the
Scotch writers, in particular, consciously Gallicised their
style, in the pursuit of that elegant plausibility which they
found so charming in French models. These reverberations of taste aided one another, and increased the facility
with which English and Continental readers acquainted
themselves mutually with the rival literature. But this
marks a condition of things hitherto unparalleled, and we
may roughly give the year 1750 as the date at which the
wall which had from the earliest times surrounded and
concealed our intellectual products, began to crumble
down and expose us to the half-admiring, half-scornful
gaze of Europe.

This communion with exotic forms of intelligence, and
the renewed sympathy for antique and romantic forms
of thought and expression, tended, no doubt, to prepare

our literature for the revolution which was coming. But even so late as 1780 there were few signs of change. Individual men of genius forced the language to say for them and through them things which had not been said before, but the pedagogic shackles were practically un-loosened. It was in the insidious forms of "sensibility," as it was called, the new species of tender and self-satisfying pity, that the rigid rules of life were being most directly broken. This warm stream of sentiment, amounting at times to something like enthusiasm, tended to melt the horny or stony crust which the recognised conditions of thought had spread over every kind of literature. Grace, eloquence, intellectual curiosity, dignity —all these were still possible under the hard formular régime ; but the more spiritual movements of the mind— lyrical passion, daring speculation, real sublimity, splendid caprice—were quite impossible within a space so cramped, and were, as a matter of fact, scarcely attempted.

When we consider, then, how unfavourable the con-ditions were in which literature was confined during the central years of the eighteenth century, we may marvel, not at the poverty, but at the richness of the actual pro-duct. If the creation of the novel was the greatest triumph of the age, it was not its only one. These years brought forth a number of men whose intellectual vitality was so commanding that it negatived the sterile qualities of the soil from which they sprang. If Butler, Gibbon, Johnson, and Gray had been born in an age which aided instead of retarding the flow of their ideas, their periods might have been fuller, their ornament more splendid. But so intense was their individuality, so definite their sense of what their gift was to the age, that they over-came their disabilities and produced work which we,

18

regarding it with deep sympathy and respect, cannot conceive being cast in a form more pertinent or more characteristic. And it is a sentimental error to suppose that the winds of God blow only through the green tree ; it is sometimes the dry tree which is peculiarly favourable to their passage.

VIII

THE AGE OF WORDSWORTH

1780–1815

THE period which immediately preceded and accompanied the French Revolution was one of violent and complete transition in English literature. The long frost of classicism broke up ; the sealed fountains of romantic expression forced their way forth, and then travelled smoothly on upon their melodious courses. The act of release, then, is the predominant interest to us in a general survey, and the progress of liberated romance the main object of our study. Poetry once more becomes the centre of critical attention, and proves the most important branch of literature cultivated in England. The solitary figure of Burke attracts towards the condition of prose an observation otherwise riveted upon the singularly numerous and varied forms in which poetry is suddenly transforming itself. As had been the case two hundred years before, verse came abruptly to the front in England, and absorbed all public attention.

Among the factors which led to the enfranchisement of the imagination, several date from the third quarter of the eighteenth century. Johnson's famous and diverting *Lives of the Poets* was raised as a bulwark against forces which that sagacious critic had long felt to be advancing, and which he was determined to withstand.

The Aristotelian rules, the monotony of versification, the insistence on abstract ideas and conventional verbiage—the whole panoply of classicism under which poetry had gone forth to battle in serried ranks since 1660 was now beginning to be discredited. The Gallic code was found insufficient, for Gray had broken up the verse ; Collins had introduced a plaintive, flute-like note ; Thomson had looked straight at nature; then the timid protest had given scandal, while Churchill and Goldsmith had gone back to the precise tradition. But 1760–70 produced a second and stronger effort in revolt, founded on archaistic research. Antiquaries had gone dimly searching after the sources of Middle English, and Chatterton had forged the Rowley poems ; Warton had glorified Spenser, and Percy had edited his inspiring *Reliques.* Most of all, the pent-up spirit of lyricism, that instinct for untrammelled song which the eighteenth century had kept so closely caged, had been stimulated to an eager beating of its wings by the mysterious deliverances of the pseudo-Ossian.

On the whole, this last, although now so tarnished and visibly so spurious, seems to have been at that time the most powerful of all the influences which made for the revival of romanticism in England. Thousands of readers, accustomed to nothing more stimulating than Young and Blair, reading the Desolation of Balclutha and Ossian's Address to the Sun with rapture, found a new hunger for song awakened in their hearts, and felt their pulses tingling with mystery and melody. They did not ask themselves too closely what the rhapsody was all about, nor quibble at the poorness of the ideas and the limited range of the images. What Gessner gave and Rousseau, what the dying century longed for in that subdued hysteria which was presently to break forth in political violence, was produced to excess by the vibrations of those shadowy harp-strings which unseen fingers plucked above the Caledonian graves of Fingal and Malvina. *Ossian* had nothing of position and solid value to present to Europe; but it washed away the old order of expression, and it prepared a clear field for Goethe, Wordsworth, and Chateaubriand.

But, in the meantime, four poets of widely various talent arrest our attention during the last years of the century. Of these, two, Cowper and Crabbe, endeavoured to support the old tradition ; Burns and Blake were entirely indifferent to it—such, at least, is the impression which their work produces on us, whatever may have been their private wish or conviction. Certain dates are of value in emphasising the practically simultaneous appearance of these poets of the transition. Cowper's *Table Talk* was published in 1782, and the *Task* in 1785. Crabbe's clearly defined first period opens with the *Candidate* of 1780, and closes with the *Newspaper* of 1785. Blake's *Poetical Sketches* date from 1783, and the *Songs of Innocence* from 1787. If the world in general is acquainted with a single bibliographical fact, it is aware that the Kilmarnock Burns was issued in 1786. Here, then, is a solid body of poetry evidently marked out for the notice of the historian, a definite group of verse inviting his inspection and his classification. Unfortunately, attractive and interesting as each of these poets is, it is exceedingly difficult to persuade ourselves that they form anything like a school, or are proceeding in approximately the same direction. If a writer less like Crabbe than Burns is to be found in literature, it is surely Blake, and a parallel between Cowper and Burns would reduce a critic to despair.

At first sight we simply see the following general phenomena. Here is WILLIAM COWPER, a writer of great elegance and amenity, the soul of gentle wit and urbane grace, engaged in continuing and extending the work of Thomson, advancing the exact observation of natural objects, without passion, without vitality, without a trace of lyrical effusion, yet distinguished from his eighteenth-century predecessors by a resistance to their affected, rhetorical diction; a very pure, limpid, tender talent, all light without fire or vapour. Then, here is GEORGE CRABBE, whom Byron would have done better to call "Dryden in worsted stockings," a dense, rough, strongly vitalised narrator, without a touch of revolt against the conventions of form, going back, indeed—across Goldsmith and Pope—to the precise prosody used by Dryden at the close of his life for telling tragical stories; a writer absolutely retrogressive, as it at first seems, rejecting all suggestion of change, and completely satisfied with the old media for his peculiar impressions, which are often vehement, often sinister, sometimes very prosaic and dull, but generally sincere and direct—Crabbe, a great, solid talent, without grace, or flexibility, or sensitiveness.

Then here is WILLIAM BLAKE, for whom the classic forms and traditions have nothing to say at all; whose ethereal imagination and mystic mind have taken their deepest impressions from the Elizabethan dramatists and from Ossian; whose aim, fitfully and feverishly accomplished, is to fling the roseate and cerulean fancies of his brain on a gossamer texture woven out of the songs of Shakespeare and the echoes of Fingal's airy hall; a poet this for whom time, and habit, and the conventions of an age do not exist; who is no more nor less at home in 1785 than he would be in 1585 or 1985; on whom his own epoch, with its tastes and limitations, has left no mark whatever; a being all sensitiveness and lyric passion, and delicate, aerial mystery.

And finally, here is ROBERT BURNS, the incarnation of natural song, the embodiment of that which is most spontaneous, most ebullient in the lyrical part of nature. With Burns the reserve and quietism of the eighteenth century broke up. There were no longer Jesuit rules of composition, no longer dread of enthusiasm, no longer a rigorous demand that reason or intellect should take the first place in poetical composition. Intellect, it must be confessed, counts for little in this amazing poetry, where instinct claims the whole being, and yields only to the imagination. After more than a century of sober, thoughtful writers, Burns appears, a song-intoxicated man, exclusively inspired by emotion and the stir of the blood. He cannot tell why he is moved. He uses the old conventional language to describe the new miracle of his sensations. "I never hear," he says, "the loud, solitary whistle of the curlew in a summer noon, or the wild mixing cadence of a troop of gray plovers in an autumnal morning, without feeling an elevation of soul like the enthusiasm of devotion or poetry." This is the prose of the eighteenth century; but when the same ideas burst forth into metre:

> " *The Muse, nae poet ever fand her,*
> *Till by himsel' he learned to wander,*
> *Adown some trotting burn's meander,*
> *And no think lang;*
> *O sweet to stray, and pensive ponder*
> *A heart-felt sang*"—

we start to discover that here is something quite novel,

a mode of writing unparalleled in its easy, buoyant emotion since the days of Elizabeth.

We have spoken of Burns as he comes to us in the sequence of the great poets of Britain. In Scottish poetry he takes a somewhat different place. Here he seems not one in a chain, but the supreme artist to whom all others are merely subsidiary. Scotch Doric verse appears to us like a single growth, starting from the rich foliage of Dunbar and his compeers, up the slender stem of Alexander Scott, of the Sempills, of Montgomery, of Allan Ramsay, of the song-writers of the eighteenth century, swelling into the fine opening bud of Fergusson, only to break into the single aloe-blossom of the perfect Burns. All local Scottish verse, from the early sixteenth century until to-day, presupposes Burns ; it all expands towards him or dwindles from him. If his works were entirely to disappear, we could re-create some idea of his genius from the light that led to it and from the light that withdraws from it. This absolute supremacy of Burns, to perfect whose amazing art the Scottish race seemed to suppress and to despoil itself, is a very remarkable phenomenon. Burns is not merely the national poet of Scotland ; he is, in a certain sense, the country itself : all elements of Scotch life and manners, all peculiarities of Scotch temperament and conviction, are found embroidered somewhere or other on Burns's variegated singing-robes.

It is obvious that these four great poets of the Eighties are not merely "great" in very various degree, but are singularly unlike one another. Cowper so literary, Crabbe so conventional, Blake so transcendental, Burns so spontaneous and passionate—there seems no sort of relation between them. The first two look backward resolutely, the third resolutely upward, the fourth broadly stretches himself on the impartial bosom of nature, careless of all rules and conventions. It appears impossible to bring them into line, to discover a direction in which all four can be seen to move together. But in reality there is to be discovered in each of them the protest against rhetoric which was to be the keynote of revolt, the protest already being made by Goethe and Wieland, and so soon to be echoed by Alfieri and André Chenier. There was in each of the four British poets, who illuminated this darkest period just before the dawn, the determination to be natural and sincere. It was this that gave Cowper his directness and his delicacy ; it was this which stamps with the harsh mark of truth the sombre vignettes of Crabbe, just as truly as it gave voluptuous ecstasy to the songs of Blake, and to the strong, homely verse of Burns its potent charm and mastery.

It was reality that was rising to drive back into oblivion the demons of conventionality, of " regular diction," of the proprieties and machinery of composition, of all the worn-out bogies with which poetical old women frightened the baby talents of the end of the eighteenth century. Not all was done, even by these admirable men : in Burns himself we constantly hear the old verbiage grating and grinding on ; in his slow movements Crabbe is not to be distinguished from his predecessors of a hundred years ; Cowper is for ever showing qualities of grace and elegant amenity which tempt us to call him, not a forerunner of the nineteenth, but the finest example of the eighteenth-century type. Yet the revolt against rhetorical convention is uppermost, and that it is which is really the characteristic common feature of this singularly dissimilar quartette ;

and when the least inspired, the least revolutionary of
the four takes us along the dismal coast that his childhood knew so well, and bids us mark how

> " *Here on its wiry stem, in rigid bloom,*
> *Grows the salt lavender that lacks perfume;*
> *Here the dwarf sallows creep, the septfoil harsh,*
> *And the soft, shiny mallow of the marsh,*"

we observe that the reign of empty verbiage is over, and
that the poets who shall for the future wish to bring
concrete ideas before us will do so in sincere and exact
language.   That position once regained, the revival of
imaginative writing is but a question of time and of
opportunity.

A very singular circumstance was the brevity of duration of this school of the Eighties, if school it can be
called.   Burns was unknown until 1786, and in 1796 he
died.   Cowper's original productions, so far as they were
not posthumous, were presented to the world in 1782
and 1785, and for nine years before his death in 1800,
he had been removed from human intercourse.   Blake
remained as completely invisible as any one of his own elemental angels, and his successive collections can scarcely
be said to have done more than exist, since even those
which were not, like the Prophetic Books, distributed
in a species of manuscript were practically unobserved.
Crabbe had a very curious literary history : his career was
divided into two distinct portions, the one extending from
1780 to 1785, the other continued from 1807 ; from his
thirty-first to his fifty-third year Crabbe was obstinately
silent.   We may say, therefore, that the transitional
period in English poetry, hanging unattached between
the classical and the romantic age, lasted from 1780 to
1786.   During these seven years a great deal of admirable

verse was brought before the observation of English readers, who had to make the best they could of it until the real romantic school began in 1798. In Cowper, Crabbe, Burns, and Blake, we look in vain for any exotic influence of any importance. Cowper was a good scholar and translated Homer, but Greek poetry left no mark on his style; the others were innocent of ancient learning, and they were united in this also, that they are exclusively, almost provincially, British.

Meanwhile, the old classical tradition did not perceive itself to be undermined. If criticism touched these poets at all—Blake evaded it, by Burns it was bewildered—it judged them complacently by the old canons. They did not possess, in the eyes of contemporaries, anything of the supreme isolation which we now award to them. The age saw them accompanied by a crowd of bards of the old class, marshalled under the laureateship of Whitehead, and of these several had an air of importance. Among these minnows, ERASMUS DARWIN was a triton who threw his preposterous scientific visions into verse of metallic brilliance, and succeeded in finishing what Dryden had begun. But with this partial and academic exception, everything that was written, except in the form of satire, between 1780 and 1798, in the old manner, merely went further to prove the absolute decadence and wretchedness to which the classical school of British poetry was reduced.

It was a happy instinct to turn once more to foreign forms of poetic utterance, and a certain credit attaches to those who now began to cultivate the sonnet. Two slender collections, the one by Thomas Russell, and the other by William Lisle Bowles, both of which appeared in 1789, exhibited the results of the study of Petrarch.

Of these two men, Russell, who died prematurely in 1788, was the better as well as the more promising poet; his *Philoctetes in Lemnos* is doubtless the finest English sonnet of the century. But he attracted little notice; while Bowles was fortunate enough to extend a powerful and, to say the truth, an unaccountable spell over Coleridge, who doubtless brought to the mild quatorzains of Bowles much more than he found there. Russell was the first English imitator of the budding romantic poetry of Germany. It is necessary to mention here the pre-Wordsworthian, or, more properly, pre-Byronic, publications of Samuel Rogers — the *Poems* of 1786, the accomplished and mellifluous *Pleasures of Memory* of 1792, the *Epistle to a Friend* of 1798. These were written in a style, or in a neutral tint of all safe styles mingled, that elegantly recalls the easier parts of Goldsmith. Here, too, there was some faint infusion of Italian influence. But truly the early Rogers survives so completely on traditional sufferance that it is not needful to say more about it here; a much later Rogers will demand a word a little further on.

But an event was now preparing of an importance in the history of English literature so momentous that all else appears insignificant by its side. In June 1797 a young Cambridge man named SAMUEL TAYLOR COLERIDGE, who was devoted to poetry, paid a visit to another young Cambridge man named WILLIAM WORDSWORTH, who was then settled with his sister Dorothy near Crewkerne, in Dorset. The Wordsworths had been deeply concerned in poetical experiment, and William showed to his guest a fragment which he had lately composed in blank verse; we may read it now as the opening of the first book of the *Excursion.* Coleridge was overwhelmed; he pronounced the poem "superior to any-thing in our language which in any way resembled it," and he threw in his lot unreservedly with Wordsworth. The brother and sister were then just in the act to move to a house called Alfoxden, in West Somerset, where they settled in July 1797. Coleridge was then living at Nether Stowey, close by, a spur of the Quantocks and two romantic coombes lying between them. On these delicious hills, in sight of the yellow Bristol Channel, English poetry was born again during the autumn months of 1797, in the endless walks and talks of the three enthusiasts—three, since Dorothy Wordsworth, though she wrote not, was a sharer, if not an originator, in all their audacities and inspirations.

Wordsworth and Coleridge had each published collec-tions of verses, containing some numbers of a certain merit, founded on the best descriptive masters of the eighteenth century. But what they had hitherto given to the public appeared to them mere dross by the glow of their new illumination. Dorothy Wordsworth appears to have long been drawn towards the minute and sensitive study of natural phenomena; William Wordsworth already divined his philosophy of land-scape; Coleridge was thus early an impassioned and imaginative metaphysician. They now distributed their gifts to one another, and kindled in each a hotter fire of impulse. A year went by, and the enthusiasts of the Quantocks published, in September 1798, the little volume of *Lyrical Ballads* which put forth in modest form the results of their combined lucubrations. Mrs. S. T. Coleridge, who was not admitted to the meditations of the poetic three, gaily announced that "the *Lyrical Ballads* are not liked at all by any," and this was, rather crudely put, the general first opinion of the public. It is proper that we should remind ourselves what this epoch-making volume contained.

It was anonymous, and nothing indicated the authorship, although the advertisements might reveal that Southey, Lamb, Lloyd, and Coleridge himself were of the confraternity to which its author or authors belonged. The contributions of Wordsworth were nineteen, of Coleridge only four ; but among these last, one, the *Rime of the Ancyent Marinere*, was of preponderating length and value, "professedly written," so the preface said, "in imitation of the *style* as well as of the spirit of the elder poets." This very wonderful poem, Coleridge's acknowledged masterpiece, had been composed in November 1797, and finished, so Dorothy records, on "a beautiful evening, very starry, the hornèd moon shining." A little later *Christabel* was begun, and, in "a lonely farmhouse between Porlock and Lynton" (probably early in 1798), *Kubla Khan*. Neither of these, however, nor the magnificent *Ode to France*, nor *Fears in Solitude*, make their appearance in the *Lyrical Ballads* of 1798. In this volume Wordsworth is predominant, and his contributions exemplify two of his chief aims in poetical revolution. He desired to destroy the pompous artificiality of verse-diction and to lower the scale of subjects deemed worthy of poetical treatment; in this he was but partly judicious, and such experiments as "Anecdote for Fathers" and the "Idiot Boy" gave scoffers an occasion to blaspheme. But Wordsworth also designed to introduce into verse an impassioned consideration of natural scenes and objects as a reflection of the complex life of man, and in this he effected a splendid revolution. To match such a lyric as the "Tables Turn'd" it was necessary to return to the age of Milton, and in the "Lines written a Few Miles above Tintern Abbey," Wordsworth somewhat shyly slipped in at the end of the volume a statement of his literary creed, and an example of the new manner of writing so noble, so full, and so momentous, that it has never been excelled, even by himself. '

Thus, in a little russet volume published at Bristol, and anonymously put forth by two struggling lads of extreme social obscurity, the old order of things literary was finally and completely changed. The romantic school began, the classic school disappeared, in the autumn of 1798. It would be a great error, of course, to suppose that this revolution was patent to the world : the incomparable originality and value of "Tintern Abbey" was noted, as is believed, by one solitary reader ; the little book passed as a collection of irregular and somewhat mediocre verse, written by two eccentric young men suspected of political disaffection. But the change was made, nevertheless ; the marvellous verses were circulated, and everywhere they created disciples. So stupendous was the importance of the verse written on the Quantocks in 1797 and 1798, that if Wordsworth and Coleridge had died at the close of the latter year we should indeed have lost a great deal of valuable poetry, especially of Wordsworth's ; but the direction taken by literature would scarcely have been modified in the slightest degree. The association of these intensely brilliant and inflammatory minds at what we call the psychological moment, produced full-blown and perfect the exquisite new flower of romantic poetry.

Burns had introduced "a natural delineation of human passions ;" Cowper had rebelled against "the gaudiness and inane phraseology" of the eighteenth century in its decay ; Crabbe had felt that "the language of conversation in the middle and lower classes of society is adapted to the purposes of poetic pleasure." These phrases, from the original preface of 1798, did not clearly enough define the objects of Wordsworth and Coleridge. To the enlarged second edition, therefore, of 1800, the former prefixed a more careful and lucid statement of their distinguishing principles. This preface, extending to nearly fifty pages, is the earliest of those disquisitions on the art of verse which would give Wordsworth high rank among critics if the lustre of his prose were not lost in the blaze of his poetry.

During these last two years of the century the absolute necessity for a radical reform of literature had impressed itself upon many minds. Wordsworth found himself the centre of a group of persons, known to him or unknown, who were anxious that "a class of poetry should be produced" on the lines indicated in "Tintern Abbey," and who believed that it would be "well adapted to interest mankind permanently," which the poetry of the older school had manifestly ceased to do. It was to these observers, these serious disciples, that the important manifesto of 1800 was addressed. This was no case of genius working without consciousness of its own aim; there was neither self-delusion nor mock-modesty about Wordsworth. He considered his mission to be one of extreme solemnity. He had determined that no "indolence" should "prevent him from endeavouring to ascertain what was his duty," and he was convinced that that duty was called to redeem poetry in England from a state of "depravity," and to start the composition of "poems materially different from those upon which general approbation is [in 1800] at present bestowed." He was determined to build up a new art on precept and example, and this is what he did achieve with astonishing completeness.

In the neighbourhood of the Quantocks, where he arrived at the very moment that his powers were at their ripest and his genius eager to expand, Wordsworth found himself surrounded by rustic types of a pathetic order, the conditions of whose life were singularly picturesque. He was in the state of transition between the ignorance of youth and that hardness and density of apprehension which invaded his early middle life. His observation was keen and yet still tender and ductile. He was accompanied and stimulated in his investigations by his incomparable sister. To them came Coleridge, swimming in a lunar radiance of sympathy and sentimental passion, casting over the more elementary instincts of the Wordsworths the distinction of his elaborate intellectual experience. Together on the ferny hills, in the deep coombes, by " Kilve's sounding shore," the wonderful trio discussed, conjectured, planned, and from the spindles of their talk there was swiftly spun the magic web of modern romantic poetry. They determined, as Wordsworth says, that "the passions of men should be incorporated with the beautiful and permanent forms of nature." All elements were there—the pathetic peasants, the pure solitudes of hill and wood and sky, the enthusiastic perception of each of these, the moment in the history of the country, the companionship and confraternity which circulate the tongues of fire—and accordingly the process of combination and creation was rapid and conclusive.

There are, perhaps, no two other English poets of anything like the same importance who resemble one

19

another so closely as do Wordsworth and Coleridge at the outset of their career. They were engaged together, to a degree which it is difficult for us to estimate to-day, in breaking down the false canons of criticism which rhetorical writers had set up, and in recurring to a proper and beautiful use of common English. In so doing and writing in close companionship, interested in the same phenomena, immersed in the same scenery, it is not extraordinary that the style that each adopted strictly resembled the style of the other. This is especially true of their blank verse, a form which both sedulously cultivated, in which both enshrined some of their most characteristic thoughts, and in which both were equally engaged in destroying that wooden uniformity of pause and cadence with which Akenside had corrupted the cold but stately verse of Thomson. Who was to decide by whom the " Nightingale " and by whom the " Night-Piece " of 1798 were written ? The accent, the attitude, were almost precisely identical.

Yet distinctions there were, and as we become familiar with the two poets these predominate more and more over the superficial likeness. Coleridge is conspicuous, to a degree beyond any other writer between Spenser and Rossetti, for a delicate, voluptuous languor, a rich melancholy, and a pitying absorption without vanity in his own conditions and frailties, carried so far that the natural objects of his verse take the qualities of the human Coleridge upon themselves. In Wordsworth we find a purer, loftier note, a species of philosophical severity which is almost store, a freshness of atmosphere which contrasts with Coleridge's opaline dream-haze, magnifying and distorting common things. Truth, sometimes pursued to the confines or past the confines of triviality, is Wordsworth's first object, and he never stoops to self-pity, rarely to self-study. Each of these marvellous poets is pre-eminently master of the phrase that charms and intoxicates, the sequence of simple words so perfect that it seems at once inevitable and miraculous. Yet here also a very distinct difference may be defined between the charm of Wordsworth and the magic of Coleridge. The former is held more under the author's control than the latter, and is less impulsive. It owes its impressiveness to a species of lofty candour which kindles at the discovery of some beautiful truth not seen before, and gives the full intensity of passion to its expression. The latter is a sort of Æolian harp (such as that with which he enlivened the street of Nether Stowey) over which the winds of emotion play, leaving the instrument often without a sound or with none but broken murmurs, yet sometimes dashing from its chords a melody, vague and transitory indeed, but of a most unearthly sweetness. Wordsworth was not a great metrist ; he essayed comparatively few and easy forms, and succeeded best when he was at his simplest. Coleridge, on the other hand, was an innovator ; his *Christabel* revolutionised English prosody and opened the door to a thousand experiments ; in *Kubla Khan* and in some of the lyrics, Coleridge attained a splendour of verbal melody which places him near the summit of the English Parnassus.

In an historical survey such as the present, it is necessary to insist on the fact that although Coleridge survived until 1834, and Wordsworth until 1850, the work which produced the revolution in poetic art was done before the close of 1800. It was done, so far as we can see, spontaneously. But in that year the Wordsworths and their friend proceeded to Germany, for the stated purpose of acquainting themselves with what the Teutonic world was achieving in literature.   In Hamburg they visited the aged Klopstock, but felt themselves far more cordially drawn towards the work of Bürger and Schiller, in whom they recognised poets of nature, who, like themselves, were fighting the monsters of an old, outworn classicism.   Wordsworth was but cautiously interested; he had just spoken scornfully of "sickly and stupid German tragedies."   Coleridge, on the other hand, was intoxicated with enthusiasm, and plunged into a detailed study of the history, language, and philosophy of Germany.   Bürger, whose *Lenore* (1774) had started European romanticism, was now dead; but Goethe and Schiller were at the height of their genius.   The last-mentioned had just produced his *Wallenstein*, and Coleridge translated or paraphrased it in two parts; these form one of the very few versions from any one language into another which may plausibly be held to excel the original.   In the younger men, with whom Coleridge should have been in more complete harmony—in Tieck, in the young, yet dying Novalis, in the Schlegels—Coleridge at this time took but little interest.   The fact is that, tempting as was to himself and Wordsworth then, and to us now, the idea of linking the German to the English revival, it was not very easy to contrive.   The movements were parallel, not correlated; the wind of revolt, passing over European poetry, struck Scandinavia and Germany first, then England, then Italy and France, but each in a manner which forced it to be independent of the rest.

For the next fifteen years poetry may be said to have been stationary in England.   It was not, for that reason, sluggish or unprolific; on the contrary, it was extremely

active. But its activity took the form of the gradual
acceptance of the new romantic ideas, the slow expul-
sion of the old classic taste, and the multiplication of
examples of what had once for all been supremely accomplished in the hollows of the Quantocks. The career
of the founders of the school during these years of settle-
ment and acceptation may be briefly given. At the very
close of 1800, Wordsworth went back to his own Cum-
brian county, and for the next half-century he resided,
practically without intermission, beside the little lakes
which he has made so famous, Grasmere and Rydal.
Here, after marrying in 1802, he lived in great simplicity and dignity, gradually becoming the centre of a
distinguished company of admirers. From 1799 to 1805
he was at work on the *Prelude,* a didactic poem in which
he elaborated his system of natural religion ; and he
began at Grasmere to use the sonnet with a persistent
mastery and with a freedom such as it had not known
since the days of Milton. In 1814 the publication of
the *Excursion* made a great sensation, at first not wholly
favourable, and gave to the service of Wordsworth some
of the pleasures of martyrdom. In 1815 the poet collected his lyrical writings.

This date, 1814–15, therefore, is critical in the career
of Wordsworth : it forced his admirers and his de-
tractors alike to consider what was the real nature of
the innovation which he had introduced, and to what
extreme it could be pushed. In 1815 he once more
put forth his views on the art of verse in a brilliant
prose essay, which may be regarded as his final, or
at least maturest utterance on the subject. At this
moment a change came over the aspect of his genius :
he was now forty-five years of age, and the freshness

of his voice, which had lasted so long, was beginning to fail.   He had a brief Virgilian period, when he wrote "Laodamia" and "Dion," and then the beautiful talent hardened into rhetoric and sing-song.   Had Wordsworth passed away in 1815 instead of 1850, English literature had scarcely been the poorer.   Of Coleridge there is even less to be said.   His career was a miserable tissue of irregularity, domestic discord, and fatal indulgence in opium.   In 1812 he recast his old drama of *Osorio* as *Remorse*, a fine romantic tragedy on Jacobean lines.   He was occasionally adding a few lines to the delicious pamphlet of poetry which at length found a publisher in 1817 as *Sibylline Leaves*.   Yet even here, all that was really important had been composed before the end of the eighteenth century.   Save for one or two pathetic and momentary revivals of lyric power, Coleridge died as a poet before he was thirty.

The name of ROBERT SOUTHEY has scarcely been mentioned yet, although it is customary to connect it indissolubly with those of his great friends.   He was slightly younger than they, but more precocious, and as early as 1793 he somewhat dazzled them by the success of his *Joan of Arc*.   From that time forth until shortly before his death, in 1843, Southey never ceased to write.   He was always closely identified in domestic relations with Wordsworth, whose neighbour he was in the Lakes for forty years, and with Coleridge, who was his brother-in-law. He early accepted what we may call the dry bones of the romantic system, and he published a series of ambitious epics—*Thalaba*, in 1801 ; *Madoc*, in 1805 ; *Kehama*, in 1810 ; *Roderick*, in 1814—which he intended as contributions to the new poetry.   His disciple and latest unflinching admirer, Sir Henry Taylor, has told us that

Southey "took no pleasure in poetic passion"—a melancholy admission. We could have guessed as much from his voluminous and vigorous writing, from which imagination is conspicuously absent, though eloquence, vehemence, fluency, and even fancy are abundant. The best part of Southey was his full admiration of some aspects of good literature, and his courageous support of unpopular specimens of these. When Wordsworth was attacked, Southey said, in his authoritative way, "A greater poet than Wordsworth there never has been, nor ever will be." He supported the original romantic movement by his praise, his weighty personality, the popular character of his contributions. But he added nothing to it; he could not do so, since, able and effective man of letters as he was, Southey was not, in any intelligible sense, himself a poet.

What effect the new ideas could produce on a perfectly ductile fancy may be observed in a very interesting way in the case of THOMAS CAMPBELL. This young Scotchman, born in 1777, had evidently seen no poetry more modern than that of Johnson, Goldsmith, and Rogers, when he published his *Pleasures of Hope* in 1799. The very name of this work discovered its adhesion to eighteenth-century tradition. It was a tame, "correct" essay, in a mode already entirely outworn. As a student it had been Campbell's pride to be styled "the Pope of Glasgow." When he became aware of them, he rejected all the proposed reforms of Wordsworth, whose work he continued to detest throughout his life; but in 1800 he proceeded to Germany, where he fell completely under the spell of the romantic poets of that nation, and in 1803 gave to the world "Lochiel," "Hohenlinden," and the "Exile of Erin." These were succeeded by other

spirited ballads, amatory and martial, and in 1809 by a
romantic epic in Spenserian stanza, *Gertrude of Wyoming*,
in which Campbell's style is wholly Teutonised. After
this Campbell wrote little that was readable, and his
fame, once far greater than that of Coleridge and Wordsworth, has now dwindled to an unjust degree. He had a
remarkable gift for lucid, rapid, and yet truly poetical
narrative ; his naval odes or descants, the " Battle of the
Baltic " and " Ye Mariners of England," are without rivals
in their own class, and Campbell deserves recognition as
a true romanticist and revolutionary force in poetry,
although fighting for his own hand, and never under the
flag of Wordsworth and Coleridge. For the time being,
however, Campbell did more than they—more, perhaps,
than any other writer save one—to break down in popular
esteem the didactic convention of the classic school.

A still greater force in popularising and fixing the
romantic tradition was Sir WALTER SCOTT in the poetry
of his early middle life—that is to say, from 1799 to
1814. From the dawn of childhood he had shown an
extraordinary passion for listening to chivalrous and
adventurous tales, and for composing the like. He was
fortunate enough to see and to be greatly moved by
Burns ; and as he advanced, the intense Scotticism of his
nature was emphasised by the longing to enshrine Scotch
prowess and nature in picturesque verse. The mode in
which this was to be done had not even dimly occurred
to him, when he met with that lodestar of romanticism,
the *Lenore* of Bürger ; he translated it, and was led to
make fresh eager inroads into German poetry, with which
he was much more in sympathy than Wordsworth was,
or even Coleridge. As early as 1799 Scott published a
version of *Goetz von Berlichingen*. Even Goethe, how-

ever, did not at this time persuade Scott to make a deep study of literature ; he was still far more eager to learn in the open school of experience. He imitated a few German ballads, and he presently began to collect the native songs of his own country ; the far-reaching result was the publication of the *Scottish Minstrelsy* (1802).

Still, nothing showed that Walter Scott was likely to become an original writer, and he was thirty-four when Europe was electrified with the appearance of the *Lay of the Last Minstrel* in 1805. Then followed *Marmion* in 1808, the *Lady of the Lake* in 1810, and the *Lord of the Isles* in 1815, not to speak of other epical narratives which were not so successful. Meanwhile, the publication of *Waverley*, in 1814, opened another and a still more splendid door to the genius of Scott, and he bade farewell to the Muses. But from 1805 to 1815 he was by far the most prominent British poet; as Wordsworth put it, Scott was "the whole world's darling," and no one, perhaps, before or since, has approached the width and intensity of his popularity. While Wordsworth distributed a few hundreds of his books, and Coleridge could not induce his to move at all, Scott's poetry sold in tens of thousands, and gave the tone to society. At the present day something of the charm of Scott's verse-narratives has certainly evaporated ; they are read for the story, a fatal thing to confess about poetry. The texture of Scott's prosody is thinner and looser than that of his great contemporaries, nor are his reflections so penetrating or so exquisite as the best of theirs. Nevertheless, the divine freshness and exuberance of Scott are perennial in several of his episodes, and many of his songs are of the highest positive excellence. Perhaps if he had possessed a more delicate ear, a subtler sense of the phases of landscape, something of that mysticism and passion which we unwillingly have to admit that we miss in his poetry, he might not have interpreted so lucidly to millions of readers the principles of the romantic revival.   With his noble disregard of self, he bade those who sought the higher qualities find them in Wordsworth; but Scott also, with his vigour of invention and his masculine sense of flowing style, took a prominent and honourable part in the reformation of English poetry.

These, then, were the influences at work during the fifteen years with which the century opened, and so completely was the old tradition overcome that poetry of the class of Johnson and Pope abruptly ceased, not, indeed, to be admired, but to be composed. A little group of pious writers, of whom Bloomfield and Grahame may be named, endeavoured to keep blank verse and the heroic couplet as they had received it from their Thomsonian forefathers.   But although the *Farmer's Boy* (1798) and the *Sabbath* (1802) had many imitators and enjoyed a preposterous popularity, their influence was quite outside the main channels of literary activity.   The critics stormed against the reforms introduced by Wordsworth, and ridiculed his splendid experiments.   But after the preface of 1800 nobody who had any genuine poetic gift could go on writing in the eighteenth-century way, and, as a curious matter of fact, no one except the satirists did attempt to do so.

But it is time to turn to the condition of prose, which, however, offers us at this juncture in our history fewer phenomena of importance.   The one great prose-writer of the close of the eighteenth century was EDMUND BURKE, and his peculiarities are to be studied to best effect in what

he wrote between 1790 and his death in 1797. Burke is
therefore strictly transitional, and it is not less rational
to consider him as the forerunner of De Quincey than
as the successor of Robertson and Gibbon. He is really
alone in the almost extravagant splendour of his oratory,
too highly coloured for the eighteenth century, too hard
and resonant for the nineteenth. When Burke is at his
best, as for instance in the *Letter to a Noble Lord* of 1796,
it is difficult to admit that any one has ever excelled him
in the melody of his sentences, the magnificence of his
invective, the trumpet-blast of his sonorous declamation.
It is said that Burke endeavoured to mould his style on
that of Dryden. No resemblance between the richly
brocaded robes of the one and the plain russet of the
other can be detected. It is not quite certain that the
influence of Burke on succeeding prose has been altogether beneficial; he has seemed to encourage a kind of
hollow vehemence, an affectation of the " grand style "
which in less gifted rhetoricians has covered poverty of
thought. We must take Burke as he is, without com-
paring him with others; he is the great exception, the
man essentially an orator whose orations were yet literature. There is an absence of emotional imagination,
however, in Burke which is truly typical of the rhetor.
In this, as in so much else, Burke is seen still to belong
to the eighteenth century. He died just when the young
folks in Western Somerset were working out their revolutionary formulas in verse; he missed even the chance
of having these presented to his attention. We may be
absolutely certain, however, that he would have rejected
them with as much scorn and anger as he evinced for the
political principles of the French Revolution. Whoever
might have smiled on Goody Blake and Betty Foy, it

would not have been the fierce and inflexible author of the letters *On a Regicide Peace*.

It was, perhaps, a fortunate thing for literature that Burke should die at that juncture and at the meridian of his powers. His last Tracts sum up the prose of the century with a magnificent burst of sincere and transcendent ardour. He retains the qualities which had adorned the dying age, its capacity in the manipulation of abstract ideas, its desire for the attainment of intellectual truth, its elegant and persuasive sobriety, its limited but exquisitely balanced sense of literary form. But Burke was a statesman too, and here he turns away from his eighteenth-century predecessors ; he will be bound by no chains of abstract reasoning. Theories of politics were to him "the great Serbonian bog" ; he refused to listen to metaphysical discussions ; when he was dealing with American taxation, " I hate the very sound of them," he said. As he grew older, his mind, always moving in the train of law and order, grew steadily more and more conservative. He rejected the principles of Rousseau with scorn, and when there arose before him a "vast, tremendous, unformed spectre" in the far more terrific guise of the French Revolution, Burke lost not a little of his self-command. He died with the prophetic shrieks of the *Regicide Peace* still echoing in men's ears ; he died without a gleam of hope for England or for Europe, his intellect blazing at its highest incandescence in what he believed to be the deepening twilight of the nations.

Against Burke there wrote the revolutionary rhetoricians, those who saw the colours of dawn, not of sunset, in the blood-red excesses of the French. Richard Price and Joseph Priestley were the leaders of this movement in idea;

but in style they remained heavy and verbose, handing down the heritage of Locke to Bentham and Godwin. Priestley, after, in 1791, having his house wrecked and his scientific instruments destroyed, as a popular punishment for his sympathy with the Revolution, lived on until 1804 to see something like a justification of his prophecies. These men were the pathetic victims of Burke's splendid indignation, but in 1791 a direct attack on the *Reflections* took up the cudgels in defence. This was the once-famous *Rights of Man*, by Tom Paine, an audacious work, the circulation of which was so enormous that it had a distinct effect in colouring public opinion. A sturdier and more modern writer of the same class was WILLIAM GODWIN, whose *Political Justice* (1793) shows a great advance in lucidity and command of logical language. He has been compared, surely to his own moral advantage, with Condorcet ; but there is no question that he was curiously related to the French precursors of the Revolution, and particularly to Rousseau and Helvetius, from whom he caught, with their republican ardour, not a little of the clear merit of their style.

The spirit of change was everywhere in the air, and it showed itself in the field of diverting literature no less than in that of political controversy. The growth of mediævalism in fiction has been traced back to Horace Walpole's *Castle of Otranto* (1764), where the supernatural was boldly introduced into pseudo-Gothic romance. This innovation was greatly admired, and presently, having been reinforced by the influence of German neo-mediæval narrative, was copiously imitated. In the last decade of the eighteenth century, Mrs. Radcliffe, M. G. Lewis, and Beckford, presently followed by Maturin, founded what has been called the School of Terror, in the form of romantic novels in which fear was treated as the dominant passion. These " bogey" stories were very widely appreciated, and they served both to free the public mind from the fetters of conventional classic imagery, and to prepare it to receive impressions of enthusiasm and wonder. After having been shut up for more than a hundred years in the cage of a sort of sceptical indifferentism, the nature of man was blinded by the light of liberty, and staggered about bewildered by very strange phenomena. These crude romance-writers had a definite and immediate influence on the poets with whom the beginning of the next chapter will deal, but they also affected the whole future of English prose romance.

The Revolutionists created, mainly in order to impress their ideas more easily upon the public, a school of fiction which is interesting as leading in the opposite direction from Mrs. Radcliffe and Maturin, namely, towards the realistic and philosophical novel as we know it to-day. Bage, Hannah More, Holcroft, and even Godwin are not read any longer, and may be considered as having ceased to occupy any prominent position in our literature. But they form a valuable link between Fielding and Smollett on the one hand, and Jane Austen and the modern naturalistic school on the other. When the age was suddenly given over to sliding panels and echoing vaults, and the touch in the dark of " the mealy and carious bones of a skeleton," these humdrum novelists restored the balance of common-sense and waited for a return to sanity. The most difficult figure to fit in to any progressive scheme of English fiction is FRANCES BURNEY, who was actually alive with Samuel Richardson and with Mr. George Meredith. She wrote seldom, and published at long intervals ; her best novels, founded on a judicious study of Marivaux and Rousseau, implanted on a strictly British soil, were produced a little earlier than the moment we have now reached. Yet the *Wanderer* was published simultaneously with *Waverley*. She is a social satirist of a very sprightly order, whose early *Evelina* and *Cecilia* were written with an ease which she afterwards unluckily abandoned for an aping of the pomposity of her favourite lexicographer. Miss Burney was a delightful novelist in her youth, but she took no part in the progressive development of English literature.

In 1800 MARIA EDGEWORTH opened, with *Castle Rackrent*, the long series of her popular, moral, and fashionable tales. Their local colouring and distinctively Irish character made them noticeable; but even the warm praise of Scott and the more durable value of her stories for children have not prevented Miss Edgeworth from becoming obsolete. She prepares the way for the one prose-writer of this period whose genius has proved absolutely perdurable, who holds no lower a place in her own class than is held in theirs by Wordsworth, Coleridge, and Scott—for that impeccable JANE AUSTEN, whose fame becomes every day more inaccessible to the devastating forces of time and shifting fashion. It has long been seen, it was noted even by Macaulay, that the only writer with whom Jane Austen can fairly be compared is Shakespeare. It is obvious that she has nothing of his width of range or sublimity of imagination ; she keeps herself to that two-inch square of ivory of which she spoke in her proud and simple way. But there is no other English writer who possesses so much of Shakespeare's inevitability, or who produces such evidence of a like omniscience. Like Balzac, like Tourgenieff at his best,

Jane Austen gives the reader an impression of knowing everything there was to know about her creations, of being incapable of error as to their acts, thoughts, or emotions. She presents an absolute illusion of reality; she exhibits an art so consummate that we mistake it for nature. She never mixes her own temperament with those of her characters, she is never swayed by them, she never loses for a moment her perfect, serene control of them. Among the creators of the world, Jane Austen takes a place that is with the highest and that is purely her own.

The dates of publication of Miss Austen's novels are misleading if we wish to discover her exact place in the evolution of English literature. Astounding as it appears to-day, these incomparable books were refused by publishers from whose shops deciduous trash was pouring week by week. The vulgar novelists of the Minerva Press, the unspeakable Musgraves and Roches and Rosa Matildas, sold their incredible romances in thousands, while *Pride and Prejudice* went a-begging in MS. for nearly twenty years. In point of fact the six immortal books were written between 1796 and 1810, although their dates of issue range from 1811 to 1818. In her time of composition, then, she is found to be exactly the contemporary of Wordsworth and Coleridge in their reform of poetry, instead of impinging on the career of Sir Walter Scott as a romance-writer. Her methods, however, in no degree resemble those of the poets, and she has no conscious lesson of renaissance to teach. She does not share their interest in landscape; with her the scenery is a mere accessory. If she is with them at all, it is in her minute adherence to truth, in her instinctive abhorrence of anything approaching rhetoric, in her minute observation and literary employment of the detail of daily life. It is difficult to say that she was influenced by any predecessor, and, most unfortunately, of the history of her mind we know almost nothing. Her reserve was great, and she died before she had become an object of curiosity even to her friends. But we see that she is of the race of Richardson and Marivaux, although she leaves their clumsy construction far behind. She was a satirist, however, not a sentimentalist. One of the few anecdotes preserved about her relates that she refused to meet Madame de Staël, and the Germanic spirit was evidently as foreign to her taste as the lyricism born of Rousseau. She was the exact opposite of all which the cosmopolitan critics of Europe were deciding that English prose fiction was and always would be. Lucid, gay, penetrating, exquisite, Jane Austen possessed precisely the qualities that English fiction needed to drag it out of the Slough of Despond and start it wholesomely on a new and vigorous career.

One curious result of the revolution in literary taste was the creation of an official criticism mainly intended to resist the new ideas, and, if possible, to rout them. The foundation of the *Edinburgh Review* in 1802 is a remarkable landmark in the history of English literature. The proposition that a literary journal should be started which should take the place of the colourless *Monthly Review* was made by Sydney Smith, but FRANCIS JEFFREY, a young Scotch advocate, was editor from the first, and held the post for six-and-twenty years. He was a half-hearted supporter of the Scoto-Teutonic reformers, but a vehement opponent, first of Coleridge and Wordsworth, afterwards of Shelley and Keats. The finer raptures of poetry were not revealed to Jeffrey, and in the criticism of their contemporaries he and his staff were often guilty

20

of extraordinary levity. Yet, on the whole, and where
the prejudices of the young reviewers were not involved,
the *Edinburgh* did good work, and it created quite a new
standard of merit in periodical writing. To counteract
its Whiggishness the Ministerial party founded in 1809
the Tory *Quarterly Review,* and put that bitter pedant and
obscurantist, Gifford, in the editorial chair. This periodical
also enjoyed a great success without injuring its rival,
which latter, at the close of the period with which we are
dealing, had reached the summit of its popularity and a
circulation in those days quite unparalleled. Readers of
the early numbers of the *Edinburgh* and the *Quarterly*
will to-day be surprised at the emotion they caused and
the power which they wielded. They are often smart,
sometimes witty, rarely sound, and the style is, as a rule,
pompous and diffuse. The modern reader is irritated by
the haughty assumption of these boyish reviewers, who
treat genius as a prisoner at the bar, and as in all probability a guilty prisoner. The *Quarterly* was in this respect a worse sinner even than the *Edinburgh:* if Jeffrey
worried the authors, Gifford positively bit them. This
unjust judging of literature, and particularly of poetry—
what is called the " slashing " style of criticism—when it
is now revived, is usually still prosecuted on the lines laid
down by Jeffrey and Gifford. It gives satisfaction to the
reviewer, pain to the author, and a faint amusement to
the public. It has no effect whatever on the ultimate
position of the book reviewed, but, exercised on occasion,
it is doubtless a useful counter-irritant to thoughtless
or venal eulogy. If so, let the credit be given to the
venerable Blue-and-yellow and Brown *Reviews.*

A book which is little regarded to-day exercised so
wide and so beneficial an influence on critical thought

at the beginning of the century that it seems imperative to mention it here. The *Curiosities of Literature*, by Isaac D'Israeli, was not a masterpiece, but its storehouses of anecdote and cultivated reflection must have familiarised with the outlines of literary history thousands who would have been repelled by a more formal work. We dare not speak here at any length of Cobbett and Combe, of Bentham and Dugald Stewart, of Horner and Mackintosh and Mary Wollstonecraft. Of all these writers, in their various ways, it may safely be said that their ideas were of more importance than their style, and that, interesting as they may severally be, they do not illustrate the evolution of English literature.

During the later years of this period romantic fiction fell into great decay. Out of its ashes sprung the historical novel, the invention of which was boldly claimed by Miss Jane Porter, whose *Thaddeus of Warsaw*, long cherished by our great-grandfathers, and not entirely unknown to our fathers, had some faint merit. Other ladies, with the courage of their sex, but with remarkably little knowledge of the subject, attacked the muse of history. But nothing was really done of importance until Sir WALTER SCOTT turned his attention from poetry to prose romance. *Waverley* was not published till 1814, and the long series of novels really belong to the subsequent chapter. They had, however, long been prepared for, and it will be convenient to consider them here. Scott had written a fragment of an historical novel (afterwards *Waverley*) in 1805, and in 1808 he had taken up the useful task of preparing for the press an antiquarian story by Strutt, called *Queenhoo Hall*. His long poems of the same decade had necessitated the approach to historical study in a romantic and yet human spirit.

From his earliest years Scott had been laying up, from Scottish and from German sources, impressions which were to be definitely useful to him in the creation of his great novels. At last, in the maturity of forty-three years, he began the gigantic work which he was not to abandon until his death in 1832.

It is difficult to speak of the novels of Sir Walter Scott in a perfectly critical spirit. They are a cherished part of the heritage of the English-speaking race, and in discussing them we cannot bring ourselves to use regarding them anything but what to foreign critics seems the language of hyperbole. The noble geniality of attitude which they discover in the author, their perennial freshness, their variety, their "magnificent train of events," make us impatient of the briefest reference to their shortcomings in execution. But it is, perhaps, not the highest loyalty to Scott to attempt to deny that his great books have patent faults : that the conduct of the story in *Rob Roy* is primitive, that the heroines of *Ivanhoe* are drawn with no psychological subtlety, that there is a great deal that is terribly heavy and unexhilarating in the pages of *Peveril of the Peak*. It is best, surely, to admit all this, to allow that Scott sometimes wrote too rapidly and too loosely, that his antiquarianism sometimes ran away with him, that his pictures of mediæval manners are not always quite convincing. He has not the inevitable perfection of Jane Austen ; he makes no effort to present himself to us as so fine an artist.

When this is admitted, let the enemy make the best they can of it. We may challenge the literatures of the world to produce a purer talent, or a writer who has with a more brilliant and sustained vivacity combined the novel with the romance, the tale of manners with the tale of wonder. Scott's early ideal was Fielding, and he began the *Waverley* series in rivalry with *Tom Jones*, but he soon left his master. If Scott has not quite the intense sympathy with humanity nor quite the warm blood of Fielding, he has resources which the earlier novelist never dreamed of. His design was to please the modern world by presenting a tale of the Middle Ages, and to do this he had to combat a wide ignorance of and lack of sympathy with history; to create, without a model, homely as well as histrionic scenes of ancient life ; to enliven and push on the narrative by incessant contrasts, high with low, tragic with facetious, philosophical with adventurous. His first idea was, doubtless, to dwell as exclusively as possible with Scottish chivalry. But *Guy Mannering*, once severely judged by the very admirers of Scott, now esteemed as one of his best books, showed what genius for humorous portraiture was possessed by the creator of Dandie Dinmont and Dominie Sampson ; while the *Antiquary*, in its pictures of seaside life in a fishing-town of Scotland, showed how close and how vivid was to be his observation of rustic society.

In all the glorious series there are but two which a lover of Scott would wish away. It is needless to mention them ; their very names recall to us that honourable tragedy of over-strain, of excessive imaginative labour, which bowed his head at length to the ground. The life of Scott, with its *splendeurs et misères*—the former so hospitably shared, the latter so heroically borne — forms a romance as thrilling as any of his fictions, and one necessary to our perfect comprehension of his labours. Great as had been the vogue of his poems, it was far exceeded by that of his novels, and when Scott died his was doubtless the strongest naturalistic influence then being exercised in Europe. All the romances of Alexandre Dumas and Victor Hugo sprang directly from him ; he had inspired Fouqué in Germany, Manzoni in Italy, and Fernan Caballero in Spain. Wherever historical fiction of a picturesque and chivalrous order was produced, it bore the stamp of Walter Scott upon its margin. Nor with the decline of the imitations is it found that the original ceases to retain its hold on the interest of the English race.

Walter Scott, so long a European force, has now, foiled by the victory of the school of Balzac, retired once more to the home he came from, but on British soil there is as yet no sign of any diminution of his honour or popularity. Continental criticism is bewildered at our unshaken loyalty to a writer whose art can be easily demonstrated to be obsolete in many of its characteristics. But English readers confess the perennial attractiveness of a writer whose "tone" is the most perfect in our national literature, who has left not a phrase which is morbid or petulant or base, who is the very type of that generous freedom of spirit which we are pleased to identify with the character of an English gentleman. Into the persistent admiration of Sir Walter Scott there enters something of the militant imperialism of our race.

IX

THE AGE OF BYRON

1815–1840

It is noticeable that the early manifestations of the reforming spirit in English literature had been accompanied by nothing revolutionary in morals or conduct. It is true that, at the very outset, Wordsworth, Southey, and Coleridge had been inclined to a "pantisocratic" sympathy with the principles of the French Revolution, and had leaned to the radical side in politics. But the spirit of revolt was very mildly awakened in them, and when the Reign of Terror came, their aspirations after democratic freedom were nipped in the bud. Early in the century Wordsworth had become, what he remained, a Church and State Tory of the extreme type; Southey, who in 1794 had, "shocking to say, wavered between deism and atheism," promptly developed a horror for every species of liberal speculation, and contributed with gusto to the *Quarterly Review*. Temperament and circumstance combined to make Scott a conservative in politics and manners. Meanwhile, it was in the hands of these peaceful men that the literary revolution was proceeding, and we look back from 1815 with a sense of the extraordinary modesty and wholesome law-abiding morality of the generation which introduced romanticism in this country.

No section of English literature is, we will not say more innocent merely, but more void of the appearance of offence than that which was produced by the romantic reformers of our poetry. The audacity of Wordsworth and Coleridge was purely artistic ; it was bounded by the determination to destroy certain conventions of style, and to introduce new elements and new aspects into the treatment of poetry. But these novelties include nothing that could unsettle, or even excite, the conscience of the least mature of readers. Both these great writers spoke much of passion, and insisted on its resumption by an art which had permitted it to escape too long. But by passion Wordsworth understood no unruly turbulence of the senses, no revolt against conventional manners, no disturbance of social custom. He conceived the term, and illustrated his conception in his poetry, as intense emotion concentrated upon some object of physical or pathetic beauty—such as a mountain, a child, a flower —and led directly by it into the channel of imaginative expression. He saw that there were aspects of beauty which might lead to danger, but from these he and Scott, and even Coleridge, resolutely turned away their eyes.

To all the principal writers of this first generation, not merely vice, but coarseness and licence were abhorrent, as they had been to no earlier race of Englishmen. The rudeness of the eighteenth century gave way to a cold refinement, exquisitely crystal in its highest expressions, a little empty and inhuman in its lower ones. What the Continental nations unite to call our "hypocrisy," our determination not to face the ugly side of nature at all, to deny the very existence of the unseemly instincts, now came to the front. In contrast to the European riot,

England held her garments high out of the mire, with a somewhat mincing air of excessive virtue. The image was created of Britannia, with her long teeth, prudishly averting her elderly eyes from the cancan of the nations. So far as this refinement was genuine it was a good thing —the spotless purity of Wordsworth and Scott is matter for national pride—but so far as it was indeed hypocritical, so far as it was an exhibition of empty spiritual pride, it was hateful. In any case, the cord was drawn so tight that it was bound to snap, and to the generation of intensely proper, conservative poets and novelists there succeeded a race of bards who rejoiced to be thought profligates, socialists, and atheists. Our literature was to become "revolutionary" at last.

In the Sixth Lord BYRON the pent-up animal spirits of the new era found the first channel for their violence, and England positively revelled in the poetry of crime and chaos. The last of a race of lawless and turbulent men, proud as Lucifer, beautiful as Apollo, sinister as Loki, Byron appeared on the scenes arrayed in every quality which could dazzle the youthful and alarm the mature. His lovely curly head moved all the women to adore him ; his melancholy attitudes were mysteriously connected with stories of his appalling wickedness ; his rank and ostentation of life, his wild exotic tastes, his defiance of restraint, the pathos of his physical infirmity, his histrionic gifts as of one, half mountebank, half archangel, all these combined to give his figure, his whole legend, a matchless fascination. Nor, though now so much of the gold is turned to tinsel, though now the lights are out upon the stage where Byron strutted, can we cease to be fascinated. Even those who most strenuously deny him imagination, style, the durable parts of literature, cannot pretend to be unmoved by the matchless romance of his career. Goethe declared that a man so pre-eminent for character had never existed in literature before, and would probably never appear again. This should give us the note for a comparative estimate of Byron: in quality of style he is most unequal, and is never, perhaps, absolutely first-rate; but as an example of the literary temperament at its boiling-point, history records no more brilliant name.

Byron was in haste to be famous, and wrote before he had learned his art. His intention was to resist the incursion of the romantic movement, and at the age of twenty-one he produced a satire, the aim of which, so far as it was not merely splenetic, was the dethronement of Wordsworth and Coleridge in favour of Dryden and Pope. In taste and conviction he was reactionary to the very last; but when he came to write, the verse poured forth like lava, and took romantic forms in spite of him. His character was formed during the two wild years of exile (June 1809 to August 1811), when, a prey to a frenzied restlessness, he scoured the Mediterranean, rescued Turkish women, visited Lady Hester Stanhope, swam across the Hellespont, rattled at the windows of seraglios, and even—so Goethe and the world believed—murdered a man with a yataghan and captured an island of the Cyclades. Before he began to sing of Lara and the Giaour he was himself a Giaour, himself Lara and Conrad; he had travelled with a disguised Gulnare, he had been beloved by Medora, he had stabbed Hassan to the heart, and fought by the side of Alp the renegade; or, if he had not done quite all this, people insisted that he had, and he was too melancholy to deny the impeachment.

Languid as Byron affected to be, and haughtily indolent, he wrote with extraordinary persistence and rapidity. Few poets have composed so much in so short a time. The first two cantos of *Childe Harold* in 1812 lead off the giddy masque of his productions, which for the next few years were far too numerous to be mentioned here in detail. Byron's verse romances, somewhat closely modelled in form on those of Scott, began with the *Giaour* in 1813, and each had a beautiful, fatal hero, "of one virtue and a thousand crimes," in whom tens of thousands of awe-struck readers believed they recognised the poet himself in masquerade. All other poetry instantly paled before the astounding success of Byron, and Scott, who had reigned unquestioned as the popular minstrel of the age, "gave over writing verse-romances" and took to prose. Scott's courtesy to his young rival was hardly more exquisite than the personal respect which Byron showed to one whom he insisted in addressing as "the Monarch of Parnassus"; but Scott's gentle chieftains were completely driven out of the field by the Turkish bandits and pirates. All this time Byron was writing exceedingly little that has stood the attacks of time; nor, indeed, up to the date of his marriage in 1815, can it be said that he had produced anything of any real poetical importance. He was now, however, to be genuinely unhappy and candidly inspired.

Adversity drove him in upon himself, and gave him something of creative sincerity. Perhaps, if he had lived, and had found peace with advancing years, he might have become a great artist. But that he never contrived to be. In 1816 he left England, shaking its dust from his feet, no longer a pinchbeck pirate, but a genuine outlaw, in open enmity with society. This enfranchisement acted upon his genius like a tonic, and in the last eight years of his tempestuous and lawless life he wrote many things of extraordinary power and even splendour. Two sections of his work approach, nearer than any others, perfection in their kind. In a species of magnificent invective, of which the *Vision of Judgment* (1822) is the finest example, Byron rose to the level of Dryden and Swift; in the picturesque satire of social life—where he boldly imitated the popular poets of Italy, and in particular Casti and Pulci—his extreme ease and versatility, his masterly blending of humour and pathos, ecstasy and misanthropy, his variegated knowledge of men and manners, gave him, as Scott observed, something of the universality of Shakespeare. Here he is to be studied in *Beppo* (1818) and in the unmatched *Don Juan* of his last six years. It is in these and the related works that we detect the only perdurable Byron, the only poetry that remains entirely worthy of the stupendous fame of the author.

It is the fatal defect of Byron that his verse is rarely exquisite. That indescribable combination of harmony in form with inevitable propriety in language which thrills the reader of Milton, of Wordsworth, of Shelley, of Tennyson—this is scarcely to be discerned in Byron. We are, in exchange, presented with a rapid volume of rough melody, burning words which are torches rather than stars, a fine impetuosity, a display of personal temperament which it has nowadays become more interesting to study in the poet than in the poetry, a great noise of trumpets and kettle-drums in which the more delicate melodies of verse are drowned. The lack of these refinements, however, is imperceptible to all but native ears, and the lack of them has not prevented Byron

from seeming to foreign critics to be by far the greatest
and the most powerful of our poets. There was no difficulty in comprehending his splendid, rolling rhetoric;
and wherever a European nation stood prepared to in-
veigh against tyranny and conventionality, the spirit of
Byron was ready to set its young poets ablaze.

Hence, while in England the influence of Byron on
poetry was not in the least degree commensurate with
his fame, and while we have here to look to prose-
writers, such as Bulwer, as his most direct disciples, his
verse inspired a whole galaxy of poets on the Continent.
The revival of Russian and Polish literature dates from
Byron; his spirit is felt in the entire attitude and in not
a few of the accents of Heine and of Leopardi; while
to the romantic writers of France he seemed the final
expression of all that was magnificent and intoxicating.
Neither Lamartine nor Vigny, Victor Hugo nor Musset,
was independent of Byron's influence, and in the last-
mentioned we have the most exact reproduction of the
peculiar Byronic gestures and passionate self-abandon-
ment which the world has seen.

In *Don Juan* Byron had said that "poetry is but
passion." This was a heresy, which it would be easy to
refute, since by passion he intended little more than a
relinquishing of the will to the instincts. But it was also
a prophecy, for it was the reassertion of the right of the
individual imagination to be a law to itself, and all subsequent emancipation of the spirit may be traced back
to the ethical upheaval of which Byron was the storm-
thrush. He finally broke up the oppressive silence which
the pure accents of Wordsworth and Coleridge had not
quite been able to conquer. With Byron the last rags of
the artificiality which had bound European expression

for a century and a half were torn off and flung to the winds. He taught roughly, melodramatically, inconsistently, but he taught a lesson of force and vitality. He was full of technical faults, drynesses, flatnesses ; he lacked the power to finish ; he offended by a hundred careless impertinences; but his whole being was an altar on which the flame of personal genius flared like a conflagration.

The experiment which Byron made was repeated with a more exquisite sincerity by PERCY BYSSHE SHELLEY, who resembled him in belonging to the aristocratic class, and in having a strong instinctive passion for liberty and toleration. The younger poet, however, showed still less caution than the elder, and while yet a boy gained a dangerous reputation for violent radical prejudices and anti-social convictions. Partly on this account, and partly because the transcendental imagination of Shelley was less easy than Byron's piratical romance for common minds to appreciate, the poetry of the former was almost completely unrecognised until many years after his death, and Byron's deference to Shelley was looked upon as a fantastic whim of friendship. The younger poet was erratic at Eton and Oxford, being expelled from the latter for a puerile outburst of atheism. Born in 1792, the productions of Shelley were already numerous when, in his *Alastor* (1816), he first showed any definite disposition for the higher parts of poetry. This majestic study in blank verse was superior in melody and in imaginative beauty to anything that had been written in English, other than by Wordsworth and Coleridge in their youth, since the romantic age began. The scholarship of Milton and Wordsworth was obvious, but *Alastor* contains passages descriptive of the transport of the soul in the presence of natural loveliness in which a return to the Hellenic genius for style is revealed.

Shelley lived only six years longer, but these were years of feverish composition, sustained, in spite of almost complete want of public sympathy, at a fiery height of intensity. He left England, and in that exile was brought immediately into contact with Byron, with whom he formed an intimacy which no eccentricity on either side sufficed to dissolve. That he was serviceable to Byron no one will deny ; that Byron depressed him he did not attempt to conceal from himself ; yet the esteem of the more popular poet was valuable to the greater one. The terror caused by the vague rumour of Shelley's rebellious convictions was not allayed by the publication of *Laon and Cythna* (1817), a wild narrative of an enthusiastic brother and sister, martyrs to liberty. In 1818 was composed, but not printed, the singularly perfect realistic poem of *Julian and Maddalo.* Shelley was now saturating himself with the finest Greek and Italian classic verse—weaving out of his thoughts and intellectual experiences a pure and noble system of æsthetics. This he illustrated in 1820 by his majestic, if diffuse and sometimes overstrained lyrical drama of *Prometheus Unbound,* with which he published a few independent lyrics which scarcely have their peer in the literature of the world ; among these the matchless *Ode to the West Wind* must be named. The same year saw the publication of the *Cenci,* the most dramatic poetic play written in English since the tragedy of *Venice Preserved.* Even here, where Shelley might expect to achieve popularity, something odious in the essence of the plot warned off the public.

He continued to publish, but without an audience ; nor

did his *Epipsychidion*, a melodious rhapsody of Platonic love, nor his *Adonais*, an elegy of high dignity and splendour, in the manner of Bion and in commemoration of Keats, nor the crystalline lyrics with which he eked out his exiguous publications, attract the slightest interest. Shelley was, more than any other English poet has been, *le banni de liesse*. Then, quite unexpectedly, on the 8th of July 1822 he was drowned while yachting in the Gulf of Spezia. He left behind him unrevised, amid a world of exquisite fragments, a noble but vague gnomic poem, the *Triumph of Life*, in which Petrarch's *Trionfi* are summed up and sometimes excelled.

A life of disappointment and a death in obscurity were gradually followed by the growth of an almost exaggerated reputation. Fifty years after his death Shelley had outshone all his contemporaries—nay, with the exception of Shakespeare, was probably the most passionately admired of all the English poets. If this extremity of fame has once more slightly receded, if Shelley holds his place among the sovereign minstrels of England, but rather abreast of than in front of them, it is because time has reduced certain of his violent paradoxes to commonplaces, and because the world, after giving several of his axioms of conduct full and respectful consideration, has determined to refrain from adopting them. Shelley, when he was not inspired and an artist, was a prophet vaguely didactic or neurotically prejudiced; his is the highest ideal of poetic art produced by the violence of the French Revolution, but we are too constantly reminded of that moral parentage, and his *sans-culottism* is no longer exhilarating, it is merely tiresome. There are elements, then, even in Shelley, which have to be pared away; but, when these are removed, the remainder is beautiful beyond the range of praise—perfect in aerial, choral melody, perfect in the splendour and purity of its imagery, perfect in the divine sweetness and magnetic tenderness of its sentiment. He is probably the English writer who has achieved the highest successes in pure lyric, whether of an elaborate and antiphonal order, or of that which springs in a stream of soaring music straight from the heart.

Closely allied as he was with Byron in several respects, both of temperament and circumstance, it is fortunate that Shelley was so very little affected by the predominance of his vehement rival. His intellectual ardour threw out, not puffs of smoke, as Byron's did, but a white vapour. He is not always transparent, but always translucent, and his mind moves ethereally among incorporeal images and pantheistic attributes, dimly at times, yet always clothed about with radiant purity. Of the gross Georgian mire not a particle stuck to the robes of Shelley. His diction is curiously compounded of forcible, fresh mintages, mingled with the verbiage of the lyric poets of the eighteenth century, so that at his best he seems like Æschylus, and at his worst merely like Akenside. For all his excessive attachment to revolutionary ideas, Shelley retains much more of the age of Gray than either Keats, Coleridge, or Wordsworth; his style, carefully considered, is seen to rest on a basis built about 1760, from which it is every moment springing and sparkling like a fountain in columns of ebullient lyricism. But sweep away from Shelley whatever gives us exquisite pleasure, and the residuum will be found to belong to the eighteenth century. Hence, paradoxical as it sounds, the attitude of Shelley to style was in the main retrograde; he was, for instance, no admirer of

21

the arabesques of the Cockney school. He was, above all else, a singer, and in the direction of song he rises at his best above all other English, perhaps above all other modern European poets. There is an ecstasy in his best lyrics and odes that claps its wings and soars until it is lost in the empyrean of transcendental melody. This rhapsodical charm is entirely inimitable ; and in point of fact Shelley, passionately admired, has been very little followed, and with success, perhaps, only by Mr. Swinburne. His genius lay outside the general trend of our poetical evolution ; he is exotic and unique, and such influence as he has had, apart from the effect on the pulse of the individual of the rutilant beauty of his strophes, has not been very advantageous. He is often hectic, and sometimes hysterical, and, to use his own singular image, those who seek for mutton-chops will discover that Shelley keeps a gin-palace.

A third influence at work in this second romantic generation was that consciously formed on Elizabethan and Italian lines. The group of poets which culminated in Keats desired to forget all that had been written in English verse since about 1625, and to continue the work of such Italianated poets as Fletcher and the disciples of Spenser. There can be no question that a very prominent part in heralding this revival was taken by Charles Lamb's *Specimens of English Dramatic Poets* (1808), a book which seemed to be unnoticed at first, but which was devoured with ecstasy by several young men of good promise, and particularly by Hunt, Keats, Procter, and Beddoes. While Leigh Hunt was being imprisoned for libelling the Prince Regent, in 1812, he made a very minute study of the *Parnaso Italiano*, and particularly of Ariosto. Between 1814 and 1818 he published several volumes, in which the Italians were closely and fervidly imitated ; among these the *Story of Rimini* holds a really important place in the evolution of English poetry. Hunt was very promptly imitated by Keats, who was eleven years his junior, and in every element of genius immeasurably his superior. A certain school of critics has never been able to forgive Leigh Hunt, who, it must be admitted, lacked distinction in his writings, and taste in his personal relations ; but Hunt was liberal and genial, and a genuine devotee of poetry.

Of the other writers who formed what was rudely called the Cockney school, under the presidency of Hunt, J. H. Reynolds and Charles Wells had talent, but JOHN KEATS was one of the greatest poets that any country has produced. The compositions which place the name of this stable-keeper's son with those of Shakespeare and Milton were written between 1817, when he first ceased to be stiff and affected, and 1820, when the failure of his health silenced his wonderful voice. Within this brief space of time he contrived to enrich English literature with several of the most perennially attractive narrative-poems in the language, not mere snatches of lyrical song, but pieces requiring sustained effort and a careful constructive scheme, *Endymion, Lamia,* the *Eve of St. Agnes,* the *Pot of Basil, Hyperion.* When he wrote his latest copy of verses, Keats had not completed twenty-five years of life, and it is the copious perfection of work accomplished so early, and under so many disadvantages, which is the wonder of biographers. He died unappreciated, not having persuaded Byron, Scott, or Wordsworth of his value, and being still further than Shelley was from attracting any public curiosity or admiration. His triumph was to be posthumous ; it began with the magnanimous tribute of *Adonais*, and it has gone on developing and extending, until, at the present moment, it is Keats, the semi-educated surgeon's apprentice, cut down in his crude youth, who obtains the most suffrages among all the great poets of the opening quarter of the century. To a career which started with so steady a splendour, no successes should have been denied. It is poor work to speculate about might-have-beens, but the probable attainments of Keats, if he could have lived, amount, as nearly as such unfulfilled prophecies can ever do, to certainty. Byron might have become a sovereign, and Shelley would probably have descended into politics ; Keats must have gone on to further and further culmination of poetic art.

Nothing in English poetry is more lovely than those passages in which Keats throws off his cockney excesses and sings in the note of classic purity. At these moments, and they were growing more and more frequent till he ceased to write, he attains a depth of rich, voluptuous melody, by the side of which Byron seems thin, and even Shelley shrill. If we define what poetry is in its fullest and deepest expression, we find ourselves describing the finest stanzas in the maturer works of Keats. His great odes, in which, perhaps, he is seen to the most advantage as an artist in verse, are Titanic and Titianic— their strength is equalled only by the glow and depth of their tone. From Spenser, from Shakespeare, from Milton, from Ariosto, he freely borrowed beauties of style, which he fused into an enamel or amalgam, no longer resembling the sources from which they were stolen, but wearing the impress of the god-like thief himself. It is probable that, marvellous as is such a fragment as *Hyperion*, it but faintly foreshadows the majesty of the style of which Keats would shortly have been master. Yet, enormous as are the disadvantages under which the existing work of Keats labours, we are scarcely conscious of them. We hold enough to prove to us how predominant the imagination was in him, how sympathetic his touch as an artist. He loved " the principle of beauty in all things," and he had already, in extreme youth, secured enough of the rich felicity of phrase and imperial illumination, which marks the maturity of great poets, to hold his own with the best. No one has lived who has known better than he how to " load every rift of his subject with ore."

It is impossible, too, not to recognise that Keats has been the master-spirit in the evolution of Victorian poetry. Both Tennyson and Browning, having in childhood been enchained by Byron, and then in adolescence by Shelley, reached manhood only to transfer their allegiance to Keats, whose influence on English poetry since 1830 has been not less universal than that of Byron on the literature of the Continent. His felicities are exactly of a kind to stimulate a youthful poet to emulation, and in spite of what he owes to the Italians—to whom he went precisely as Chaucer did, to gain richness of poetical texture—the speech of Keats is full of a true British raciness. No poet, save Shakespeare himself, is more English than Keats ; none presents to us in the harmony of his verse, his personal character, his letters and his general tradition, a figure more completely attractive, nor better calculated to fire the dreams of a generous successor.

The friend and biographer of Byron, THOMAS MOORE, was in sympathy with the poets of revolution, and was long associated with them in popular estimation. At the present moment Moore is extremely disdained by the critics, and has the greatest possible difficulty in obtaining a fair hearing. He is scarcely mentioned, save to be decried and ridiculed. This is a reaction against the reputation which Moore long continued to enjoy on rather slight grounds, but it is excessive. As a lyrical satirist, his lightness of touch and buoyant wit give an Horatian flavour to those collections of epistles and fables of which the *Fudge Family in Paris* (1818) began a series. But the little giddy bard had a serious side ; he was profoundly incensed at the unsympathetic treatment of his native island by England, and he seized the "dear harp of his country" in an amiable frenzy of Hibernian sentiment. The result was a huge body of songs and ballads, the bulk of which are now, indeed, worthless, but out of which a careful hand can select eight or ten that defy the action of time, and preserve their wild, undulating melancholy, their sound as of bells dying away in the distance. The artificial prettiness and smoothness of Moore are seen to perfection in his chain of Oriental romances, *Lalla Rookh* (1817), and these, it is to be feared, are tarnished beyond all recovery.

The five years from 1816 to 1821 were the culminating years of the romantic movement. The spirit of poetry invaded every department of English ; there were birds in every bush, and wild music burdened every bough. In particular, several writers of an older school, whom the early movement of Wordsworth and Coleridge had silenced, felt themselves irresistibly moved to sing once more, and swell the new choir with their old voices ; it was *cras amet qui nunquam amavit, quique amavit cras amet.* Among those who had loved more than twenty years before was Samuel Rogers, who came forward with a *Jacqueline* bound up with Byron's *Lara*—strange incongruity, a Methody spinster on the arm of a dashing dragoon. Save on this solitary occasion, however, the amiable Muse of Rogers never forgot what was due to her self-respect, and clung close to the manner of Goldsmith, slowly and faintly relaxing the rigour of versification in a blank verse *Italy*, but never, in a single graceful line, quite reaching the point of poetry. The other revenant, GEORGE CRABBE, did better. After a silence almost unbroken for two-and-twenty years, he resumed his sturdy rhyming in 1807, and in 1810 enriched the language with a poem of really solid merit, the *Borough*, a picture of social and physical conditions in a seaside town on the Eastern Coast. Crabbe never excelled, perhaps never equalled, this saturnine study of the miseries of provincial life ; like his own watchman, the poet seems to have no other design than to " let in truth, terror, and the day." Crabbe was essentially a writer of the eighteenth century, bound close by the versification of Churchill and those who, looking past Pope, tried to revive the vehement music of Dryden ; his attitude to life and experience, too, was of the age of 1780. Yet he showed the influence of romanticism and of his contemporaries in the exactitude of his natural observation and his Dutch niceness in the choice of nouns. He avoided, almost as carefully as Wordsworth himself, the vague sonorous synonym which continues the sound while adding nothing to the sense. As Tennyson used to say, " Crabbe has a world of his own," and his plain, strong, unaffected poetry will always retain a certain number of admirers.

This second generation of romanticism was marked

by a development of critical writing which was of the very highest importance. It may indeed be said, without much exaggeration, that at this time literary criticism, in the modern sense, was first seriously exercised in England. In other words, the old pseudo-classic philosophy of literature, founded on the misinterpretation of Aristotle, was completely obsolete; while the rude, positive expression of baseless opinion with which the *Edinburgh* and the *Quarterly* had started, had broken down, leaving room for a new sensitive criticism founded on comparison with ancient and exotic types of style, a sympathetic study of nature, and a genuine desire to appreciate the writer's contribution on its own merits. Of this new and fertile school of critics, Coleridge, Hazlitt, Leigh Hunt, and Lamb were the leaders.

It is noticeable that the utterances of these writers which have made their names famous were, as a rule, written on occasion, and in consequence of an opportunity which came seldom and as a rule came late. Hunt's best work in criticism dates from 1808 until 1840 indeed, but only because during those years he possessed or influenced successive journals in which he was free to speak his mind. Hazlitt, on the other hand, was thirty-five years of age before his introduction to the *Edinburgh Review* enabled him in 1814 to begin his articles on the English comic writers. To the accident that Hazlitt was invited to lecture at the Surrey Institution we owe his *English Poets* and his essays on Elizabethan literature. Lamb and De Quincey found little vehicle for their ideas until the periodical called *London* was issued in 1820; here the *Essays of Elia* and the *Opium-Eater* were published, and here lesser writers, and later Carlyle himself with his *Life and Writings of Schiller,* found a sympathetic asylum. It was therefore to the development and the increased refinement of periodical literature that the new criticism was most indebted, and newspapers of a comparatively humble order, without wealth or influence behind them, did that for literature which the great Quarterly Reviews, with their insolence and their sciolism, had conspicuously failed to achieve.

With the definite analysis of literary productions we combine here, as being closely allied to it, the criticism of life contributed by all these essayists, but pre-eminently by CHARLES LAMB. This, perhaps the most beloved of English authors, with all his sufferings bravely borne, his long-drawn sorrows made light of in a fantastic jest, was the associate of the Lake poets at the outset of their career. He accepted their principles although he wholly lacked their exaltation in the presence of nature, and was essentially an urban, not a rural talent, though the tale of *Rosamund Gray* may seem to belie the judgment. The poetry of his youth was not very successful, and in the first decade of the century Lamb sank to contributing facetious ana to the newspapers at sixpence a joke. His delicate *Tales from Shakespeare* (1807), and the *Specimens* of 1808, of which we have already spoken, kept his memory before the minds of his friends, and helped to bring in a new era of thought by influencing a few young minds. Meanwhile he was sending to certain fortunate correspondents those divine epistles which, since their publication in 1837, have placed Lamb in the front rank of English letter-writers. But still he was unknown, and remained so until in 1818 the young publisher Ollier was persuaded to venture on a collection of Lamb's scattered writings. At last, at the age of forty-five, he began to immortalise himself with those *Essays of Elia,* of which the opening series was ultimately given to the world as a volume in 1823.

The career of THOMAS DE QUINCEY began even later, and was even more obscure. Ten years younger than Lamb, and like him an admirer and disciple of Wordsworth and Coleridge, De Quincey made no serious attempt to excel in verse, and started in prose not earlier than, as has been already noted, 1821, the book of the *Opium-Eater* appearing anonymously the following year. He had now put out from shore, and we find him for the future, practically until his death in 1859, swimming " in the midst of a German Ocean of literature," and rarely consenting to quit the pen. His collected works, with difficulty saved, just before his end, out of a chaos of anonymity, first revealed to the general public the quality of this astonishing author. In the same way, to chronicle what Wilson contributed to literature is mainly to hunt for *Noctes Ambrosianæ* in the file of *Blackwood's Magazine.* To each of these critical writers, diverse in taste and character, yet all the children of the new romantic movement, the advance of the higher journalism was the accident which brought that to the surface which might otherwise have died in them unfertilised and unperceived.

Of this group of writers, two are now found to be predominant—Lamb for the humour and humanity of his substance, De Quincey for the extraordinary opportunity given by his form for the discussion of the elements of style. Of the latter writer it has been said that " he languished with a sort of despairing nympholepsy after intellectual pleasures." His manner of writing was at once extremely splendid and extremely precise. He added to literature several branches or provinces which had up to his day scarcely been cultivated in English ; among these, impassioned autobiography, distinguished by an exquisite minuteness in the analysis of recollected sensations, is pre-eminent. He revelled in presenting impressions of intellectual self-consciousness in phrases of what he might have called sequacious splendour. De Quincey was but little enamoured of the naked truth, and a suspicion of the fabulous hangs, like a mist, over all his narrations. The most elaborate of them, the *Revolt of the Tartars*, a large canvas covered with groups of hurrying figures in sustained and painful flight, is now understood to be pure romance. The first example of his direct criticism is *Whiggism in its Relations to Literature*, which might be called the Anatomy of a Pedant.

De Quincey is sometimes noisy and flatulent, sometimes trivial, sometimes unpardonably discursive. But when he is at his best, the rapidity of his mind, its lucidity, its humour and good sense, the writer's passionate loyalty to letters, and his organ-melody of style command our deep respect. He does not, like the majority of his critical colleagues, approach literature for purposes of research, but to obtain moral effects. De Quincey, a dreamer of beautiful dreams, disdained an obstinate vassalage to mere matters of fact, but sought with intense concentration of effort after a conscientious and profound psychology of letters.

With this group of literary critics may be mentioned one who was not without relation with them, and who was yet widely distinct. The men of whom we have been speaking sought their inspiration mainly in the newly recovered treasures of early national poetry and prose. These were also formative elements in the mind of WALTER SAVAGE LANDOR; but he imitated more closely than they the great classics of antiquity, and, in particular, Pindar, Æschylus, and Cicero. As early as 1795 he had occasionally published poetry; his concentrated and majestic *Gebir* (1798) is certainly one of the pioneers of English romanticism. But Landor, with his tumultuous passions and angry self-sufficiency, led a youth tormented by too much emotional and social tempest and too little public encouragement to become prominent in prose or verse. It was in the comparative serenity of middle age, and during his happy stay in or near Florence from 1821 to 1828, that he wrote the *Imaginary Conversations*, and became one of the great English men of letters. No ôther work of Landor's has achieved popularity, although much of his occasional prose and verse has called forth the impassioned praise of individuals.

The *Conversations* display, in stiff and Attic form, dramatic aptitudes, for confirmation of which we search in vain the pages of his academic plays. These historic dialogues, strange as it seems, were refused by publisher after publisher; but, at length, in 1824, two volumes of them were issued, and the world was gained. This great series of stately colloquies holds a unique position in English literature. The style of Landor is too austere, too little provided with ornament, too strenuously allusive to please the running reader. But in a mingling of dignity and delicacy, purity and vehemence, into what is an amalgam of all the rarer qualities of thought and expression, Landor ranks only just below the greatest masters of language. His genius is impeded by a certain haughty stiffness; he approaches majestically, and sometimes nimbly, but always protected from the reader by a suit of mail, always rendered inaccessible by an unconquerable shyness.

The second romantic generation was marked by the rise of a school of historians inferior only to the great classic group of Hume, Robertson, and Gibbon. In the full tide of monarchical reaction, William Mitford completed, in 1810, his *History of Greece*, a book eloquent and meritorious in its way, but to be superseded by the labours of Grote. Sharon Turner, a careful imitator of Gibbon, illustrated the Anglo-Saxon period of our chronicles, and the Scottish metaphysician, Sir James Mackintosh, towards the close of his life, occupied himself with the constitutional history of England. Of more importance was the broad and competent English history of Lingard, a Catholic priest at Ushaw, whose work, though bitterly attacked from the partisan point of view, has been proved to be in the main loyal and accurate. These excellent volumes appeared in 1819, and deserve the praise which should be given in rhetorical times to histories of modest learning and research. It was the ambition of Southey, who was an admirable biographer, to excel in history also. In Brazil and in the Peninsular war he found excellent subjects, but his treatment was not brilliant enough to save his books from becoming obsolete. The second of these was, indeed, almost immediately superseded by Sir W. Napier's *History of the War in the Peninsula* (1828), a masterpiece of military erudition.

These names, however, merely lead us up to that of HENRY HALLAM, whose *View of the Middle Ages*, in 1818, announced to the world a brilliantly gifted writer on political history. His *Constitutional History of*

England came nine years later. In his old age Hallam made a track through the previously pathless waste of general European literature. His gravity is supported by a vast basis of solid knowledge, his judgment is sane and balanced, and to his immediate contemporaries his style appeared remarkable for "succinctness and perspicuous beauty." But the modern writer is not so well pleased with Hallam, who begins to be the Georgian type of the falsely impressive. His felicities are those which Macaulay emphasised and carried to a further precision ; his faults are his own, and they are a want of intuitive sympathy with the subject under discussion, and a monotonous and barren pomp of delivery which never becomes easy or flexible. The far-famed "judgment," too, of Hallam is not as wide as we could wish. He is safe only in the discussion of recognised types, and the reader searches his critical pages in vain for signs of the recognition of an eccentric or abnormal talent. The most laudable tendency of the historians of this age, seen in Hallam, indeed, but even more plainly in secondary writers, such as P. F. Tytler, Coxe, and James Mill, was towards the adoption of a scientific accuracy. It was the aim of these men to reject mere legend and rhetorical superstition, and to build, as one of them said, "the history of a country upon unquestionable muniments." In this way they pointed directly to that scientific school of history which has been one of the glories of the later years of the nineteenth century.

The splendid achievements of Miss Austen in the novel and Sir Walter Scott in romance tended somewhat to the discouragement of their immediate successors. The Waverley Novels continued to be poured forth, in rapid and splendid succession, throughout the years which we are now considering, and they obscured the fame of all possible rivals. Yet there were, during this period, secondary writers, independent of the influence of Scott, whose novels possessed sterling merit. From that interesting Scottish author, Mary Brunton, whose *Self-Control* (1811) and *Discipline* (1814) are excellent precursors of a long series of " kail-yard " fiction, there naturally descended the delightful Miss Ferrier, whose *Marriage* (1818) charmed not only the author of *Waverley*, but a host of lesser readers, by its lively humour and its delicious satire of many types of Scotch womanhood. Miss Ferrier would be a Doric Jane Austen, were her skill in the evolution of a plot a little better trained, and her delineation of character a little more sternly restrained from caricature. The story of her delicate tact in soothing the shattered faculties of Sir Walter Scott has endeared Miss Ferrier to thousands who never read her three amusing novels. J. G. Lockhart, though Scott's son-in-law, was not his disciple in four novels of a modern and more or less psychological class. *Adam Blair* (1822) is the best of these, and escapes the frigidity of the author's one classical romance, *Valerius* (1821), a highly accomplished attempt to resuscitate domestic society under Trajan.

Romance was continued on somewhat the same lines which had made Mrs. Radcliffe and Lewis so popular. The grisly story of *Melmoth the Wanderer*, by Maturin, with its horrible commerce with demons, and its scenes of bombastic passion, dates from 1820. Mrs. Percy Shelley, as befitted the widow of so great a magician of language, reached a purer style and a more impressive imagination in her ghastly romance of *Frankenstein*, which has given an image (usually misquoted) to everyday English speech, and may still be read with genuine terror and pity. A very spirited and yet gloomy novel, the *Anastatius* of Hope (1819) appeared at a time when the public were ablaze with the pretensions of Byron; the hero of this daring, piratical romance is all that the noble poet desired himself to be supposed to be. James Morier opened a series of tales of Oriental manners by the publication of *Hajji Baba* in 1824; the satire of Persian manners was brilliant enough and keen enough to call forth a remonstrance against this "very foolish business" from the Shah himself. Morier was anxious to turn the enormous success of this his first book to account, but in further publications he was less successful. He tried to be serious, while his genius led him to the laughable.

Native talent and a hopeless absence of taste and judgment were never more strangely mingled than in John Galt, who, after vainly essaying every department of letters, published in middle life an admirable comic novel, the *Annals of the Parish* (1821), and set all Scotland laughing. It is the autobiography of a country minister, and describes the development of society in a thriving lowland village with inimitable humour and whimsicality. Galt went on pouring forth novels almost until his death in 1839, but he never hit the target again so plainly in the bull's eye.

Byron was scarcely dead before his influence began to display itself in the work of a multitude of writers of "fashionable" novels, dealing mainly with criminals of high birth, into the desperate texture of whose lives there was woven a thread of the ideal. In this school of fiction two young men rose to the highest distinction, and "thrilled the boys with dandy pathos" in a lavish profusion. Of these elegant and fluent novelists the younger made his appearance first, with *Vivian Gray*, in 1826, but his rival was close behind him with *Falkland* in 1827 and *Pelham* in 1828. Through the next twenty years they raced neck by neck for the suffrages of the polite. In that day EDWARD LYTTON BULWER, afterwards the first Lord LYTTON, seemed a genius of the very highest order, but it was early perceived that his dandiacal attitude was not perfectly sincere, that the graces of his style were too laboured and prolix, and that the tone of his novels fostered national conceit and prejudice at the expense of truth. His sentiment was mawkish, his creations were unsubstantial and often preposterous. But the public liked the fastidious elaborateness of a gentleman who catered for their pleasures "with his fingers covered with dazzling rings, and his feet delightfully pinched in a pair of looking-glass boots"; and Bulwer Lytton certainly possessed extraordinary gifts of activity, versatility, and sensitiveness to the requirements of his readers. What has shattered the once-glittering dome of his reputation is what early readers of *Zanoni* called his "fearfully beautiful word-painting," his hollow rhetoric, his puerile horrors. Towards the end of his glorious career Lord Lytton contrived to prune his literary extravagances, and his latest works are his best.

To early contemporaries the novels of BENJAMIN DISRAELI, long afterwards Earl of BEACONSFIELD, seemed more extravagant and whimsical than even those of Bulwer. Disraeli, too, belonged to the great company of the dandies—to the Brummels and Lauzuns of literature. His early novels were baffling miscellanies of the wildest and the most foppish folly combined with

22

rare political wit and a singular clairvoyance. A like inconsistency marked their style, which is now almost crazy in its incoherence, and now of a florid but restrained beauty to which Bulwer, with all his machinery of rhetoric, never attained. *Contarini Fleming* (1832) may be said to record a step towards the emancipation of English romance, in its extraordinary buoyancy of Byronic stimulus. But as a writer, Disraeli was at his best and steadily improving from *Venetia* (1837) to *Tancred* (1847). In these novels he is less tawdry in his ornament, less glittering in his affectation of Voltairean epigram, less inflated and impracticable than in his earlier, and certainly than in his two latest novels, those curious fruits of his old age. The dandy style, of which Barbey d'Aurevilly was the contemporary type in France, is best studied in England in Disraeli, whose novels, though they no longer appeal to the masses, preserve better than Bulwer's the attention of cultivated readers. In these Byronic novelists, who preserved for their heroes "the dear corsair expression, half savage, half soft," love of the romance of pure adventure was handed down, across Dickens and Thackeray, and in an indirect way Bulwer and Disraeli are the progenitors of the Ouidas and Rider Haggards of a later age.

A very peculiar talent—in its fantastic nature, perhaps, more delicate and original than any of these—was that of THOMAS LOVE PEACOCK, the learned friend and correspondent of Shelley. This interesting satirist displayed a survival of the eighteenth-century temper in nineteenth-century forms, and thought of Voltaire when the rest of the world was thinking of Scott, whom Peacock considered "amusing only because he misrepresented everything." The new was singularly odious

to him ; it was only in the old, the classical, the Attic,
that he could take any pleasure. The poetry of Peacock,
both serious and ludicrous, has a charm of extreme
elegance ; but the qualities of his distinguished mind
are best observed in his curious satirical or grotesque
romances, seven in number, of which *Headlong Hall*
(1816) was the first, and *Nightmare Abbey* (1818) doubtless
the most entertaining. His latest novel, *Gryll Grange*,
appeared so late as 1860, and Peacock outlived all his
contemporaries, dying at a great age in 1862. He totally
disregarded English traditions of romance-writing, and
followed the eighteenth-century type of French *conte*.
In his eccentric, discursive way, he is the wittiest English
writer of the age, and after almost passing into oblivion,
he is once more becoming a prominent favourite with
readers of fastidious taste.

The fourth decade of this century was, on the whole,
a period of rest and exhaustion in the literature of this
country. In poetry it was marked by the disappearance
into silence of those who had done most to make the
age what it was, a time of progress and revolt. The
younger poets were dead, their elder brethren were
beginning to pass away, and those who survived the
longest, in particular Wordsworth and Landor, continued to add to the bulk, but not signally to the value
of their works. Yet Tennyson, little observed or praised,
was now producing the most exquisite and the most
brilliantly varied of his lyrics. Discouraged at his recep-
tion, he had published, when this chapter closes, nothing
since 1833. The solitary young poet who deserved to be
mentioned in the same breath, Elizabeth Barrett, was
famous before 1840, but not for those pieces of which
her riper taste chiefly approved, or those for which

posterity is still admiring her after sixty years. In this lull
of the poetic world the voice of Robert Browning was
yet unheard, though it had spoken out in *Paracelsus* and
Strafford. But the sportive fancy of Hood, already near-
ing the close of his brief life, was highly appreciated,
and Praed, though still uncollected, had left a splendid
memory to his friends. Where poets were so few, the
pure talent of Hartley Coleridge, the greater S. T. Coleridge's eldest, unhappy son, may claim a word. A group
of dramatists and lyrical writers, among whom Beddoes
is by far the greatest, link the generation of Keats and
Shelley with that of Tennyson and the Brownings ; but
most of them are nebulous, and the most eminent mere
asteroids in comparison with the planets which preceded
and followed them.

In prose more vigorous influences were at work. In
1825 Macaulay marked an epoch in criticism by contributing to the *Edinburgh Review* his elaborate article on
Milton, the earliest example in English of the modern
étude, or monograph in miniature, which has since
become so popular a province of letters. When our
period closes, Macaulay is a Cabinet minister. His
career as an essayist was mainly prior to 1840, at which
date he had shown himself neither ballad-writer nor
historian. In his famous reviews he created a species
of literature, partly biographical, partly critical, which
had an unrivalled effect in raising the average of cultivation. Countless readers found in the pages of
Macaulay's *Essays* their earliest stimulus to independent
thought and the humane study of letters. Carlyle, five
years the senior of Macaulay, had been much slower in
reaching the great mass of the public. His graceful
Life of Schiller (1825) having failed to achieve a world-

wide sensation, Carlyle deliberately and most successfully set himself to insist upon attention by adopting a
style of extreme eccentricity, full of Germanisms, violently abrupt and tortuously parenthetical, a lingo which
had to be learned like a foreign language. In the recep-
tion ultimately given to *Sartor Resartus* (1834) he was
assured of the success of his stratagem, and he continued,
to his eminent personal advantage, to write, not in English, but in Carlylese for the remainder of his life.

The names crowd upon us as we endeavour to distinguish what literature was when Queen Victoria
ascended the throne. Marryat was at the climax of
his rapidly won nautical fame ; the cavaliers of G. P. R.
James were riding down innumerable lonely roads ; the
first Lord Lytton was in the midst of the series of his
elaborately heroical romances, not cast in gold, perhaps,
but richly parcel-gilt ; Disraeli had just culminated in
Henrietta Temple. Such were the forces which up to
1840 were the most active in purely popular literature.
None of them, perhaps, was of the highest order either
in imagination or in style, but each in his own way was
repeating and emphasising the lesson of the romantic
revolution of 1798.

X

THE EARLY VICTORIAN AGE

1840–1870

IN spite of the interesting elements which we have just endeavoured to indicate, the history of English literature between 1825 and 1840 was comparatively uneventful. The romantic revolution was complete: the new spirit had penetrated every corner of literary production, and the various strains introduced from Germany, from Celtic sources, from the resuscitated study of natural landscape, from the habit of contemplating radical changes in political, religious, and social ideas, had settled down into an accepted intellectual attitude, which itself threatened to become humdrum and conventional. But this menace of a new classicism passed away under the mental storm and stress which culminated in 1848, a second and less radical revolution on the lines of that which was then half a century old, a revolution which had, in English literature, the effect of unsettling nothing that was valuable in the new romantic tradition, but of scouring it, as it were, of the dust and cobwebs which were beginning to cloud its surface, and of polishing it to the reflection of more brilliant and delicate aspects of nature.

In this second revival of thought and active expression the practice of publishing books grew with a celerity which baffles so succinct a chronicle as ours. It becomes, therefore, impossible from this point forwards to discuss with any approach to detail the careers of individual authors. All that we can now hope to do is to show in some degree what was the general trend and what were the main branches of this refreshed and giant body of literature. Between the accession of the Queen and the breaking out of the war with Russia the profession of letters flourished in this country as it had never done before. It is noticeable that in the first years of the century the men of genius are sharply distinguished from the herd of negligible men of talent. We recognise some ten or twelve names so far isolated from all the rest that, with little injustice, criticism may concentrate its attention on these alone. But in the second revival this was not the case : the gradations are infinitely slow, and a sort of accomplished cleverness, highly baffling to the comparative critic, brings us down from the summit, along innumerable slopes and invidiously gentle undulations. Nowhere is it more difficult to know whom to mention and whom to omit.

In poetry, a body of writing which had been kept back by the persistent public neglect of its immediate inspirers, Shelley and Keats, took advantage of the growing fame of those authors to insist on recognition for itself. Hence, although Alfred Tennyson had been a published author since 1826, the real date of his efflorescence as a great, indisputable power in poetry is 1842 ; Elizabeth Barrett, whose first volume appeared in 1825, does not make her definite mark until 1844; and Robert Browning, whose *Pauline* is of 1833, begins to find readers and a discreet recognition in 1846, at the close of the series of his *Bells and Pomegranates*. These three

writers, then, formed a group which it is convenient to
consider together : greatly dissimilar in detail, they possessed distinctive qualities in common ; we may regard
them as we do Wordsworth, Coleridge, and Southey, or
Byron, Shelley, and Keats.   The vogue, however, of this
latest cluster of poets was destined to develop more
slowly, perhaps, but much more steadily and for a
longer period than that of any previous trio.   After fifty
years of production and increasing popularity two of
them were still amongst us, in the enjoyment of an
almost unparalleled celebrity.   It is important, so far
as possible, to clear away from our minds the impression
which half a century of glory has produced, and to see
how these poets struck their first candid admirers in the
forties.

In the first place, it is obvious that their unquestionable merits were dimmed by what were taken to be
serious defects of style.   Oddly enough, it was ALFRED
TENNYSON who was particularly assailed for faults which
we now cheerfully admit in Miss Barrett, who to her
own contemporaries seemed the most normal of the
three.   That Keats was "misdirected" and "unripe"
had been an unchallenged axiom of the critical faculty;
but here were three young writers who were calmly
accepting the formulas of Keats and of "his deplorable
friend Mr. Shelley," and throwing contempt on those
so authoritatively laid down by the *Edinburgh Review.*
Tennyson was accused of triviality, affectation, and
quaintness.   But his two volumes of 1842 were published
at a moment when public taste was undergoing a radical
change.   The namby-pamby of the thirties was disgusting
the younger men, and the new burden imposed by the
Quarterlies was being tossed from impatient shoulders.

When R. H. Horne, in 1844, called upon Englishmen to set aside "the thin gruel of Kirke White" and put to their lips "the pure Greek wine of Keats," he not only expressed a daring conviction to which many timider spirits responded, but he enunciated a critical opinion which the discussions of fifty years have not superseded.

What such candid spirits delighted in in the Tennyson of 1842 was the sensuous comprehensiveness of his verse. He seemed to sum up, in a composite style to which he gradually gave a magic peculiarly his own, the finest qualities of the school that had preceded him. He studied natural phenomena as closely as Wordsworth had, his melodies were almost as liquid and aerial as those of Coleridge, he could tell a story as well as Campbell, his songs were as pure and ecstatic as Shelley's, and for depth and splendour of colour Keats hardly surpassed him. As soon, therefore, as the general public came to recognise him, he enchanted it. To an enthusiastic listener the verse of Tennyson presently appeared to sum up every fascinating pleasure which poetry was competent to offer, or if anything was absent, it was supposed to be the vigour of Byron or the manly freshness of Scott. To the elements he collected from his predecessors he added a sense of decorative beauty, faintly archaic and Italian, an unprecedented refinement and high finish in the execution of verse, and a philosophical sympathy with the broad outlines of such social and religious problems as were engaging the best minds of the age. Those who approached the poetry of Tennyson, then, were flattered by its polished and distinguished beauty, which added to their own self-respect, and were repelled by none of those austerities and

violences which had estranged the early readers of
Wordsworth and Shelley.

ELIZABETH BARRETT, also, pleased a wide and influential circle.   Although her work was less pure than
Tennyson's, and has proved to be less perennial, there
were many readers of deliberate judgment who preferred
it to his.   Their nerves were pleasurely excited by the
choral tumult of Miss Barrett's verse, by her generous
and humane enthusiasm, and by the spontaneous im-
pulsiveness of her emotion.   They easily forgave the
slipshod execution, the hysterical violence, the Pythian
vagueness and the Pythian shriek.   More critical readers
were astonished that one who approached the composition of poetry with an almost religious sense of responsi-
bility, whose whole life was dedicated to the highest aims
of verse, who studied with eclectic passion the first
classics of every age, should miss the initial charm, and
should, fresh from Sophocles and Dante, convey her
thoughts in a stream which was seldom translucent and
never calm.   In some of her lyrics, however, and more
rarely in her sonnets, she rose to heights of passionate
humanity which place her only just below the great
poets of her country.

About the year 1850, when, as Mrs. Browning, she was
writing at her best, all but a few were to be excused
if they considered her the typical *vates*, the inspired
poet of human suffering and human aspiration.   But
her art, from this point onward, declined, and much of
her late work was formless, spasmodic, singularly tuneless and harsh, nor is it probable that what seemed
her premature death, in 1861, was a real deprivation to
English literature.   Mrs. Browning, with great afflatus
and vigour, considerable beauty of diction, and not a

little capacity for tender felicity of fanciful thought, had
the radical fault of mistaking convulsion for strength, and
of believing that sublimity involved a disordered and
fitful frenzy. She was injured by the humanitarian sentimentality which was just coming into vogue, and by
a misconception of the uses of language somewhat analogous to that to which Carlyle had resigned himself.
She suffered from contortions produced by the fumes of
what she oddly called

> " *The lighted altar booming o'er*
> *The clouds of incense dim and hoar*";

and if " the art of poetry had been a less earnest object
to " her, if she had taken it more quietly, she might have
done greater justice to her own superb ambition.

When the youthful ROBERT BROWNING, in 1846,
carried off in clandestine marriage the most eminent
poetess of the age, not a friend suspected that his fame
would ever surpass hers. Then, and long afterwards, he
was to the world merely "the man who married Elizabeth
Barrett," although he had already published most of his
dramas, and above all the divine miracle-play of *Pippa
Passes*. By his second book, *Paracelsus* (1835), he had
attracted to him a group of admirers, small in number,
but of high discernment ; these fell off from what seemed
the stoniness of *Strafford* and the dense obscurity of
Sordello. At thirty-five Robert Browning found himself
almost without a reader. The fifteen years of his married
life, spent mainly in Italy, were years of development, of
clarification, of increasing selective power. When he
published *Men and Women* (1855), whatever the critics
and the quidnuncs might say, Browning had surpassed
his wife and had no living rival except Tennyson. He

continued, for nearly forty years, to write and publish verse ; he had no other occupation; and the results of his even industry grew into a mountain. After 1864 he was rarely exquisite ; but *The Ring and the Book,* an immense poem in which one incident of Italian crime is shown reflected on a dozen successive mental facets, interested everybody, and ushered Browning for the first time to the great public.

Browning was in advance of his age until he had become an elderly man. His great vogue did not begin until after the period which we deal with in this chapter. From 1870 to 1889 he was an intellectual force of the first class ; from 1850 to 1870 he was a curiosity, an eccentric product more wondered at than loved or followed. His analysis was too subtle, and his habit of expression too rapid and transient, for the simple early Victorian mind ; before his readers knew what he was saying, he had passed on to some other mood or subject. The question of Browning's obscurity is one which has been discussed until the flesh is weary. He is often difficult to follow ; not unfrequently neglectful, in the swift evolution of his thought, whether the listener can follow him or not ; we know that he liked "to dock the smaller parts-o'-speech." In those earlier years of which we speak, he pursued with dignity, but with some disappointment, the rôle of a man moved to sing to others in what they persisted in considering no better than a very exasperating mode of pedestrian speech. So that the pure style in Browning, his exquisite melody when he is melodious, his beauty of diction when he bends to classic forms, the freshness and variety of his pictures— all this was unobserved, or noted only with grudging and inadequate praise.

The one prose-writer who in years was the exact contemporary of these poets, but who was enjoying a universal popularity while they were still obscure, the greatest novelist since Scott, the earliest, and in some ways still the most typical of Victorian writers, was CHARLES DICKENS. English fiction had been straying further and further from the peculiarly national type of Ben Jonson and Smollett — the study, that is, of "humours," oddities, extravagant peculiarities of incident and character—when the publication of the *Pickwick Papers*, which began in 1836, at once revealed a new writer of colossal genius, and resuscitated that obsolete order of fiction. Here was evident not merely an extraordinary power of invention and bustle of movement, but a spirit of such boundless merriment as the literature of the world had never seen before. From the book-publication of *Pickwick*, in 1838, until his death, in 1870, Dickens enjoyed a popularity greater than that of any other living writer. The world early made up its mind to laugh as soon as he spoke, and he therefore chose that his second novel, *Oliver Twist*, should be a study in melodramatic sentiment almost entirely without humour. *Nicholas Nickleby* combined the comic and the sensational elements for the first time, and is still the type of Dickens's longer books, in which the strain of violent pathos or sinister mystery is incessantly relieved by farce, either of incident or description. In this novel, too, the easy-going, old-fashioned air of *Pickwick* is abandoned in favour of a humanitarian attitude more in keeping with the access of puritanism which the new reign had brought with it, and from this time forth a certain squeamishness in dealing with moral problems and a certain "gush" of unreal sentiment obscured the finer qualities of the novelist's genius. The rose-coloured innocence of the Pinches, the pathetic deaths, to slow music, of Little Nell and Little Dombey, these are examples of a weakness which endeared Dickens to his enormous public, but which add nothing to his posthumous glory.

The peculiarity of the manner of Dickens is its excessive and minute consistency within certain arbitrary limits of belief. Realistic he usually is, real he is scarcely ever. He builds up, out of the storehouse of his memory, artificial conditions of life, macrocosms swarming with human vitality, but not actuated by truly human instincts. Into one of these vivaria we gaze, at Dickens's bidding, and see it teeming with movement; he puts a microscope into our hands, and we watch, with excited attention, the perfectly consistent, if often strangely violent and grotesque adventures of the beings comprised in the world of his fancy. His vivacity, his versatility, his comic vigour are so extraordinary that our interest in the show never flags. We do not inquire whether Mr. Toots and Joe Gargery are "possible" characters, whether they move and breathe in a common atmosphere; we are perfectly satisfied with the evolutions through which their fascinating showman puts them. But real imitative vitality, such as the characters of Fielding and Jane Austen possess, the enchanting marionettes of Dickens never display: in all but their oddities, they are strangely incorporeal. Dickens leads us rapidly through the thronged mazes of a fairy-land, now comic, now sentimental, now horrific, of which we know him all the time to be the creator, and it is merely part of his originality and cleverness that he manages to clothe these radically phantasmal figures with the richest motley robes of actual, humdrum, "realistic" observation.

For the first ten years of the Victorian era, Dickens was so prominent as practically to overshadow all competitors. When we look back hastily, we see nothing but his prolific puppet-show, and hear nothing but the peals of laughter of his audience. There were not wanting those who, in the very blaze of his early genius, saw reason to fear that his mannerisms and his exaggerations would grow upon him. But until 1847 he had no serious rival; for Bulwer, sunken between his first brilliancy and his final solidity, was producing nothing but frothy *Zanonis* and dreary *Lucretias*, while the other popular favourites of the moment had nothing of the master's buoyant fecundity. High spirits and reckless adventure gave attractiveness to the early and most rollicking novels of CHARLES LEVER; but even *Charles O'Malley*, the best of them, needs to be read very light - heartedly to be convincing. FREDERICK MARRYAT wrote of sailors as Lever did of dragoons, but with a salt breeziness that has kept *Peter Simple* and *Mr. Midshipman Easy* fresh for sixty years. Marryat and Lever, indeed, come next to Dickens among the masculine novelists of this age, and they, as he is, are of the school and following of Smollett. Gay caricature, sudden bursts of sentiment, lively description, broken up by still livelier anecdote, with a great nonchalance as to the evolution of a story and the propriety of its ornament—these are the qualities which characterise the novelists of the early Victorian age. In our rapid sketch we must not even name the fashionable ladies who undertook at this time, in large numbers, to reproduce the foibles and frivolities of "society."

The name of THOMAS CARLYLE was mentioned in the last chapter, and he went on writing until about 1877, but the central part of his influence and labour was early Victorian. No section of Carlyle's life was so important, from a literary point of view, as the first period of twelve years in London. In 1833, discomfited by persistent want of success, he was on the point of abandoning the effort. " I shall quit literature ; it does not invite me," he wrote. But in this depressed mood he sat down to the solid architecture, toil "stern and grim," of the *French Revolution*, composed at Cheyne Walk in a sour atmosphere of "bitter thrift." In 1837 it appeared with great éclat, was followed in 1838 by the despised and thitherto unreprinted *Sartor Resartus*, and by the four famous series of Carlyle's public lectures. Of these last, *Hero Worship* was alone preserved. But all this prolonged activity achieved for the disappointed Carlyle a tardy modicum of fame and fee. He pushed the "painting of heroisms" still further in the brilliant improvisation called *Past and Future*, in 1843, and with this book his first period closes. He had worked down, through the volcanic radicalism of youth, to a finished incredulity as to the value of democracy. He now turned again to history for a confirmation of his views.

But meanwhile he had revealed the force that was in him, and the general nature of his message to mankind. His bleak and rustic spirit, moaning, shrieking, roaring, like a wild wind in some inhospitable northern woodland, had caught the ear of the age, and sang to it a fierce song which it found singularly attractive. First, in subject ; after the express materialism of Bentham, Owen, and Fourier, prophets of the body, the ideal part of man was happy to be reminded again of its existence, even if by a prophet whose inconsistency and whose personal dissatisfaction with things in general tended to dismay the soul of the minute disciple. It was best not to follow the thought of Carlyle too implicitly, to consider him less as a guide than as a stimulus, to allow his tempestuous and vague nobility of instinct to sweep away the coverings of habit and convention, and then to begin life anew. Emerson, an early and fervent scholar, defined the master's faculty as being to " clap wings to the sides of all the solid old lumber of the world." Carlyle's amorphous aspirations excited young and generous minds, and it was natural that the preacher of so much lawless praise of law should seem a law-giver himself. Yet it is difficult to decide what Carlyle has bequeathed to us, now that the echoes of his sonorous denunciations are at last dying away. Standing between the Infinite and the individual, he recognises no gradations, no massing of the species; he compares the two incomparable objects of his attention, and scolds the finite for its lack of infinitude as if for a preventable fault. Unjust to human effort, he barks at mankind like an ill-tempered dog, angry if it is still, yet more angry if it moves. A most unhelpful physician, a prophet with no gospel, but vague stir and turbulence of contradiction. We are beginning now to admit a voice and nothing more, yet at worst what a resonant and imperial clarion of a voice !

For, secondly, in manner he surprised and delighted his age. Beginning with a clear and simple use of English, very much like that of Jeffrey, Carlyle deliberately created and adopted an eccentric language of his own, which he brought to perfection in *Sartor Resartus.*

23

Founded on a careful selection of certain Greek and German constructions, introduced so as to produce an irregular but recurrent effect of emphasis, and at poignant moments an impression as of a *vox humana* stop in language, skilfully led up to and sustained, the euphuism of Carlyle was one of the most remarkable instances on record of a deliberately artificial style adopted purely and solely for purposes of parade, but preserved with such absolute consistency as soon to become the only form of speech possible to the speaker. Early critics described it as a mere chaos of capitals and compounds and broken English ; but a chaos it was not —on the contrary, it was a labyrinth, of which the powerful and insolent inventor was most careful to preserve the thread.

We have hitherto been speaking of a solvent Carlyle as essayist, lecturer, critic, and stripper-off of social raiment. It was presently discovered that on one side his genius was really constructive. He became the finest historian England had possessed since Gibbon. The brilliant, episodical *French Revolution* was followed by a less sensational but more evenly finished *Cromwell* in 1845, and by that profoundly elaborated essay in the eighteenth-century history of Germany, the *Life of Friedrich II.*, in 1858. By this later work Carlyle outstripped, in the judgment of serious critics, his only possible rival, Macaulay, and took his place as the first scientific historian of the early Victorian period. His method in this class of work is characteristic of him as an individualist ; he endeavours, in all conjunctions, to see the man moving, breathing, burning in the glow and flutter of adventure. This gives an extraordinary vitality to portions of Carlyle's narrative, if it also tends to disturb the reader's conception of the general progress of events. After the publication of the *Friedrich*, Carlyle continued to live for nearly twenty years, writing occasionally, but adding nothing to his intellectual stature, which, however, as time passed on, grew to seem gigantic, and was, indeed, not a little exaggerated by the terror and amazement which the grim old Tartar prophet contrived to inspire in his disciples and the world in general.

Born after Carlyle, and dying some twenty years before him, THOMAS BABINGTON MACAULAY pressed into a short life, feverishly filled with various activity, as much work as Carlyle achieved in all his length of days. The two writers present a curious parallelism and contrast, and a positive temptation to paradoxical criticism. Their popularity, the subjects they chose, their encyclopædic interest in letters, unite their names, but in all essentials they were absolutely opposed. Carlyle, with whatever faults, was a seer and a philosopher; English literature has seen no great writer more unspiritual than Macaulay, more unimaginative, more demurely satisfied with the phenomenal aspect of life. In Carlyle the appeal is incessant—*sursum corda;* in Macaulay the absence of mystery, of any recognition of the divine, is remarkable. Macaulay is satisfied with surfaces, he observes them with extraordinary liveliness. He is prepared to be entertaining, instructive, even exhaustive, on almost every legitimate subject of human thought; but the one thing he never reaches is to be suggestive. What he knows he tells in a clear, positive, pleasing way; and he knows so much that often, especially in youth, we desire no other guide. But he is without vision of unseen things; he has no message to the heart; the waters of the soul are never troubled by his copious and admirable flow of information.

Yet it is a narrow judgment which sweeps Macaulay aside. He has been, and probably will long continue to be, a most valuable factor in the cultivation of the race. His *Essays* are not merely the best of their kind in existence, but they are put together with so much skill that they are permanent types of a certain species of literary architecture. They have not the delicate, palpitating life of the essays of Lamb or of Stevenson, but taken as pieces of constructed art built to a certain measure, fitted up with appropriate intellectual upholstery, and adapted to the highest educational requirements, there is nothing like them elsewhere in literature. The most restive of juvenile minds, if induced to enter one of Macaulay's essays, is almost certain to reappear at the other end of it gratified, and, to an appreciable extent, cultivated. Vast numbers of persons in the middle Victorian period were mainly equipped for serious conversation from the armouries of these delightful volumes. The didactic purpose is concealed in them by so genuine and so constant a flow of animal spirits, the writer is so conspicuously a master of intelligible and appropriate illustration, his tone and manner are so uniformly attractive, and so little strain to the feelings is involved in his oratorical flourishes, that readers are captivated in their thousands, and much to their permanent advantage. Macaulay heightened the art of his work as he progressed; the essays he wrote after his return from India in 1838 are particularly excellent. To study the construction and machinery of the two great Proconsular essays, is to observe literature of the objective and phenomenal order carried almost to its highest possible perfection.

In 1828, in the *Edinburgh Review*, Macaulay laid down a new theory of history. It was to be pictorial and vivid; it was to resemble (this one feels was his idea) the Waverley Novels. To this conception of history he remained faithful throughout his career; he probably owed it, though he never admits the fact, to the reading of Augustin Thierry's *Conquête d'Angleterre*. Macaulay had been a popular essayist and orator for a quarter of a century, when, in 1849, he achieved a new reputation as an historian, and from this date to 1852, when his health began to give way, he was at the head of living English letters. In his history there meet us the same qualities that we find in his essays. He is copious, brilliant, everlastingly entertaining, but never profound or suggestive. His view of an historical period is always more organic than Carlyle's, because of the uniformity of his detail. His architectonics are excellent; the fabric of the scheme rises slowly before us; to its last pinnacle and moulding there it stands, the master-builder expressing his delight in it by an ebullition of pure animal spirits. For half the pleasure we take in Macaulay's writing arises from the author's sincere and convinced satisfaction with it himself. Of the debated matter of Macaulay's style, once almost superstitiously admired, now unduly depreciated, the truth seems to be that it was as natural as Carlyle's was artificial; it represented the author closely and unaffectedly in his faults and in his merits. Its monotonous regularity of cadence and mechanical balance of periods have the same faculty for alternately captivating and exasperating us that the intellect of the writer has. After all, Macaulay lies a little outside the scope of those who seek an esoteric and mysterious pleasure from style. He loved crowds, and it is to the populace that his life's work is addressed.

If the strongly accentuated and opposed styles of Carlyle and Macaulay attracted the majority of lively pens during the early Victorian period, there were not wanting those who were anxious to return to the unadorned practice of an English that should entirely forget its form in the earnest desire to say in clear and simple tones exactly what it wanted to say. Every generation possesses such writers, but from the very fact of their lack of ambition and their heedlessness of the technical parts of composition they seldom attain eminence. Perhaps the most striking exception in our literature is JOHN HENRY NEWMAN, whose best sermons and controversial essays display a delicate and flexible treatment of language, without emphasis, without oddity, which hardly arrests any attention at first—the reader being absorbed in the argument or statement—but which in course of time fascinates, and at last somewhat overbalances the judgment, as a thing miraculous in its limpid grace and suavity. The style which Newman employs is the more admired because of its rarity in English ; it would attract less wonder if the writer were a Frenchman. If we banish the curious intimidation which the harmony of Newman exercises, at one time or another, over almost every reader, and examine his methods closely, we see that the faults to which his writing became in measure a victim in later years—the redundancy, the excess of colour, the languor and inelasticity of the periods—were not incompatible with what we admire so much in the *Sermons at St. Mary's Church* and in the pamphlets of the Oxford Movement.

These imperfections in the later works of Newman—

obvious enough, surely, though ignored by his blind
admirers—were the result of his preoccupation with other
matters than form. His native manner, cultivated to a
high pitch of perfection in the Common Room at Oriel,
was abundant, elegant, polished, rising to sublimity when
the speaker was inspired by religious fervour, sinking to
an almost piercing melancholy when the frail tenor of
human hopes affected him, barbed with wit and ironic
humour when the passion of battle seized him. His intellect, so aristocratic and so subtle, was admirably served
through its period of storm and stress by the armour of
this academic style. But when the doubts left Newman,
when he settled down at Edgbaston among his worshippers, when all the sovereign questions which his soul
had put to him were answered, he resigned not a little
of the purity of his style. It was Newman's danger, perhaps, to be a little too intelligent ; he was tempted to
indulge a certain mental indolence, which assailed him,
with mere refinements and facilities of thought. Hence,
in his middle life, it was only when roused to battle,
it was in the *Apologia* of 1864 and *A Grammar of Assent*
of 1870, that the Fénelon of our day rose, a prince of
religious letters, and shamed the enemies of his communion by the dignity of his golden voice. But on other
occasions, taking no thought what he should put on, he
clothed his speech in what he supposed would best
please or most directly edify his immediate audience,
and so, as a mere writer, he gradually fell behind those
to whose revolutionary experiments his pure and styptic
style had in early days offered so efficient a rivalry.
But the influence of the Anglican Newman, now suf-
fused through journalism, though never concentrated
in any one powerful disciple, has been of inestimable

service in preserving the tradition of sound, unemphatic English.

The fifth decade of the century was a period of singular revival in every branch of moral and intellectual life. Although the dew fell all over the rest of the threshing-floor, the fleece of literature was not unmoistened by it. The years 1847–49 were the most fertile in great books which England had seen since 1818–22. It was in the department of the novel that this quickening of vitality was most readily conspicuous. Fiction took a new and brilliant turn ; it became vivid, impassioned, complicated ; in the hands of three or four persons of great genius, it rose to such a prominent place in the serious life of the nation as it had not taken since the middle career of Scott. Among these new novelists who were also great writers, the first position was taken by WILLIAM MAKEPEACE THACKERAY, who, though born so long before as 1811, did not achieve his due rank in letters until *Vanity Fair* was completed in 1848. Yet much earlier than this Thackeray had displayed those very qualities of wit, versatility, and sentiment, cooked together in that fascinating and cunning manner which it is so difficult to analyse, which were now hailed as an absolute discovery. *Barry Lyndon* (1840) should have been enough, alone, to prove that an author of the first class had arisen, who was prepared to offer to the sickly taste of the age, to its false optimism, its superficiality, the alterative of a caustic drollery and a scrupulous study of nature. But the fact was that Thackeray had not, in any of those early sketches to which we now turn back with so much delight, mastered the technical art of story-telling. The study of Fielding appeared to reveal to him the sort of evolution, the constructive pertinacity, which had hitherto been lacking. He read *Jonathan Wild* and wrote *Barry Lyndon;* by a still severer act of self-command, he studied *Tom Jones* and composed *Vanity Fair.* The lesson was now learned. Thackeray was a finished novelist; but, alas! he was nearly forty years of age, and he was to die at fifty-two. The brief remainder of his existence was crowded with splendid work; but Thackeray is unquestionably one of those writers who give us the impression of having more in them than accident ever permitted them to produce.

Fielding had escorted the genius of Thackeray to the doors of success, and it became convenient to use the name in contrasting the new novelist with Dickens, who was obviously of the tribe of Smollett. But Thackeray was no consistent disciple of Fielding, and when we reach his masterpieces—*Esmond,* for instance—the resemblance between the two writers has become purely superficial. Thackeray is more difficult to describe in a few words than perhaps any other author of his merit. He is a bundle of contradictions—slipshod in style, and yet exquisitely mannered; a student of reality in conduct, and yet carried away by every romantic mirage of sentiment and prejudice; a cynic with a tear in his eye, a pessimist that believes the best of everybody. The fame of Thackeray largely depends on his palpitating and almost pathetic vitality; he suffers, laughs, reflects, sentimentalises, and meanwhile we run beside the giant figure, and, looking up at the gleam of the great spectacles, we share his emotion. His extraordinary power. of entering into the life of the eighteenth century, and reconstructing it before us, is the most definite of his purely intellectual claims to our regard. But it is the character of the man himself — plaintive, affectionate, protean in its moods, like April weather in its changes —that, fused with unusual completeness into his works, preserves for us the human intensity which is Thackeray's perennial charm as a writer.

Two women of diverse destiny, but united in certain of their characteristics, share with Thackeray the glory of representing the most vivid qualities of this mid-Victorian school of fiction. In 1847 the world was startled by the publication of a story of modern life named *Jane Eyre*, by an anonymous author. Here were a sweep of tragic passion, a broad delineation of elemental hatred and love, a fusion of romantic intrigue with grave and sinister landscape, such as had never been experienced in fiction before ; to find their parallel it was necessary to go back to the wild drama of Elizabeth. Two years later *Shirley*, and in 1852 *Villette*, continued, but did not increase, the wonder produced by *Jane Eyre;* and just when the world was awakening to the fact that these stupendous books were written by Miss CHARLOTTE BRONTË, a schoolmistress, one of the three daughters of an impoverished clergyman on the Yorkshire wolds, she died, early in 1855, having recently married her father's curate. The story of her grey and grim existence at Haworth, the struggles which her genius made to disengage itself, the support she received from sisters but little less gifted than herself, all these, constantly revived, form the iron framework to one of the most splendid and most durable of English literary reputations.

Neither Charlotte Brontë, however, nor her sisters, Emily and Anne, possessed such mechanical skill in the construction of a plot as could enable them to develop their stories on a firm epical plan. They usually preferred the autobiographic method, because it enabled them to evade the constructive difficulty; and when, as in *Shirley*, Charlotte adopted the direct form of narrative, she had to fall back upon the artifice of a schoolroom diary. This reserve has in fairness to be made; and if we desire to observe the faults as well as the splendid merits of the Brontean school of fiction, they are displayed glaringly before us in the *Wuthering Heights* of Emily, that sinister and incongruous, but infinitely fascinating tragedy.

Much more of the art of building a consistent plot was possessed by ELIZABETH CLEGHORN GASKELL; indeed, she has written one or two short books which are technically faultless, and might be taken as types of the novel form. Strange to say, the recognition of her delicate and many-sided genius has never been quite universal, and has endured periods of obscuration. Her work has not the personal interest of Thackeray's, nor the intense unity and compression of Charlotte Brontë's. It may even be said that Mrs Gaskell suffers from having done well too many things. She wrote, perhaps, a purer and a more exquisite English than either of her rivals, but she exercised it in too many fields. Having in *Mary Barton* (1848) treated social problems admirably, she threw off a masterpiece of humorous observation in *Cranford*, returned in a different mood to manufacturing life in *North and South*, conquered the pastoral episode in *Cousin Phillis*, and died, more than rivalling Anthony Trollope, in the social-provincial novel of *Wives and Daughters*. Each of these books might have sustained a reputation; they were so different that they have stood somewhat in one another's way. But the absence of the personal magnetism—emphasised by the fact that all particulars regarding the life and character of Mrs. Gaskell have been sedulously concealed from public knowledge—has determined a persistent under-valuation of this writer's gifts, which were of a very high, although a too miscellaneous order.

It is impossible, while dealing with these glories of the middle Victorian period, to omit, although he still lives, all mention of one more glorious still. Full of intellectual shortcomings and moral inconsistencies as is the matter of Mr. JOHN RUSKIN, his manner at its best is simply incomparable. If the student rejects for the moment, as of secondary or even tertiary importance, all that Mr. Ruskin has written for the last forty years, and confines his attention to those solid achievements, the first three volumes of *Modern Painters*, the *Stones of Venice*, and the *Seven Lamps of Architecture*, he will find himself in presence of a virtuoso whose dexterity in the mechanical part of prose style has never been exceeded. The methods which he adopted almost in childhood—he was a finished writer by 1837—were composite ; he began by mingling with the romantic freshness of Scott qualities derived from the poets and the painters, " vial-fuls, as it were, of Wordsworth's reverence, Shelley's sensitiveness, Turner's accuracy." Later on, to these he added technical elements, combining with the music of the English Bible the reckless richness of the seventeenth-century divines perhaps, but most certainly and fatally the eccentric force of Carlyle. If, however, this olla-podrida' of divergent mannerisms goes to make up the style of Ruskin, that style itself is one of the most definite and characteristic possible.

What it was which Mr. Ruskin gave to the world under the pomp and procession of his effulgent style, it is, perhaps, too early yet for us to realise. But it is plain that he was the greatest phenomenal teacher of the age ; that, dowered with unsurpassed delicacy and swiftness of observation, and with a mind singularly unfettered by convention, the book of the physical world lay open before him.as it had lain before no previous poet or painter, and that he could not cease from the ecstasy of sharing with the public his wonder and his joy in its revelations. It will, perhaps, ultimately be discovered that his elaborate, but often whimsical and sometimes even incoherent disquisitions on art resolve themselves into this—the rapture of a man who sees, on clouds alike and on canvases, in a flower or in a missal, visions of illuminating beauty, which he has the unparalleled accomplishment of being able instantly and effectively to translate into words.

The happy life being that in which illusion is most prevalent, and Mr. Ruskin's enthusiasm having fired more minds to the instinctive quest of beauty than that of any other man who ever lived, we are guilty of no exaggeration if we hail him as one of the first of benefactors. Yet his intellectual nature was from the start imperfect, his sympathies always violent and paradoxical ; there were whole areas of life from which he was excluded ; and nothing but the splendour and fulness of his golden trumpets concealed the fact that some important instruments were lacking to his orchestra. It is as a purely descriptive writer that he has always been seen at his best, and here he is distinguished from exotic rivals—at home he has had none—by the vivid moral excitement that dances, an incessant sheet-lightning, over the background of each gorgeous passage. In this effect of the metaphysical temperament, Mr. Ruskin is sharply differentiated from Continental masters of description and art initiation — from Fromentin, for instance, with whom he may be instructively contrasted.

The excessive popularity enjoyed by the writings of JOHN STUART MILL at the time of his death has already undergone great diminution, and will probably continue to shrink. This eminent empirical philosopher was a very honest man, no sophist, no rhetorician, but one who, in a lucid, intelligible, convincing style, placed before English readers views of an advanced character, with the value of which he was sincerely impressed. The world has since smiled at the precocious artificiality of his education, and has shrunk from something arid and adust in the character of the man. Early associated with Carlyle, he did not allow himself to be infected by Carlylese, but carefully studied and imitated the French philosophers. His *System of Logic* (1843) and his *Political Economy* (1848) placed his scientific reputation on a firm basis. But Mill could be excited, and even violent, in the cause of his convictions, and he produced a wider, if not a deeper impression by his remarkable sociological essays on *Liberty* (1859) and the *Subjection of Women.* He is, unfortunately for the durability of his writings, fervid without being exhilarating. Sceptical and dry, precise and plain, his works inspire respect, but do not attract new generations of admirers.

The greatest of Victorian natural philosophers, CHARLES DARWIN, was a man of totally different calibre. He had not the neatness of Mill's mind, nor its careful literary training, and he remained rather unfortunately indifferent to literary expression. But he is one of the great artificers of human thought, a noble figure destined, in utter simplicity and abnegation of self, to perform one of the most stirring and inspiring acts ever carried out by a single intelligence, and to reawaken the sources of human enthusiasm. Darwin's great suggestion, of life evolved by the process of natural selection, is so far-reaching in its effects as to cover not science only, but art and literature as well; and he had the genius to carry this suggested idea, past all objections and obstacles, up to the station of a biological system the most generally accepted of any put forth in recent times. In the years of his youth there was a general curiosity excited among men of science as to the real origins of life; it became the glory of Charles Darwin to sum up these inquiries in the form of a theory which was slowly hailed in all parts of the world of thought as the only tenable one. From 1831 to 1836 he had the inestimable privilege of attending, as collecting naturalist, a scientific expedition in the waters of the southern hemisphere. After long meditation, in 1859 his famous *Origin of Species* was given to the public, and awakened a furious controversy. In 1871 it was followed by the *Descent of Man*, which, although more defiant of theological prejudice, was, owing to the progress of evolutionary ideas in the meanwhile, more tamely received. Darwin lived long enough to see the great biological revolution, which he had inaugurated, completely successful, and—if that was of importance to a spirit all composed of humble simplicity—his name the most famous in the intellectual world.

XI

THE AGE OF TENNYSON

THE record of half a century of poetic work performed by ALFRED TENNYSON between 1842, when he took his position as the leading poet after Wordsworth, and 1892, when he died, is one of unequalled persistency and sustained evenness of flight. If Shakespeare had continued to write on into the Commonwealth, or if Goldsmith had survived to welcome the publication of *Sense and Sensibility*, these might have been parallel cases. The force of Tennyson was twofold: he did not yield his pre-eminence before any younger writer to the very last, and he preserved a singular uniformity in public taste in poetry by the tact with which he produced his contributions at welcome moments, not too often, nor too irregularly, nor so fantastically as to endanger his hold on the popular suffrage. He suffered no perceptible mental decay, even in the extremity of age, and on his deathbed, in his eighty-fourth year, composed a lyric as perfect in its technical delicacy of form as any which he had written in his prime. Tennyson, therefore, was a power of a static species: he was able, by the vigour and uniformity of his gifts, to hold English poetry stationary for sixty years, a feat absolutely unparalleled elsewhere ; and the result of various revolutionary movements in prosody and style made during the Victorian age was merely in every case temporary. There was an explosion, the smoke rolled away, and Tennyson's statue stood exactly where it did before.

In this pacific and triumphant career certain critical moments may be mentioned. In each of his principal writings Tennyson loved to sum up a movement of popular speculation. In 1847 feminine education was in the air, and the poet published his serio-comic or sentimentalist-satiric educational narrative of the *Princess*, the most artificial of his works, a piece of long-drawn exquisite *marivaudage* in the most softly gorgeous blank verse. In 1850, by inevitable selection, Tennyson succeeded Wordsworth as Laureate, and published anonymously the monumental elegy of *In Memoriam*. This poem had been repeatedly taken up since the death, seventeen years before, of its accomplished and beloved subject, Arthur Hallam. As it finally appeared, the anguish of bereavement was toned down by time, and an atmosphere of philosophic resignation tempered the whole. What began in a spasmodic record of memories and intolerable regret, closed in a confession of faith and a repudiation of the right to despair. The skill of Tennyson enabled him to conceal this irregular and fragmentary construction ; but *In Memoriam* remains a disjointed edifice, with exquisitely carved chambers and echoing corridors that lead to nothing. It introduced into general recognition a metrical form, perhaps invented by Ben Jonson, at once so simple and so salient, that few since Tennyson have ventured to repeat it, in spite of his extreme success.

The Crimean war deeply stirred the nature of Tennyson, and his agitations are reflected in the most feverish and irregular of all his principal compositions, the *Maud*

24

of 1855. This volume contains ample evidence of a hectic condition of feeling. It is strangely experimental; in it the poet passes on occasion further from the classical standards of style than anywhere else, and yet he rises here and there into a rose-flushed ecstasy of plastic beauty that reminds us of what the statue must have seemed a moment after the breath of the Goddess enflamed it. The volume of 1855 is an epitome of all Tennyson in quintessence—the sumptuous, the simple, the artificial, the eccentric qualities are here; the passionately and brilliantly uplifted, the morbidly and caustically harsh moods find alternate expression; the notes of nightingale and night-jar are detected in the strange antiphonies of this infinitely varied collection.

For the remainder of his long life Tennyson concentrated his talents mainly on one or two themes or classes of work. He desired to excel in epic narrative and in the drama. It will be found that most of his exertions in these last five-and-twenty years took this direction. From his early youth he had nourished the design of accomplishing that task which so many of the great poets of England had vainly desired to carry out, namely, the celebration of the national exploits of King Arthur. In 1859 the first instalment of *Idylls of the King* was, after many tentative experiments, fairly placed before the public, and in 1872 the series closed. In 1875 Tennyson issued his first drama, *Queen Mary;* and in spite of the opposition of critical opinion, on the stage and off it, he persisted in the successive production of six highly elaborated versified plays, of which, at length, one, *Becket,* proved a practical success on the boards. That the enforced issue of these somewhat unwelcome dramas lessened the poet's-hold over the public was obvious, and almost any other man in his seventy-sixth year would have acquiesced. But the artistic energy of Tennyson was unconquerable, and with a juvenile gusto and a marvellous combination of politic tact and artistic passion the aged poet called the public back to him with the four irresistible volumes of ballads, idyls, songs, and narratives of which the *Tiresias* of 1885 was the first, and the *Death of Œnone* of 1892 the fourth. It would be idle to pretend that the enchanting colours were not a little faded, the romantic music slightly dulled, in these last accomplishments; yet, if they showed something of the wear and tear of years, they were no "dotages," to use Dryden's phrase, but the characteristic and still admirable exercises of a very great poet who simply was no longer young. When, at length, Tennyson passed away, it was in the midst of such a paroxysm of national grief as has marked the demise of no other English author. With the just and reverent sorrow for so dear a head, something of exaggeration and false enthusiasm doubtless mingled. The fame of Tennyson is still, and must for some years continue to be, an element of disturbance in our literary history. A generation not under the spell of his personal magnificence of mien will be called upon to decide what his final position among the English poets is to be, and before that happens the greatest of the Victorian luminaries will probably, for a moment at least, be shorn of some of his beams.

The long-drawn popularity of the mellifluous and polished poetry of Tennyson would probably have resulted, in the hands of his imitators, in a fatal laxity and fluidity of style. But it was happily counteracted by the example of ROBERT BROWNING, who asserted the predominance of the intellect in analytic production,

and adopted forms which by their rapidity and nakedness were specially designed not to cover up the mental
process. If the poetry of the one was like a velvety
lawn, that of the other resembled the rocky bed of a
river, testifying in every inch to the volume and velocity
of the intellectual torrent which formed it. So, a couple
of centuries before, the tumultuous brain of Donne had
been created to counterpoise and correct the voluptuous
sweetness of the school of Spenser. If any mind more
original and powerful than Browning's had appeared in
English poetry since Donne, it was Dryden, in whose
masculine solidity, and daring, hurrying progression of
ideas, not a little of the author of *The Ring and the
Book* may be divined. But if Donne had subtlety and
Dryden weight, in Browning alone can be found, combined with these qualities, a skill in psychological
analysis probably unrivalled elsewhere save by Shakespeare, but exerted, not in dramatic relation of character
with character, but in self-dissecting monologue or web
of intricate lyrical speculation.

In Browning and Tennyson alike, the descent from
the romantic writers of the beginning of the century was
direct and close. Each, even Browning with his cosmopolitan tendencies, was singularly English in his line of
descendence, and but little affected by exotic forces.
Each had gaped at Byron and respected Wordsworth ;
each had been dazzled by Shelley and had given his
heart to Keats. There is no more interesting object-
lesson in literature than this example of the different
paths along which the same studies directed two poets
of identical aims. Even the study of the Greeks, to
which each poet gave his serious attention, led them
further and further from one another, and we may

find what resemblance we may between *Tithonus* and *Cleon*, where the technical form is, for once, identical. Tennyson, loving the phrase, the expression, passionately, and smoothing it and caressing it as a sculptor touches and retouches the marmoreal bosom of a nymph, stands at the very poles from Browning, to whom the verbiage is an imperfect conductor of thoughts too fiery and too irreconcilable for balanced speech, and in whom the craving to pour forth redundant ideas, half-molten in the lava turmoil, is not to be resisted. There have been sculptors of this class, too—Michelangelo, Rodin—hardly to be recognised as of the same species as their brethren, from Praxiteles to Chapu. But the plastic art embraces them all, as poetry is glad to own, not the *Lotus - Eaters* only, but *Sordello* also, and even *Fifine at the Fair*.

The course of Browning's fame did not run with the Tennysonian smoothness any more than that of his prosody. After early successes, in a modified degree—*Paracelsus* (1835), even *Strafford* (1837)—the strenuous epic narrative of *Sordello* (1840), written in a sort of crabbed shorthand which even the elect could hardly penetrate, delayed his appreciation and cast him back for many years. The name of Robert Browning became a byword for wilful eccentricity and inter-lunar darkness of style. The successive numbers of *Bells and Pomegranates* (1841–46) found him few admirers in a cautious public thus forewarned against his "obscurity," and even *Pippa Passes*, in spite of its enchanting moral and physical beauty, was eyed askance. Not till 1855 did Robert Browning escape from the designation of "that unintelligible man who married the poet"; but the publication of the two volumes of *Men and Women*, in which the lyrical and impassioned part of his genius absolutely culminated, displayed, to the few who have eyes to see, a poet absolutely independent and of the highest rank.

Then began, and lasted for fifteen years, a period in which Browning, to a partial and fluctuating degree, was accepted as a power in English verse, with his little band of devotees, his wayside altars blazing with half-prohibited sacrifice ; the official criticism of the hour no longer absolutely scandalised, but anxious, so far as possible, to minimise the effect of all this rough and eccentric, yet not " spasmodic " verse. In *Dramatis Personæ* (1864), published after the death of his wife, some numbers seemed glaringly intended to increase the scandal of obscurity ; in others, notably in *Rabbi Ben Ezra*, heights were scaled of melodious and luminous thought, which could, by the dullest, be no longer overlooked ; and circumstances were gradually preparing for the great event of 1868, when the publication of the first volume of *The Ring and the Book* saw the fame of Browning, so long smouldering in vapour, burst forth in a glare that for a moment drowned the pure light of Tennyson himself.

From this point Browning was sustained at the height of reputation until his death. He was at no moment within hailing distance of Tennyson in popularity, but among the ruling class of cultivated persons he enjoyed the splendours of extreme celebrity. He was, at last, cultivated and worshipped in a mode unparalleled, studied during his lifetime as a classic, made the object of honours in their very essence, it might have been presupposed, posthumous. After 1868 he lived for more than twenty years, publishing a vast amount of verse, contained in eighteen volumes, mostly of the old analytic kind, and varying in subject rather than in character. In these he showed over and over again the durable force of his vitality, which in a very unusual degree paralleled that of Tennyson. But although so constantly repeating the stroke, he cannot be said to have changed its direction, and the volume of the blow grew less. The publication of these late books was chiefly valuable as keeping alive popular interest in the writer, and as thus leading fresh generations of readers to what he had published up to 1868.

As a poet and as a prose-writer MATTHEW ARNOLD really addressed two different generations. It is not explained why Arnold waited until his thirty-eighth year before opening with a political pamphlet the extensive series of his prose works. As a matter of fact it was not until 1865 that, with his *Essays in Criticism,* he first caught the ear of the public. But by that time his career as a poet was almost finished. It is by the verses he printed between 1849 and 1855 that Matthew Arnold put his stamp upon English poetry, although he added characteristic things at intervals almost until the time of his death in 1888. But to comprehend his place in the history of literature we ought to consider Arnold twice over—firstly as a poet mature in 1850, secondly as a prose-writer whose masterpieces date from 1865 to 1873. In the former capacity, after a long struggle on the part of the critics to exclude him from Parnassus altogether, it becomes generally admitted that his is considerably the largest name between the generation of Tennyson and Browning and that of the so-called pre-Raphaelites. Besides the exquisite novelty of the voice, something was distinctly gained in the matter of Arnold's early poetry—

a new atmosphere of serene thought was here, a philosophical quality less passionate and tumultuous, the music of life deepened and strengthened. Such absolute purity as his is rare in English poetry ; Arnold in his gravity and distinction is like a translucent tarn among the mountains. Much of his verse is a highly finished study in the manner of Wordsworth, tempered with the love of Goethe and of the Greeks, carefully avoiding the perilous Tennysonian note. His efforts to obtain the Greek effect led Matthew Arnold into amorphous choral experiments, and, on the whole, he was an indifferent metrist. But his devotion to beauty, the composure, simplicity, and dignity of his temper, and his deep moral sincerity, gave to his poetry a singular charm which may prove as durable as any element in modern verse.

The Arnold of the prose was superficially a very different writer. Conceiving that the English controversialists, on whatever subject, had of late been chiefly engaged in " beating the bush with deep emotion, but never starting the hare," he made the discovery of the hare his object. In other words, in literature, in politics, in theology, he set himself to divide faith from superstition, to preach a sweet reasonableness, to seize the essence of things, to war against prejudice and ignorance and national self-conceit. He was full of that " amour des choses de l'esprit" which Guizot had early perceived in him ; he was armed with a delicious style, trenchant, swift, radiantly humorous ; but something made him inaccessible, his instincts were fine and kindly without being really sympathetic, and he was drawn away from his early lucidity to the use of specious turns of thought and sophisms. We live too close to him, and in an intellectual atmosphere of which he is too much a component part, to be certain how far his beautiful ironic prose-writings will have durable influence. At the present moment his prestige suffers from the publication of two posthumous volumes of letters, in which the excellence of Matthew Arnold's heart is illustrated, but which are almost without a flash of genius. But his best verses are incomparable, and they will float him into immortality.

Charlotte Brontë died in 1855, Thackeray in 1862, Elizabeth Gaskell in 1865. GEORGE ELIOT (Marian Evans), although born in the same decade, began to write so late in life and survived so long that she seemed to be part of a later generation. From the death of Dickens in 1870 to her own in 1880, she was manifestly the most prominent novelist in England. Yet it is important to realise that, like all the other Victorian novelists of eminence until we reach Mr. George Meredith, she was born in the rich second decade of the century. It was not until some years after the death of Charlotte Brontë that *Scenes of Clerical Life* revealed a talent which owed much to the bold, innovating spirit of that great woman, but which was evidently exercised by a more academic hand. The style of these short episodes was so delicately brilliant that their hardness was scarcely apparent.

The *Scenes* certainly gave promise of a writer in the first rank. In *Adam Bede*, an elaborate romance of bygone provincial manners, this promise was repeated, although, by an attentive ear, the under-tone of the mechanism was now to be detected. In the *Mill on the Floss* and *Silas Marner* a curious phenomenon appeared—George Eliot divided into two personages. The close observer of nature, mistress of laughter and tears, exquisite in the intensity of cumulative emotion, was present still, but she receded ; the mechanician, overloading her page with pretentious matter, working out her scheme as if she were building a steam-engine, came more and more to the front. In *Felix Holt* and on to *Daniel Deronda* the second personage preponderated, and our ears were deafened by the hum of the philosophical machine, the balance of scenes and sentences, the intolerable artificiality of the whole construction.

George Eliot is a very curious instance of the danger of self-cultivation. No writer was ever more anxious to improve herself and conquer an absolute mastery over her material. But she did not observe, as she entertained the laborious process, that she was losing those natural accomplishments which infinitely outshone the philosophy and science which she so painfully acquired. She was born to please, but unhappily she persuaded herself, or was persuaded, that her mission was to teach the world, to lift its moral tone, and, in consequence, an agreeable rustic writer, with a charming humour and very fine sympathetic nature, found herself gradually uplifted until, about 1875, she sat enthroned on an educational tripod, an almost ludicrous pythoness. From the very first she had been weak in that quality which more than any other is needed by a novelist, imaginative invention. So long as she was humble, and was content to reproduce, with the skilful subtlety of her art, what she had personally heard and seen, her work had delightful merit. But it was an unhappy day when she concluded that strenuous effort, references to a hundred abstruse writers, and a whole technical system of rhetoric would do the wild-wood business of native imagination. The intellectual self-sufficiency of George Eliot has suffered severe chastisement. At the present day scant justice is done to her unquestionable distinction of intellect or to the emotional intensity of much of her early work.

Two writers of less pretension exceeded George Eliot as narrators, though neither equalled her in essential genius at her best. In ANTHONY TROLLOPE English middle-class life found a close and loving portrait-painter, not too critical to be indulgent nor too accommodating to have flashes of refreshing satire. The talent of Trollope forms a link between the closer, more perspicuous naturalism of Jane Austen and the realism of a later and coarser school. The cardinal merit of the irregular novels of CHARLES READE was their intrepidity; the insipid tendency of the early Victorians to deny the existence of instinct received its death-blow from the sturdy author of *Griffith Gaunt*, who tore the pillows from all armholes, and, by his hatred of what was artificial, sacerdotal, and effeminate, prepared the way for a freer treatment of experience. His style, although not without serious blemishes, and ill sustained, has vigorous merits. Through the virile directness of Charles Reade runs the chain which binds Mr. George Meredith and Mr. Hardy to the early Victorian novelists.

A certain tendency to the chivalric and athletic ideals in life, combining a sort of vigorous Young Englandism with enthusiastic discipleship of Carlyle, culminated in the breezy, militant talent of CHARLES KINGSLEY. He was full of knightly hopes and generous illusions, a leader of "Christian Socialists," a tilter against windmills of all sorts. He worked as a radical and sporting parson in the country, finding leisure to write incessantly on a hundred themes. His early novels, and some of his miscellaneous treatises, written half in jest and half in earnest, enjoyed an overwhelming success. But Kingsley had no judgment, and he overestimated the range of his aptitudes. He fancied himself to be a controversialist and an historian. He engaged in public contest with a strong man better armed than himself, and he accepted a professorial chair for which nothing in his training had fitted him. His glory was somewhat tarnished, and he died sadly and prematurely in 1871. But his best books have shown an extraordinary tenacity of life, and though he failed in many branches of literature, his successes in one or two seem permanent. In verse, his ballads are excellent, and he made an experiment in hexameters which remains the best in English. If his early socialistic novels begin to be obsolete, *Hypatia* and *Westward Ho!* have borne the strain of forty years, and are as fresh as ever. The vivid style of Kingsley was characteristic of his violent and ill-balanced, but exquisitely cheery nature.

With Kingsley's should be mentioned a name which, dragged down in the revulsion following upon an excessive reputation, is now threatened by an equally unjust neglect. With Kingsley there came into vogue a species of descriptive writing, sometimes very appropriate and beautiful, sometimes a mere shredding of the cabbage into the pot. To achieve success in this kind of literature very rare gifts have to be combined, and not all who essay to "describe" present an image to our mental vision. In the more gorgeous and flamboyant class Mr. Ruskin had early been predominant; in a quieter kind, there was no surer eye than that of ARTHUR PENRYN STANLEY. Quite early in his career he attracted notice by an excellent *Life of Dr. Arnold* (1844); but the peculiar phenomenal faculty of which we are here speaking began to be displayed much later in his *Sinai and Palestine*—where, save in the use of colour, he may be compared with M. Pierre Loti—and in his extremely vivid posthumous correspondence. It will be a pity if, in the natural decay of what was ephemeral in Stanley's influence, this rare visual endowment be permitted to escape attention.

A group of historians of unusual vivacity and merit gave to the central Victorian period a character quite their own. Of these writers—warm friends or bitter enemies in personal matters, but closely related in the manner of their work—five rose to particular eminence. Two of them are happily still with us, and are thus excluded from consideration here. This is the less important, perhaps, in that the purely literary elements of this school of history are to be sought much less in the Bishop of Oxford and Dr. S. R. Gardiner than in Froude, Freeman, and Green. Of the group, JAMES ANTHONY FROUDE was the oldest, and he was at Oxford just at the time when the Tractarian Movement was exciting all generous minds. Greatly under the influence of Newman in the forties, Froude took orders, and was closely connected with the High Church party. With this group Freeman also, though less prominently, was and remained allied, and his anger was excited when Froude, instead of following Newman to Rome, or staying with the agitated Anglican remnant, announced his entire defection from the religious system by the publication of the *Nemesis of Faith* in 1849. From this time forth the indignation of Freeman was concentrated and implacable, and lasted without intermission for more than forty years. The duel between these men was a matter of such constant public entertainment that it claims mention in a history, and distinctly moulded the work of both these interesting artists.

In the line taken up by Froude he owed something to the advice of Carlyle, more to the spirit of close and sympathetic research inculcated by Sir Francis Palgrave. He set himself to a *History of England from the Fall of Wolsey to the Destruction of the Spanish Armada*, and this huge work, in twelve volumes, was completed in 1870. Attacked by specialists from the very first, this book was welcomed with ever-increasing warmth by the general public. Froude had an extraordinary power of holding the interest of the reader, and he appealed directly, and with seldom-failing success, to the instincts of the average man. He was curiously unaffected by those masters of popular history who held the ear of the world during his youth; he bears little trace of Macaulay and none of Carlyle in the construction of his sentences. He held history to be an account of the actions of men, and he surpassed all his English pre-decessors in the exactitude with which he seemed to re-embody the characters and emotions of humanity, blowing the dust away from the annals of the past. That he was a partisan, that he was violently swayed (as pre-eminently in his magnificent rehabilitation of Henry VIII.) not so much by a passion for facts as by philosophical prejudices, took away from the durable value of his writing, but not from its immediate charm. Froude possessed in high degree that faculty of imaginative and reproductive insight which he recognised as being one of the rarest of qualities; unhappily, it cannot be said that he possessed what he himself has described as "the moral determination to use it for purposes of truth only."

But if it is impossible to admit that Froude had the infatuation for veracity which may coexist with an inveterate tendency to blunder about details, there are yet very sterling merits in Froude's work which the attacks of his enemies entirely fail to obscure. If we compare him with Hallam and Macaulay, we see a regular advance in method. With all his judicial attitude, Hallam seldom comprehends the political situation, and never realises personal character ; Macaulay, though still unable to achieve the second, accurately measures the first ; Froude, with astonishing completeness, is master of both. It is this which, together with the supple and harmonious beauty of his periods, gives him the advantage over that estimable and learned, but somewhat crabbed writer, EDWARD AUGUSTUS FREEMAN, whose great *History of the Norman Conquest* was completed in 1876. It is said that Froude worked up his authorities, inflamed his imagination, and then, with scarcely a note to help his memory, covered his canvas with a flowing brush. Freeman, on the other hand, is never out of sight of his authorities, and in many instances, through pages and pages, his volumes are simply a cento of paraphrases from the original chroniclers. He gained freshness, and, when his text was trustworthy, an extreme exactitude ; but he missed the charm of the fluid oratory of narrative, the flushed and glowing improvisation of Froude. In consequence, the style of Freeman varies so extremely that it is difficult to offer any general criticism of it. In certain portions of the *Harold*, for instance, it reaches the very nadir of dreariness ; while his famous "night which was to usher in the ever-memorable morn of Saint Calixtus" suggests how finely he might have persuaded himself to see and to describe.

The cardinal gift of Freeman, however, was certainly not his painstaking treatment of documents, but the remarkable breadth of his historic view. I have heard that he once said that he never could decide whether modern history should begin with Napoleon I. or with the prophet Abraham. In one or the other case he saw the great map of history outrolled before his mental vision as perhaps no other man has seen it; and when to a portion of the vast subject so sanely comprehended he applied his rare analytical genius, the result was surprisingly convincing. The utterances of Freeman on the large trend of historical philosophy are therefore of particular value, and it is regrettable that that they are comparatively few. It is on this side of his genius that his influence on younger historians has been so great. In JOHN RICHARD GREEN a poet in history combined the picturesqueness of Froude with something of the exactitude and breadth of Freeman. The *Short History of the English People*, in 1874, produced a sensation such as is rarely effected in these days by any book that is not a masterpiece of imaginative art. It treated history in a new vein, easily, brightly, keenly, sometimes with an almost jaunty vivacity. The danger of Green lay in his excess of poetic sensibility, his tendency to be carried away by his flow of animal spirits, to confound what was with what must or should have been; but he was a delightful populariser of history, a man of strongly emphasised character who contrived to fascinate a world of readers by charging his work with evidences of his own gay subjectivity.

A tradition, handed down, perhaps, from the practice of the schoolmen, encourages philosophy to dispense with all æsthetic aids to expression. The names of Berkeley and Hume are sufficient to remind us that these barren and rigid forms of technical language are not obligatory, but Locke and Butler are almost excluded from mention in the history of style by the repulsive bareness of their diction. Nor is the greatest philosopher of these latest times in any way solicitous about the form of his address, which is yet at times, and when he warms to his subject, sympathetic and persuasive. But there are two reasons, among many, why the name of Mr. HERBERT SPENCER must not be omitted from such a summary as ours : firstly, because no Englishman of his age has made so deep an intellectual impression on foreign thought, or is so widely known throughout Europe ; and, secondly, because of the stimulating effect which his theories have exercised over almost every native author of the last twenty years.

Mr. Spencer adopted from Auguste Comte, who invented the term, the word "sociology," which implies a science of politics and society. He started from the position of Comte, but he soon went much further. His central theory is that society is an organism, a form of vital evolution, not to be separated from the general growth of Man. It follows that Mr. Spencer is an ultra-individualist, who brings, not biology only, but all precedent forces of knowledge to the aid of his ideas. He summons us to witness, in all phases of existence, the vast cosmical process of evolution proceeding. His admirers have not failed to point out that in his *Principles of Psychology* (1855) the theory of Darwin was foreseen. But Mr. Spencer did not become a power in thought until long after that time. His most famous works appeared between 1872 and 1884. The world, unable to grasp his grander conceptions, has been greatly entertained by his lighter essays, in

25

which his personal style appears to most advantage. He warns us of the perils the individual runs in the extension of the responsibilities of the State. He fights against the coming slavery of socialism. He sharply distinguishes the duty of the family from the charge of the State, and has even dared to attack the divine right of Parliaments. But these are but straws floating on the flood of his enormous theory of sociological phenomena.

From the large class who have adorned and enriched the natural sciences with their investigations and observations, there project two men whose gift for elegant and forcible expression was so great as to win for them a purely literary reputation also. Such men grow rare and rarer, as the statement of scientific fact tends to become more and more abstruse and algebraic. JOHN TYNDALL, the physicist, conciliated critical opinion by the courage with which he insisted on the value of the imagination in the pursuit of scientific inquiry. He had remarkable rhetorical gifts, and in his early publications on mountain structure he cultivated a highly coloured style, influenced by Ruskin, and even by Tennyson. Perhaps the best-written of his philosophical treatises is the *Forms of Water* (1872), where his tendency to polychromatic rodomontade is kept in some check. A purer and a manlier style was that of THOMAS HENRY HUXLEY, the biologist, whose contributions to controversy, in which he showed a remarkable courage and adroitness, were published as *Lay Sermons, Addresses, and Reviews*, in 1870. It was Huxley's passion to " war upon the lions in the wood;" and his whole life through he was attacking the enemies of thought, as he conceived them, and defending the pioneers of evolution. In the arena of a sort of militant philosophical essay, the colour of which he borrowed in measure from his beloved Hume, Huxley was ready for all comers, and acquitted himself with unrivalled athletic prowess. Of his morphological and physiographical work this is no place to speak.

The wealth of secondary verse in the central Victorian period was great, but it is not possible to preserve the proportion which regulates this volume and yet record its features here in detail. Certainly, on the face of things, no poet (except Arnold) between Browning and the pre-Raphaelites constrains our attention. The tendency to be affected by the polished amenity of Tennyson's style was successively experienced by generations, not one of which found itself strong enough to rise in successful revolt. In the middle of the century a group of writers, inspired by the study of Goethe's *Faust*, and anxious to enlarge the emotional as well as the intellectual scope of British verse, attempted a revolution which preserves some historical interest. Both Tennyson and Browning were violently affected by their experiments, which closely resembled those of the much later Symbolists in France. The more impressionist and irregular passages of *Maud* are, in fact, the most salient records in English literature of "spasmodic" poetry, the actual leaders of which are now of little note.

The Tennysonian tradition, however, put a great strain on the loyalty of young writers, and at length a movement was organised which involved no rebellion against the Laureate, but a very valuable modification of the monotony of his methods. The emergence of a compact body of four poets of high rank between 1865 and 1870 is a fact of picturesque importance in our literary history.

The impulse seems to have been given to them, in the first instance, by the writings and the personal teachings of Mr. Ruskin ; on their style may be traced the stamp of a pamphlet, long disdained, which becomes every year more prominent in its results. It would be difficult to say what was exactly the effect on the pre-Raphaelites of the paraphrase of the *Rubaiyat* of Omar Khayyám published in 1859 by Edward Fitz-Gerald, but the melody of this translation, and its peculiar fragrance, were the most original elements introduced into English verse for forty ,years. The strange genius of Fitz-Gerald, so fitfully and coyly revealed, has given a new quality to English verse, almost all recent manifestations of which it pervades.

If, however, the quickening effect of the frail leaf of intoxicating perfume put forth by Fitz-Gerald is manifest on the prosody of the poets of 1870, far different influences are to be traced in the texture of their style. Their genius was particularly open to such influences, for their charm was the composite charm of a highly elaborated and cultivated product, by the side of which even the polish of Tennyson at first appeared crude and primitive. The attraction of the French romances of chivalry for William Morris, of Tuscan painting for D. G. Rossetti, of the spirit of English Gothic architecture for Christina Rossetti, of the combination of all these with Greek and Elizabethan elements for Mr. Swinburne, were to be traced back to start-words given by the prophetic author of the *Seven Lamps of Architecture*. In each case, finding that the wine of imaginative writing had become watered in England, their design was to crush anew in a fiery vintage what Keats had called " Joy's grape."

These poets were all mediæval in their spirit, but with a mediævalism that swept them on, not to asceticisms of an intellectual species, but to a plastic expansion in which they achieved a sort of new renaissance. In them all, even in the saintly Christina, the instinct of physical beauty was very strongly developed ; each of them was a phenomenal and sensuous being, dried up in the east wind of mere moral speculation, and turning to pure, material art, with its technical and corporeal qualities, for relief and satisfaction. They found the texture of those species of poetry in which they desired to excel. much relaxed by the imitation of imitations of Tennyson. That great poet himself was in some danger of succumbing to flattery of what was least admirable in his talent. The date of their first books—the *Defence of Guenevere* (1858), *Goblin Market*, the *Early Italian Poets*, and the *Queen Mother and Rosamond* (all 1861)—gives a false impression of the place the four poets occupy in the history of influence, for these volumes hardly attracted even the astonishment of the public, and the publication of *Atalanta in Calydon* (1865) really marked the beginning of a sensation which culminated in the overwhelming success of D. G. Rossetti's *Poems* in 1870.

For a moment the victory of the four, exacerbating the public mind in some cases with elements of mystery, scandal, and picturesque inscrutability, tended to confuse the real development of Victorian poetry. At first, in their blaze of colour and blare of trumpets, nothing else was heard or seen. Then, as the landscape quieted again, the great figures were rediscovered in the background— Tennyson as dominant as ever, with a new freshness of tint ; Browning extremely advanced, lifted from the position of an eccentricity to be an object of worship ; Matthew Arnold the poet dragged from the obscurity to which his prose successes had condemned him ; while a number of small celebrities who had been enjoying an exaggerated esteem found themselves fatally relegated to a surprising inferiority. In short, what had been conceived to be the disturbing introduction of these young people of genius, of this generation of knockers at the door, had set the critical balance of matters straight again, and had given the really considerable .personages of an elder time an opportunity to assert their individual forces.

But another matter of importance, which was hardly perceived at the time, now calls for emphatic statement in the briefest survey of Victorian poetry. It was in the verse of these so-called revolutionaries that the dogmas of the original naturalists of 1795 found their fullest and most conservative echo. No poet since Coleridge's day, not even Tennyson, had understood the song, as that master had conceived it, with more completeness than Christina Rossetti; no poet since Keats, not even Tennyson, had understood the mission of Keats better than D. G. Rossetti did. And in these writers of 1865 the school of ecstasy and revolt, with its intermixture of mysticism, colour, melody, and elaboration of form, reached its consistent and deliberate culmination. Into the question of their relative degree of merit it would be premature to inquire here; we are chiefly concerned with the extraordinary note of vitality which these four poets combined to introduce into English imaginative literature, founded, in the truest spirit of evolution, on an apprehension and adaptation of various elements in precedent art and letters.

Almost immediately upon the apparition of the so-called "pre-Raphaelite" poets, and in many cases in positive connection with them, there happened a great

and salutary quickening of the spirit of literary criticism
in England. It remained largely individualist, and therefore liable to an excess of praise and blame which was
not philosophical in character or founded upon a just
conception of the natural growth of literary history.
But the individual judgments became, to a marked degree, more fresh, more suggestive, more penetrating, and
were justified by greater knowledge. The influence of
French methods was apparent and wholly beneficial.
The severer spirits read Sainte Beuve to their healing, and
as years went on the more gorgeous pages of Théophile
Gautier and Paul de St. Victor were studied in England
by those who undertook most conscientiously the task
of literary criticism. The time has, happily, not come
to discuss with any fulness the merits and shortcomings
of a school still labouring among us; but the most original
and the most philosophical of the group, Walter Pater,
has been too remarkable a force in our generation to
remain unnamed here. During his lifetime of more than
fifty years, Pater never succeeded in achieving more than
a grudging and uncertain recognition from his contemporaries. He died, almost obscure, in 1894, and since
that time his fame, and above all his influence, have
been rising by leaps and bounds. As it was till lately
desirable to demand attention for the splendid propor-
tions of his prose, so full and stately in its ornate harmony,
so successful in its avoidance of the worn and obvious
tricks of diction, its slender capitals so thickly studded
with the volutes and spirals of concentrated ornament,
so now a word seems no less to be needed lest Pater
should be ignorantly imitated, a word of warning against
something heavy, almost pulpy, in his soft magnificence
of style. His deliberate aim was the extraction from

literature, from art, of " the quickened sense of life."
As he loved to say with Novalis, *philosophiren ist vivi-
ficiren,* and the task of the best criticism is to maintain
the ecstasy of intellectual experience. The mind of
Pater underwent an austere metamorphosis in advancing
years, but this elevated hedonism of his youth enclosed
his main gift to his generation.

We are, however, in danger of entangling our impressions with one another if we pursue too low down the
threads which we have attempted to hold through more
than five centuries from Langland and Chaucer to Huxley
and Pater.   We must drop them here, leaving them loose,
for they are parts of a living organism, and we cannot
presume to say in what direction their natural growth
will lead them next, nor what relative value their parts
may take in fuller perspective.   We have spoken of nothing
which was not revealed in its general aspect and direction
at least five-and-twenty years ago.   In periods of very
rapid literary development this would be a time long
enough to bring about the most startling changes.   Within
the boundaries of one quarter of a century the English
drama did not exist, and *Hamlet* was complete.   In 1773
Dr. Johnson accompanied Boswell to the Hebrides, and
in 1798 the *Lyrical Ballads* were published.   But there is
no evidence to show that the twenty-five years through
which we have just passed have been years of a very
experimental tendency.   Fifteen or twenty of them were
overshadowed, and their production stunted, by the per-
manence of great, authoritative personages, still in full
activity.   The age was the age of Tennyson, and he held
his kingship, an absolute monarch, against all comers,
until his death in 1892.   We may anticipate that future
historians may make that date the starting-point for a

new era, but this is for us scarcely matter even for speculation. Up to 1892, certainly, we can affirm the maintenance, without radical change of any kind, of the original romantic system, now just one hundred years old. With a myriad minor variations and adaptations, poetry in England, and therefore prose, is still what it became when Wordsworth and Coleridge remodelled it in 1797 in the coombes of the Quantocks.

EPILOGUE

IN attempting to follow the course of a great literature
and to survey the process of its growth, one reflection can
never escape the historian, however little it may gratify his
vanity. He forms his opinions, if he be fairly instructed
and tolerably conscientious, on a series of æsthetic principles, guided in their interpretation by the dictates of
his own temperament. There has as yet been discovered no surer method of creating a critical estimate
of literature ; and yet the fragility and vacillation of this
standard is patent to every one whose brains have not
become ossified by vain and dictatorial processes of
"teaching." Nowhere is an arrogant dogmatism so
thoroughly out of place than in a critical history of style.
In our own day we have read, in the private letters of
Matthew Arnold—one of the most clairvoyant observers
of the last generation—judgments on current books and
men which are already seen to be patently incorrect.
The history of literary criticism is a record of conflicting
opinion, of blind prejudice, of violent *volte-faces*, of
discord and misapprehension. If we could possess the
sincere opinions of Ben Jonson, Dryden, Addison, Voltaire, Hazlitt, Goethe, and M. Jules Lemaître on *Hamlet*,
we should probably doubt that the same production
could be the subject of them all. In the seventeenth
century Shakespeare was regarded as one of a multi-

tude, a little more careless and sometimes a little more felicitous than his fellows. To the eighteenth century he became a Gothic savage, in whose "wood-notes wild" the sovereignty of Nature was reasserted, as if by accident. It was left to the nineteenth century to discover in him the most magnificent of the conscious poetic artists of the world. But what will the twentieth century think ?

We are not, I think, so helpless as these admissions and examples would indicate, nor is there the least valid reason why we should withdraw from the expression of critical opinion because of the dangers which attend it. I must hold, in spite of the censure of writers of an older school who possess every claim upon my gratitude and my esteem, that certain changes have recently passed over human thought which alter the whole nature of the atmosphere in which criticism breathes. A French professor of high repute has attacked, as an instance of effrontery and charlatanism, the idea that we can borrow for the study of literature help from the methods of Darwin and Häckel. He scoffs at the notion of applying to poetry and prose the theory which supposes all plant and animal forms to be the result of slow and organic modification. With every respect for the authority of so severe a censor, I venture to dissent entirely from his views. I believe, on the contrary, that what delays the progress of criticism in England, where it is still so primitive and so empirical, is a failure to employ the immense light thrown on the subject by the illustrations of evolution. I believe that a sensible observation of what Darwin and Mr. Herbert Spencer have demonstrated ought to aid us extremely in learning our trade as critics and in conducting it in a business-like manner.

In the days of the Jesuits, when modern criticism
began in Europe, it was the general opinion that
literature had been created, fully armed, in polite antiquity ; that Homer—especially Homer as explained by
Aristotle—had presented the final perfection of literature.
If any variation from this original archaic type was ever
observed, it must be watched with the greatest care ; for
if it was important, it must be dangerous and false.   The
only salvation for style was to be incessantly on one's
guard to reject any offshoots or excrescences which,
however beautiful they might seem in themselves, were
not measurable by the faultless canon of antiquity.   The
French critics, such as Rapin and Bossu, were saved by
their suppleness of intelligence and by dealing solely
with a Latin people from the monstrosities which befell
their Teutonic and English adherents.   But it is instructive to see where persistence in this theory of the
unalterable criterium lands an obstinate writer like
Rymer.   He measures everybody, Shakespeare among
the rest, on the bed of Procrustes, and lops our giants
at the neck and the knees.

The pent-up spirit of independence broke forth in
that Battle of the Ancients and Moderns which is of so
much secondary interest in the chronicles of literature.
People saw that we could not admit that there had been
in extreme antiquity a single act of special literary creation constituting once for all a set of rigid types.   But
the Jesuits had at least possessed the advantage of an
idea, monstrous though it might be.   Their opponents
simply rejected their view, and had nothing definite to
put in its place.   Nothing can be more invertebrate than
the criticism of the early eighteenth century.   Happy,
vague ideas, glimmering through the mist, supplied a

little momentary light and passed away. Shaftesbury, amid a great deal of foppery about the Dæmon which inspires the Author with the Beautiful and the Amiable, contrived to perceive the relation between poetry and the plastic arts, and faintly to formulate a system of literary æsthetics. Dennis had the really important intuition that we ought to find out what an author desires to do before we condemn him for what he has not done. Addison pierced the bubble of several preposterous and exclusive formulas. But England was as far as the rest of Europe from possessing any criterium of literary production which could take the place of the rules of the Jesuits. Meanwhile, the individualist method began to come into vogue, and to a consideration of this a few words must be spared.

The individualist method in literary criticism has been in favour with us for at least a century, and it is still in vogue in most of our principal reviews. It possesses in adroit hands considerable effectiveness, and in its primary results may be entirely happy. It is in its secondary results that it leads to a chaotic state of opinion. It is, after all, an adaptation of the old theory of the unalterable type, but it merely alternates for the one "authority of the Ancients" an equal rigidity in a multitude of isolated modern instances. It consists in making a certain author, or fashion, or set of æsthetic opinions the momentary centre of the universe, and in judging all other literary phenomena by their nearness to or remoteness from that arbitrary point. At the beginning of the present century it seduced some of the finest minds of the day into ludicrous and grotesque excesses. It led Keats into his foolish outburst about Boileau, because his mind was fixed on Beaumont and Fletcher. It led De Quincey to say that both the thought and expression of one of Pope's most perfect passages were "scandalously vicious," because his mind was fixed on Wordsworth. In these cases Wordsworth and Fletcher were beautiful and right; but Pope and Boileau were, on the surface, absolutely in opposition to them; Pope and Boileau were therefore hideous and wrong. Yet admirers of classic poetry have never ceased to retort from their own equally individualist point of view, and to a general principle of literary taste we find ourselves none the nearer. What wonder if the outside world treats all critical discussion as the mere babble of contending flute-players?

But what if a scientific theory be suggested which shall enable us at once to take an intelligent pleasure in Pope and in Wordsworth, in Spenser and in Swift? Mr. Herbert Spencer has, with infinite courage, opened the entire world of phenomena to the principles of evolution, but we seem slow to admit them into the little province of æsthetics. We cling to the individualist manner, to that intense eulogy which concentrates its rays on the particular object of notice and relegates all others to proportional obscurity. There are critics, of considerable acumen and energy, who seem to know no other mode of nourishing a talent or a taste than that which is pursued by the cultivators of gigantic gooseberries. They do their best to nip off all other buds, that the juices of the tree of fame may be concentrated on their favourite fruit. Such a plan may be convenient for the purposes of malevolence, and in earlier times our general ignorance of the principles of growth might well excuse it. But it is surely time that we should recognise only two criteria of literary judgment. The first is primitive, and merely clears the ground of rubbish; it is, Does the work before us, or the author, perform what he sets out to perform with a distinguished skill in the direction in which his powers are exercised? If not, he interests the higher criticism not at all; but if yes, then follows the second test: Where, in the vast and ever-shifting scheme of literary evolution, does he take his place, and in what relation does he stand, not to those who are least like him, but to those who are of his own kith and kin?

At the close, then, of a rapid summary of the features of literary expression in England, I desire to state my conviction that the only way to approach the subject with instruction is to regard it as part of the history of a vast living organism, directed in its manifestations by a definite, though obscure and even inscrutable law of growth. A monument of poetry, like that which Tennyson has bequeathed to us, is interesting, indeed, as the variegated product of one human brain, strongly individualised by certain qualities from all other brains working in the same generation. But we see little if we see no more than the lofty idiosyncrasy of Tennyson. Born in 1550 or in 1720, he would have possessed the same personality, but his poetry, had he written in verse, could have had scarcely a remote resemblance to what we have now received from his hand. What we are in the habit of describing as "originality" in a great modern poet is largely an aggregation of elements which he has received by inheritance from those who have preceded him, and his "genius" consists of the faculty he possesses of selecting and rearranging, as in a new pattern or harmony, those elements from many predecessors which most admirably suit the only "new" thing about him, his unique set of personal characteristics. Tennyson is himself; his work bears upon it the plain stamp of a recurrent, consistent individuality. Yet it is none the less almost an amalgam of modified adaptations from others. The colour of Tennyson would not be what it is if Keats had never lived, nor does his delicacy of observation take its line of light without a reference to that of Wordsworth. The serried and nervous expression of Pope and the melodic prosody of Milton have passed, by a hereditary process, into the veins of their intellectual descendant. He is a complex instance of natural selection, obvious and almost geometrical, yet interfering not a whit with that counter-principle of individual variation which is needful to make the poet, not a parasite upon his artistic ancestors, but an independent output from the main growing organism. And what is patently true of this great representative poet of our days is in measure true also of the smallest and apparently the most eccentric writer in prose or verse, if he writes well enough to exist at all. Every producer of vital literature adds an offshoot to the unrolling and unfolding organism of literary history in its ceaseless processes of growth.

BIOGRAPHICAL LIST

OF AUTHORS MENTIONED IN THIS VOLUME

ADDISON, JOSEPH	1672–1719
AKENSIDE, MARK	1721–1770
ARBUTHNOT, JOHN	1667–1735
ARNOLD, MATTHEW	1822–1888
ASCHAM, ROGER	1515–1568
AUSTEN, JANE	1775–1817
BACON, FRANCIS, VISCOUNT ST. ALBANS	1560–1626
BAGE, ROBERT	1728–1801
BARBOUR, JOHN	1316(?)–1395
BARCLAY, ALEXANDER	1475(?)–1552
BARROW, ISAAC	1630–1677
BEAUMONT, FRANCIS	1584–1616
BEAUMONT, SIR JOHN	1582–1627
BEDDOES, THOMAS LOVELL	1803–1849
BENTLEY, RICHARD	1662–1742
BERKELEY, GEORGE	1685–1753
BERNERS, JOHN BOURCHIER, LORD	1467–1533
BLAIR, ROBERT	1699–1746
BLAKE, WILLIAM	1757–1827
BLIND HARRY	fl. 15th Cent.
BOLINGBROKE, VISCOUNT	1678–1751
BOSWELL, JAMES	1740–1795
BOWLES, WILLIAM LISLE	1762–1850

BROKE, ARTHUR	*d.* 1563
BRONTË, CHARLOTTE	1816–1855
BRONTË, EMILY	1818–1848
BROWNE, SIR THOMAS	1605–1682
BROWNING, ELIZABETH BARRETT	1809–1861
BROWNING, ROBERT	1812–1889
BRUNTON, MARY	1778–1818
BUNYAN, JOHN	1628–1688
BURKE, EDMUND	1729–1797
BURNEY, FANNY	1752–1840
BURNS, ROBERT	1759–1796
BURTON, ROBERT	1577–1640
BUTLER, JOSEPH	1692–1752
BUTLER, SAMUEL	1612–1680
BYRON, LORD	1788–1824
CAMPBELL, THOMAS	1777–1844
CAMPION, THOMAS	1567(?)–1620
CAPGRAVE, JOHN	1393–1464
CAREW, THOMAS	1598(?)–1639(?)
CARLYLE, THOMAS	1795–1881
CARTE, THOMAS	1686–1754
CARTWRIGHT, WILLIAM	1611–1643
CAVENDISH, GEORGE	1500–1561(?)
CAXTON, WILLIAM	1422(?)–1491
CHAPMAN, GEORGE	1559(?)–1634
CHATTERTON, THOMAS	1752–1770
CHAUCER, GEOFFREY	1340(?)–1400
CHESTERFIELD, EARL OF	1694–1773
CHILLINGWORTH, WILLIAM	1602–1644
CHURCHILL, CHARLES	1731–1764
CHURCHYARD, THOMAS	1520(?)–1604
CLANVOWE, SIR THOMAS	*fl. circa* 1400

CLARENDON, EARL OF	1608–1674
CLARKE, SAMUEL	1675–1729
COLERIDGE, HARTLEY	1796–1849
COLERIDGE, SAMUEL TAYLOR	1772–1834
COLLINS, WILLIAM	1721–1759
CONGREVE, WILLIAM	1670–1729
CONSTABLE, HENRY	1562–1613
COVERDALE, MILES	1488–1568
COWLEY, ABRAHAM	1618–1667
COWPER, WILLIAM	1731–1800
CRABBE, GEORGE	1754–1832
CRANMER, THOMAS	1489–1556
CRASHAW, RICHARD	1612–1649
DANIEL, SAMUEL	1562–1619
DARWIN, CHARLES	1809–1882
DARWIN, ERASMUS	1731–1802
DAVENANT, SIR WILLIAM	1606–1668
DAVYS, SIR JOHN	1565 (?)–1618
DEFOE, DANIEL	1661 (?)–1731
DEKKER, THOMAS	1570 (?)–1641 (?)
DENHAM, SIR JOHN	1615–1669
DENNIS, JOHN	1657–1734
DE QUINCEY, THOMAS	1785–1859
DICKENS, CHARLES	1812–1870
DISRAELI, BENJAMIN	1804–1881
D'ISRAELI, ISAAC	1766–1848
DONNE, JOHN	1573–1631
DOUGLAS, GAWIN	1474 (?)–1522
DRAYTON, MICHAEL	1563–1631
DRUMMOND, WILLIAM	1585–1649
DRYDEN, JOHN	1631–1700
DUNBAR, WILLIAM	1460 (?)–1520 (?)

EDGEWORTH, MARIA 1767–1849
ELIOT, GEORGE (EVANS, MARIAN) . . 1819–1880
ETHEREDGE, SIR GEORGE . . 1634–1693 (?)
EVELYN, JOHN 1620–1706

FARQUHAR, GEORGE 1678–1707
FERGUSSON, ROBERT 1750–1774
FERRIER, SUSAN 1782–1854
FIELDING, HENRY 1707–1754
FITZ-GERALD, EDWARD 1809–1883
FLETCHER, GILES . . . . 1585 (?)–1623
FLETCHER, JOHN 1579–1625
FLETCHER, PHINEAS 1582–1650
FORD, JOHN . . . . . 1586 (?)–1639
FORTESCUE, SIR JOHN . . . 1394 (?)–1476 (?)
FOXE, JOHN 1517–1587
FREEMAN, EDWARD AUGUSTUS . . 1823–1892
FROUDE, JAMES ANTHONY . . . 1818–1894
FULLER, THOMAS 1608–1661

GALT, JOHN 1779–1839
GARTH, SIR SAMUEL 1661–1719
GASCOIGNE, GEORGE . . . 1525 (?)–1577
GASKELL, ELIZABETH CLEGHORN . 1810–1865
GAY, JOHN 1685–1732
GIBBON, EDWARD 1737–1794
GIFFORD, WILLIAM 1756–1826
GILPIN, WILLIAM 1724–1804
GODWIN, WILLIAM 1756–1836
GOLDING, ARTHUR . . . . *fl.* 16th Cent.
GOLDSMITH, OLIVER 1728–1774
GOOGE, BARNABEE 1540–1594
GOWER, JOHN . . . . . 1325 (?)–1408

GRAY, THOMAS 1716-1771
GREEN, JOHN RICHARD 1837-1883
GREENE, ROBERT . . . . 1560 (?)-1592
GRIMALD, NICHOLAS. 1519-1562

HABINGTON, WILLIAM 1605-1654
HALIFAX, GEORGE SAVILE, MARQUIS OF. 1633-1695
HALL, JOSEPH 1574-1656
HALLAM, HENRY 1777-1859
HAWES, STEPHEN . . . . . d. 1523 (?)
HAZLITT, WILLIAM 1778-1830
HENRYSON, ROBERT. . . . 1430 (?)-1506 (?)
HERBERT, GEORGE 1593-1633
HEREFORD, NICHOLAS OF . . . fl. 1390
HERRICK, ROBERT 1591-1674
HEYWOOD, JOHN . . . . 1497 (?)-1580 (?)
HEYWOOD, THOMAS . . . . 1570 (?)-1650 (?)
HOBBES, THOMAS 1588-1679
HOLINSHED, RAPHAEL . . . . d. 1580 (?)
HOOD, THOMAS 1799-1845
HOOKER, RICHARD 1554-1600
HOPE, THOMAS. . . . . 1770 (?)-1831
HORNE, RICHARD HENGIST . . . 1803-1884
HOWELL, JAMES . . . . 1594 (?)-1666
HUME, DAVID 1711-1776
HUNT, LEIGH 1784-1859
HUXLEY, THOMAS HENRY . . . 1825-1895

JAMES I. OF SCOTLAND 1394-1437
JAMES, G. P. R. 1801-1860
JEFFREY, FRANCIS, LORD. . . . 1773-1850
JOHNSON, SAMUEL 1709-1784
JONSON, BENJAMIN 1574-1637

MILTON, JOHN 1608–1674
MITFORD, WILLIAM 1744–1827
MOORE, THOMAS 1779–1852
MORE, SIR THOMAS 1478–1535
MORIER, JAMES JUSTINIAN . . . 1780–1849
MORRIS, WILLIAM 1834–1896

NAPIER, SIR WILLIAM FRANCIS PATRICK 1785–1860
NASH, THOMAS 1567–1601
NEWMAN, JOHN HENRY 1801–1890
NORTH, SIR THOMAS . . . *fl.* 16th Cent.
NORTON, THOMAS 1532–1584

OCCLEVE, THOMAS . . . . 1370 (?)–1450 (?)
OLDHAM, JOHN 1653–1683
ORRERY, ROGER BOYLE, EARL OF . . 1621–1679
OTWAY, THOMAS 1652–1685
OVERBURY, SIR THOMAS 1581–1613

PAINE, THOMAS 1737–1809
PALGRAVE, SIR FRANCIS 1788–1861
PARNELL, THOMAS 1679–1718
PATER, WALTER HORATIO . . . 1839–1894
PEACOCK, THOMAS LOVE 1785–1866
PEARSON, JOHN 1613–1686
PECOCK, REGINALD 1390–1460
PEELE, GEORGE . . . . 1550(?)–1598
PEPYS, SAMUEL 1633–1703
PERCY, THOMAS 1729–1811
PHAER, THOMAS . . . . 1510 (?)–1560
POPE, ALEXANDER 1688–1744
PORTER, JANE 1776–1850
PRAED, WINTHROP MACKWORTH . . 1802–1839

BIBLIOGRAPHICAL NOTE

To a sketch of the history of English literature it is hardly possible to append a useful bibliography which shall not be of extravagant dimensions. Merely to chronicle what has been performed by native scholars and critics would require a volume in itself. But it may possibly be of some service to readers to indicate briefly what has been most recently published in the earlier provinces of the subject, and what books will aid the student in obtaining an exact acquaintance with particular epochs and lives. I make no scruple in mentioning first, for this particular purpose, those popular collections prepared by many hands, the *English Poets* (1880–94), edited, in five volumes, by Mr. T. Humphrey Ward, and *English Prose Selections* (1893–97), edited, also in five volumes, by Sir Henry Craik. We must face the fact that the body of English literature is of immense extent, and that the general reader has not the time to study every department of it. These books offer to him selected extracts. If he is born to read, a specimen will tempt him on to a whole book, and a book to a whole author. Nor is merely partial information, in a reader whose professional attention has to be directed elsewhere, worthy of so much scorn as professors are apt to give it. Common-sense abhors a system which should exclude from the enjoyment of English literature any one who cannot pass an examination on the *Treatise of the Astrolabe*, and it is a pleasure to quote the courageous words of Mr. Arthur James Balfour : " So far from a little knowledge being undesirable, a little knowledge is all that on most subjects any of us can hope to attain ; and as a source, not of worldly profit, but of personal pleasure, it may be of incalculable value to its possessor."

The author of a general treatise, however, would be indeed tame-spirited if he satisfied himself with the prospect of such unambitious readers as these, and of no others.   For those who desire to proceed further and deeper, certain guides, especially in the earlier parts of the history of modern English literature, must be named.   Within the last fifteen years an immense progress has been made in mediæval study.   In preparing for a literary estimate of the later Middle Age in England, no living man has performed so much as Professor Skeat, to whom we owe an absolute revision of the texts of Chaucer, and of several of his leading poetical contemporaries, based upon scientific principles of philology.   Mr. Skeat's final edition of Chaucer, in six volumes (1896), is invaluable to the student, and supersedes all previous work in the same field.   In obtaining a correct text, the copies of the MSS. published by the Chaucer Society have been found serviceable.   For thirty years, moreover, Mr. Skeat had been giving his attention to William Langland, and after having produced, for the Early English Text Society, an edition of *Piers. Plowman,* in four volumes (1867–84), he went over the whole work again in what is now the standard text, issued at Oxford, in two volumes, in 1886.   In 1897 he collected the principal pieces, in prose and verse, which criticism had gradually rejected from the canon of Chaucer, into a single volume. This includes Usk's *Testament of Love*, the *Plowman's Tale*, and most of the poems formerly attributed to Chaucer, but now proved not to be his. The labours of Mr. Skeat are of inestimable value to students of the fourteenth and fifteenth century, but they must be reminded that he has chosen to leave the purely literary aspect almost untouched, and to concentrate himself mainly on grammar and philology.

The publications of the English Text Society include Barbour, Wycliffe, and many of the verse-romance writers. Blind Harry, Dunbar, the *Kingis Quair*, Rolland, and others have been carefully edited by the Scottish Text Society (1883-97). Gower's *Confessio Amantis* has still to be read in Reinhold Pauli's three volumes of 1857. Lydgate, although Dr. Schick has lately printed and annotated the *Temple of Glass*, and Dr. Koeppel the *Story of Thebes*, awaits a general editor. The minor poems of Occleve (or Hoccleve) were dealt with by Dr. Furnivall in 1892. Miss L. Toulmin Smith transcribed and edited the York Mystery Plays in 1885. Mr. I. Gollancz printed the poem called *Pearl*, with a paraphrase, in 1891. The vast researches of the late Professor Child of Harvard College resulted in his *English and Scottish Popular Ballads* (1882-94), by far the most important contribution to this difficult subject. Mr. J. J. Jusserand, in *L'Epopée Mystique de William Langland* (1893) and *Le Roman d'un Roi d'Écosse* (1895), has thrown light on the temper of the English Middle Ages. Professor McCormick has been specially engaged on the text of *Troilus and Cressida*. Wycliffe and his associates have attracted the notice of Mr. T. Arnold, who edited the *Select English Works* in

1869-71, and of Mr. Skeat. The Wycliffe Society has also done good work. The sixteenth century has not of late greatly appealed to English scholars. Hawes must still be read in the imperfect edition of the Percy Society (1845), Skelton still where Dyce left him in 1843, while a critical text and commentary of Surrey is a real desideratum. Mr. Arber's useful reprints have placed several of the minor writers of the early years of Elizabeth within reach. Before leaving the mediæval period, moreover, the names of Professors Lounsbury and Ten Brink must be mentioned.

From the end of the sixteenth century onwards, almost every department of English literature has received the attention of students, and there are few authors, even of the third or fourth order, who have not found at least one recent editor. It would manifestly be impossible to give in this place a list of these editions which should have any pretence to completeness. The lives of Spenser and of Bacon have been treated by Dean Church, that of Sidney by Symonds, and that of Shakespeare by a hundred writers, among whom Professor Dowden and Mr. Sidney Lee (in the *Dictionary of National Biography*) must be mentioned. Mr. Bullen has edited Campion, Marlowe, Middleton, Day, and several of the important lyrical collections of the Elizabethan age. The labours of Dr. Grosart are too numerous to be named in detail. The text of Shakespeare was edited by W. G. Clark and Dr. W. Aldis Wright, and has recently been revised by the latter; the editions of Furness, Furnivall, and Gollancz have each a peculiarity and a merit. Mr. Swinburne has published critical volumes on Ben Jonson, on George Chapman, and on Shakespeare. The vast compilations of Mr. Fleay deserve respect. The *Letters and Life of Francis Bacon*, which occupied Spedding from 1861 to 1874, still retains its authority. The most recent texts of Spenser are those of Dr. Grosart, and (the *Faerie Queen* alone) of Mr. T. J. Wise.

Milton occupied almost simultaneously the attention of a great number of adequate biographers and editors. Among the former are pre-eminent Masson (1859–80), Mark Pattison (1879), Stopford Brooke (1879), and Adolf Stern (1877–79). The text of Milton's prose works has been neglected, and the edition of Symmons (1806) is still the best ; to that of the poems far more attention has been given by Prof. Masson, by Prof. Hales, and still more recently by Mr. Verity. A valuable contribution to a knowledge of the prosody of Milton is the treatise by Mr. Robert Bridges (1893). Dryden, whose works, with an admirable life, were edited by Sir Walter Scott in 1808, was carefully revised by Professor Saintsbury (1882–93), who had already published a life of Dryden in 1881. The poetical works of Butler were edited, with a new biography, by Mr. R. B. Johnson in 1893. The life of Locke has been written by Dr. Fowler (1880), and that philosopher has found a recent editor in Mr. A. C. Fraser. In connection with Bunyan, the excellent work of Mr. J. Brown must be recorded. Cowley, Crashaw, Quarles, and Henry More have been edited by Dr. Grosart, Waller by Mr. Drury, Donne by Mr. E. K. Chambers, Marvell by Mr. Aitken, and Herrick by five or six competing scholars. With the exception of Dryden, the Restoration dramatists have not as yet received their full meed of critical attention, although an Edinburgh reprint gives us, among others, Wilson, Davenant, and Crowne ; Mr. Ward's Sir John Vanbrugh (1893) is a model for what yet remains to be done in this direction.

With the opening of the eighteenth century, it becomes almost impossible to follow the minute progress of bibliography. It is desirable, however, to remember that the action of a great body of careful revisers is for ever modifying both the biography and the text of our principal classics. Professor Courthope has completed the editing of Pope, on the basis of materials collected by Croker, and partly manipulated by Mr. Elwin. Mr. Austin Dobson, besides what he has definitely done for Prior, Gay, Goldsmith, and Horace Walpole, has, in the general course of his essays, elucidated the minute literary history of the eighteenth century in a multitude of ways. Steele and Arbuthnot owe much to the industry of Mr. Aitken. The great Johnsonian of recent years has been Dr. G. Birkbeck Hill. Mr. A. C. Fraser's labours on Berkeley, those of Sir Henry Craik on Swift, those of Mr. Gladstone on Bishop Butler, and those of Mr. Bury on Gibbon, deserve careful attention. This list is so imperfect as to offer to numberless students of the eighteenth century a positive injustice, for which the writer of this little volume apologises on the ground of the very limited space at his command. An examination, however, of the books thus discursively mentioned will suffice to save readers from many of those mistakes which are repeated from handbook to handbook by the unwary.

INDEX

THE END

CPSIA information can be obtained at www.ICGtesting.com
Printed in the USA
LVOW06s0445180813

348392LV00001B/389/A